FROM A SICK TO SOBER SUPERMAN

ADAM JABLIN

Lotsaholic: From a Sick to Sober Superman

For information about this title or to order other books and/or electronic media, contact the publisher:

Lotsaholic, LLC
9100 South Dadeland Boulevard, Suite 1701
Miami, FL 33156

www.adamjablin.com
adamjablin@mac.com

Twitter: @Adamjablin
Facebook: https://www.facebook.com/Adam-Jablin
Instagram: @adamjablin

ISBN: 978-0-9988299-0-6 (Print)
978-0-9988299-1-3 (eBook)
978-0-9988299-2-0 (Audio Book)

Printed in the United States of America

PRAISE FOR LOTSAHOLIC

Adam Jablin is traveling on an ancient path of wisdom providing substantial insight and tools needed to make changes in our lives. He shows you how overcome obstacles–no matter how large–and to live a life rich in beauty, meaning, and purpose. You are going to love this book!

—Dion DiMucci – singer & songwriter, Grammy Hall of Fame artist

I met Adam Jablin when I was newly sober, and he made being in recovery genuinely appealing. I've stayed tight with him, and we've helped each other ever since. I'm thrilled to see that he's able help so many more people with this book. Bravo!

—Steve-O – comedian, actor, *New York Times* Bestselling Author

Adam Jablin is a man on a mission to leave his divine fingerprint on the hearts of the people that hear him speak. His story is powerful, his heart is big, and his gifts are plenty.

—Steve Weatherford–Super Bowl Champion and NFL's Fittest Man

I've known Adam Jablin the past 14 years, and in that time we have become family. We have shared some of life's most special landmarks and have had sacred conversations. Adam does truly live this life, and I am proud to call him my brother. You'll love this book.

—Michael Yormark
CEO of Roc Nation Unified and President of
Business Operations & Strategy

Adam came into my life and I can say without a doubt he mad w massive impact. He's never stopped doing that. He's done it with his words and his heart. That experience is what you will feel when you read this book.

—Los Silva (Hustle)
Founder of SVG MEDIA & #1 Social Media Influencer

Adam Jablin is a leader, sober advocate, and all around good guy. I met him in early sobriety when he shared his experience, strength, and hope with a bunch of us. I was moved by further conversations with him over the next couple of months where he helped me immensely in all aspects of life, relationships and business. He has a big heart, gives back to the community with a tremendous amount of service, and my wife and I are grateful to have him in our lives.

—Matt Williams
Creator of FROPRO, Wake Up the Sun Podcast and Recovery Warrior

It's no mistake that you are reading this sentence. Adam Jablin has been instrumental in changing my ideas, my attitudes, and my emotions in how I navigate life and continue to build momentum. This book is the gift he has provided to those seeking solutions that will take you on the amazing journey from hopeless to hero that only Adam can tell. Read this book. Then read it again!!!

—Scott Jeffries
ScottyJArt—Best Selling Artist

I met Adam Jablin twelve years ago when I was 17 years old. Since then, no man has impacted my life more than Adam. His ability to see my inner truth when I could not, his naturally outpouring positivity, and his earned trust has saved my life and kept my life on track scores of times throughout the years. So many times I have wanted to give up on dreams and Adam brought me back to my destiny. If I was down to my last phone call, I would call Adam.

—Zach Cohen
CEO Onstage Studios and Frontman of RedrumSociety

AUTHOR'S NOTE

WHETHER YOU'RE READY to take the next step in your life, feel stuck, in pain, or don't know how to turn your life around, I want you to know that you are not alone and THERE IS HOPE. I am here to help you move out of the despair and self-sabotaging patterns and begin to experience more joy and more power in your life–everyday!

TO MY FAMILY

TABLE OF CONTENTS

FOREWORD

By Dion DiMucci

I FIRST MET ADAM JABLIN when I visited his elementary school to give a motivational talk and sing some songs. He made an impression on me, because he was that kind of kid. He's still that way today. He walks into the room, and the room is better off for his presence. He lights the place up with his enthusiasm.

He came by his gifts honestly. His grandfather and his great-grandfather were pious and generous men who tried to change their corner of the world through prayer and personal influence. His father is an entrepreneurial genius who built a manufacturing powerhouse from the ground up.

Adam has taken all these gifts into another generation and up to a higher level. He's found a way to succeed in life — and not only succeed in business, but also in the areas that matter more: family, social action, spirituality, and the life of the mind. Now he spends his life teaching others how to succeed in all the same ways.

He's not making this stuff up. In fact, Adam Jablin is traveling on an ancient path of wisdom. The founding fathers of America, and so have many other sages and saints and historical game-changers. What Adam does, though, is to share that ancient wisdom in simple, practical ways. He's always substantial, yet he's always entertaining.

One of those long-ago sages once said that the glory of God is a man fully alive. I believe that's what Adam is. And that's the kind of life he's sharing with us in this book. It's a life rich in beauty, meaning, and purpose.

So much of it depends on our relationships. Our lives are constantly caught up in other lives: family members, next-door neighbors, employers, employees, customers, clients, suppliers, contractors, competitors, and rivals. We fail in life when we fail in these relationships — when we treat these people like something other than persons, when we treat people like things.

Adam knows that relationships aren't easy, but he's managed to make them simpler for us. He teaches us never to lose sight of the others and never to forget what and who they are.

Again, this isn't easy, but it can be simple. And it can be done. I know because I've been watching Adam Jablin live this way for a long time. I've known him now for thirty years.

The proof of the principles can be seen in his life. I've seen it, and I'm here to testify. You're going to love this book, and it's going to change your life for the better.

Rock on!

—Dion DiMucci – legendary singer & songwriter, Grammy Hall of Fame artist, and Rock & Roll Hall of Fame inductee

PROLOGUE

My Secret Identity

"What can I getcha?" our server asked. She casually rested her left hand on the table while her right hand grabbed for a pen from inside the pocket of her apron over her clean, white-collared shirt. I took in her appearance for a moment. She was dressed in the official uniform of Burt & Max's—a new, hip restaurant in Delray Beach, Florida. Black and gray tribal Japanese tattoos ran from her neck down her arms, and her punk, short hair was styled up in a red headband. Although she was polite, her happiness seemed contrived and I sensed that she didn't have the easiest life.

"Do you have Blue Moon?" my wife, Michelle, asked. She loved that popular Belgian beer.

"We do!" The server's enthusiasm was phony.

Michelle ordered the beer, and then the server turned to me. "What's your poison, sir?"

"Can I please have a water and an iced tea with lemon?" *I'm still double fisting.*

She studied me and then nodded and grinned. "A drinker and a nondrinker, hmm?" She asked as if she knew our history.

I looked at Michelle, and we read each other's eyes. We both knew that this girl was going through it. Michelle smirked, tossing her long, straight, dark-brown hair, and nodded, signaling that it was okay for me to be a bit forthright. My anonymity was a sensitive subject for Michelle.

"I'm retired," I said.

Michelle giggled. "Yeah, don't worry. He's had enough for a few lifetimes."

We all introduced ourselves and shook hands. Her name was Bernice. She had recently gotten pregnant and changed jobs. Her boyfriend, Jake, the baby's father, had moved to Texas for a new employment opportunity, so she had moved back in with her mother. Jake had recently detoxed off methadone and whiskey, and the disease of alcoholism and addiction had torn up their lives like a tornado. Bernice had left Jake several times, only to get back together with him, hoping that she could fix him. Each time she came to our table to refill drinks, bring out food, or make sure we were satisfied, we'd dig a little deeper into Bernice's life and my sobriety.

She was curious about what had gotten me sober, how I surrendered, and what exactly Michelle had done during that time.

"I love Adam, don't get me wrong . . . but I just couldn't allow my child to be raised in an unstable and dangerous home. He had to get better or leave."

I watched my gorgeous wife tell our story. With her big, bold, brown eyes, perfectly sculpted face, and deep-olive skin tone, she could pass for Latin, Egyptian, or Italian—She looked exotic. As I listened and observed, a wave of gratitude washed over me. Michelle explained that the birth of our

daughter was what finally gave her the courage to say that enough was enough.

Bernice leaned in toward me. "And you just quit?"

"Not exactly." I explained just how far my family had gone to see that I got well, how I could see that Michelle was as serious as a heart attack about protecting our daughter from my troubled ways.

"He made me so nervous. I was afraid he'd drop her, or worse. I pictured an accident in the bathtub, with him slipping and snapping her neck . . . or I'd imagine him driving home sloshed and hitting her in the driveway with his car."

I swallowed hard as I saw those pictures in my mind. I thought of my kids—my dynamic, dancing daughter, Sloan and my larger-than-life son, Miles. I could have lost it all to my drinking and drugging.

"In the beginning, I didn't do it for me, to be sober or find a 'higher power.'" I made quotation marks in the air with my index and middle fingers. "It was all about wanting to stay with my family. Wanting to watch my children grow up. Later, the spirituality and sanity became important to me."

TWO DAYS LATER, my childhood friend John and I met for coffee. John sat in front of me, and his six-foot-two, muscle-bound physique took up most of the table. But he looked like a beaten man—pale, jaundiced, and terribly wrinkled from years of abusing alcohol and drugs. His hairline had receded, and his face looked swollen. From my years in bodybuilding and fitness, as both an avid exerciser and a scholar of these topics, I could tell from the size of his muscles and his paunch that he'd been using growth hormone and other performance-enhancing drugs. His fashionably unshaven two-day beard didn't hide his yellowish, bloodshot eyes with big, black circles underneath. Deep in thought and worried, he repeated, "I can't believe this is happening to me." Smoke curled off the cigarette in his left hand.

John had hit bottom. His fiancée had caught him forging fake prescriptions for pharmaceutical narcotics, "which was a felony," and found needles for opiates and steroids in his gym bag. In addition, she had intercepted his credit card statements, which showed he'd been drinking in bars and strip clubs when he was supposed to be at business dinners. Panicked and furious, she had told John's mother. Together, screaming and hollering, they had barged into the middle of the Fortune 500 corporation where he worked. In front of his boss and coworkers, they had confronted him with his lies.

"Adam, I'm so embarrassed to go back to work." He looked ashamed. About two years earlier, I'd run into John at the gym. Happy, successful, fit, and energized, he had told me about his new job, English bulldogs, and new house. Now he was a shaken, hopeless, nervous wreck.

We were sitting outside at the Starbucks in Boca Raton. It was a beautiful day, with the temperature hovering in the low eighties, surprisingly low humidity, and not a cloud in the sky. I took a sip of my Venti iced green tea and asked him, "Have you ever tried to quit drinking and pharmaceutical drugs?"

He made eye contact with me, scrunched his mouth, and rubbed his neck. "Hundreds of times . . ." He took a drag from his cigarette. "But the pain, the sweats. My heart raced, I got tremors, nausea with throwing up, and diarrhea." He exhaled the smoke as he recalled those feelings.

"I'd get awful headaches, anxiety to the point I became paranoid and hallucinated. I was constantly irritable. . . . Yuck! It was the worst."

I grimaced, thinking of when I had struggled and fought to get sober.

He took a long sip from his iced coffee and then sighed. "I just couldn't take it."

I felt my own stomach clench. I could see the suffering in his eyes, and I remembered—too well—the hell of alcoholism and addiction.

Although usually quiet, John wouldn't shut up today. He trembled and seemed confused. He spoke a million miles a minute, spitting out one crazy thought after another, the thoughts rolling on top of one another. "My fiancée . . . her pregnancy . . . my job . . . my car payments . . . my mortgage . . . my awful boss . . . my nagging parents . . . my muscles . . ." He had excuse after excuse. One giant, raw nerve, John saw himself as terminally unique.

I had to make him stop telling me his sad story about how life treated him unfairly. I had to remind him of why we were sitting across from each other. "Brother, I've been there. I've been in your shoes. Acting and saying exactly what you just told me." Like a surgeon, I gently cut through his denial and despair. I explained how baffled I had been when I learned that I was a sick man and how my drinking and drug use had progressed over the years.

We reminisced about old rah-rah drinking stories from back in the day and how much fun we'd had. Like the time we threw up in the men's room at the Empire Bar to empty our stomachs for more alcohol. "But did I ever tell you that when I went home that night, I slammed back six more drinks and popped a sleeping pill and some Advil?"

"No!" He looked shocked. "How did you meet me the next morning to work out?

I smirked. "I drank a couple huge energy drinks with some uppers and painkillers for the hangover."

I showed him how I had slowly crossed an imaginary line and gone from someone who could have a few drinks to someone who needed to drink and, more than that, how extreme my behavior had gotten.

I walked him through some of my war stories, to shed light on how alcohol and drugs destroyed my body, twisted my mind, and killed my spirit. Then I revealed some of the consequences of my actions. "Yeah, in college I had a DUI, but not remembering how badly I'd yelled at my mother-in-law in an alcoholic fit that night was way worse!"

He pulled his legs in underneath the small table and sat up straight. "You did?"

"Yeah." I nodded slowly. "I still thought I was okay. Just a little out of control and hit some bad luck. My denial was thick, pal, but I needed help in the worst way."

I told him how I'd believed that with enough discipline, dedication, and willpower I could beat this thing myself, and then I told him about the intervention and the twenty-eight days I'd spent in rehab at the Hanley Center. "I wrestled with myself for nine torturous days in that place, over whether I was an alcoholic and addict or not. The word 'surrender' wasn't in my vocabulary, and I thought I was better than everyone else in there." I described my moment of clarity and how that awakening had transformed rehab, for me, from a prison to

a spiritual camp. In that awakening, my entire perception of life had changed. "Hands down, it was the greatest thing I've ever done for my family and for myself."

John took another drag from his cigarette. "Why is this happening to me?" It almost felt as if he were speaking more to himself than to me. But the tone in his voice held a glint of hope. He looked me in the eye. "Adam, I'm about to lose everything—all of it. What can I do?"

"You need help." He needed to detox safely. The detox process can be grueling and painful—and deadly if not done properly. He also needed tools—a blueprint of how to live a sober life. My old friend needed a new beginning, a do-over like when we were six years old and playing kickball. "Don't worry. I'm sure you'll be able to keep what's really important, what truly matters in your life. There's help out there." I grabbed his boulder of a shoulder and squeezed it tightly, like a coach would do to a player in the last seconds of a game. "You want me to see if they have an open spot at the rehab I went to?"

He nodded.

ONCE OR TWICE A WEEK, I have conversations like this one, helping someone who has hit bottom to reach for recovery. About fifteen times a week, I support someone who's already in the process of recovering. Throughout the year, I speak to athletes and schoolchildren, from fifth grade to college, about alcoholism and addiction. By day, I'm a mild-mannered vice president of operations for a lace manufacturer. It's my secret identity. In between lace production meetings and Skyping with customers, I'm trying to save lives.

TWO FREE BONUSES

Bonus #1: 2 Free Lotsaholic Lessons Videos!
Adam's Lotaholic Lessons bring to life some of the life changing exercises written in this book. The video lessons are magnetic, and Adam uses an online questionnaire that helps you learn the skills he teaches in the book. He will slowly build your faith and recharge your batteries. Adam's enthusiasm is contagious and has an effect on your mental, physical, emotional, spiritual and financial well-being!

Bonus #2: Download A Free Week Adam's Program—The Hero Project
Adam's The Hero Project is life changing. He developed a method that has a synergistic effect on your mental, physical, emotional, spiritual and financial well-being! This is a free week outline from early in the program. It reveals a formula for being accountable and truly becoming the HERO of your own life.

https://www.adamjablin.com/

PART I

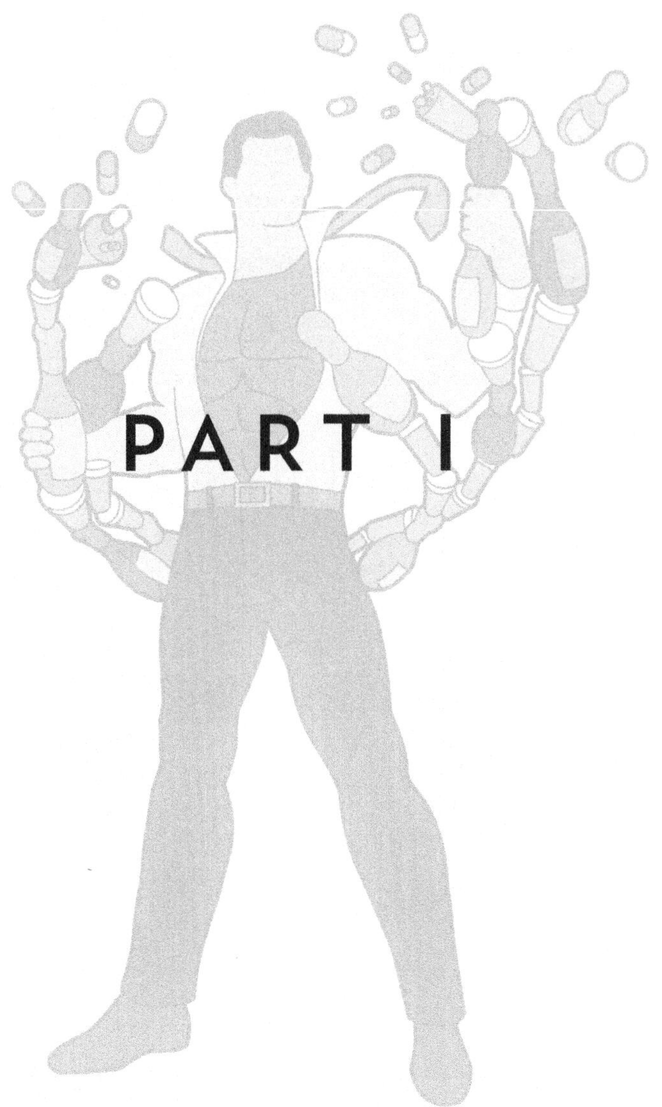

CHAPTER 1

MY BRILLIANT DISGUISE

WAITING FOR ME WAS my usual—a big brandy snifter glass filled to the rim with Patron Silver, a premium, top-shelf tequila, on the rocks, meaning poured over giant, crescent-shaped ice cubes, with just enough room for a dash of Rose's lime juice. Five shots in one glass. *Delicious.* I had arrived at the restaurant prepared to be a good boy and not drink too much. I had set my limit at two cocktails, just enough to calm my nerves for socializing.

I had business associates in from out of town—three yarn suppliers and two lace purchasers, ranging in age from thirty-eight to sixty-four. Because my father was in New York on business, entertaining them had fallen to me. *My pleasure.* I invited them to dinner at New York Prime, which was the hottest restaurant in South Florida and had been voted the

"Best Steakhouse under the Sun." My father and I ate and drank there regularly, and we knew the staff.

Jimmy, our usual waiter, greeted us at the entrance. "Hey, Adam! Great to see you again. Your table is ready." He reached out his right arm for a handshake while he used his left hand to pull me in for a hug. After we embraced, he patted me on the back twice and then led me to my traditional table next to the upscale bar. The energy inside the packed restaurant was electric. Frank Sinatra's "New York, New York" blared from the speakers. We walked by cheery tables of people drinking, eating, and enjoying the ambiance. As we crossed the dining room, I delivered fist bumps to a couple guys I'd seen earlier at my 5 AM workout at the gym. "Yo, pal! Good to see you training this morning. You look good."

"You, too, Adam. Keep it up." It felt like the TV show *Cheers,* "where everybody knows your name, and they're always glad you came."

As we approached our red mahogany Victorian table, I stared at my drink and then looked over toward the bar with a shit-eating grin. The bartenders, Billy and John, winked at me and yelled, "Ayo, Adam!" It felt like a welcoming party.

"Yo, boys! You da men!" I yelled across the restaurant. I felt like such a big shot.

Okay, Adam, only two drinks. But I drank fast. Half an hour later and two megadrinks in, I told myself, *Just one more.* I excused myself to the men's room. Knowing that the drinks might fatigue me, I'd brought two tablets of ephedrine to help me stay alert and peppy. Although it's illegal now, at that time the stimulant and appetite suppressant was popular in health and nutrition stores. I popped both tablets into my

mouth, the whole time silently bargaining with myself: *Order a Diet Coke for caffeine. That'll get you up. Sip your last drink, go home, give Michelle her shot, let her fall asleep, and then you can get it on with a few beers there.*

I'd promised Michelle I'd return home by 9:00 PM to give her the second shot of the day. Michelle and I were undergoing in vitro fertilization (IVF) in an attempt to get pregnant. It was exhausting, tedious, and frightening. Ninety-nine point nine percent of the hardship is on the woman. Daily shots, blood tests, sonograms, X-rays, habitual doctor appointments, nurse meetings, pharmacy trips, drugs, mixing the drugs, drug schedules, and countless syringes for more shots! It felt as if a day didn't go by where Michelle didn't get poked and prodded. And that wasn't a great combination for someone who feared needles and medical devices. But she faced every fear with the courage of a soldier. Michelle had become my hero.

I followed through with my plan. A couple Diet Cokes and one big-ass Patron later, I excused myself from dinner to get home to Michelle, right on time for her shot. Michelle hated my drinking, one never being enough for me, and there was no excuse for me to drink when she needed me to stick a needle in her. My anxiety grew as I focused on acting sober.

At the time, I had a black Hummer H2—my dream car. Next to the empty water bottles in the cup holder, the center compartment held mouthwash, breath mints, and a variety of prescription pills (amphetamines, or uppers, and barbiturates, or downers). Because all of them were legal, I felt some degree of justification for my consumption of alcohol and pills. I also knew many people, from the gym, work, and other social settings, who popped pills and drank in excess. I found it easy to tell myself that I was normal.

The pocket in the back of the driver's seat held vitamins, empty beer bottles—from Coors Light to Heineken to Stella Artois—and a variety of bodybuilding supplements—from vitamins and minerals to fat burners to digestive enzymes and herbal cleanses. The backseat was covered with sweaty workout clothes, more empty water bottles, and protein shake cans. On the floor were scattered *Flex, Muscle,* and *Fitness* magazines; IVF documentation; lace samples with spec sheets; and random beer bottle caps. In the trunk, I had hidden a half bottle of Belvedere vodka and an assortment of energy drinks.

I'd begun to conceal my exercise habits, just as I did my drinking. I worked out whenever I felt hurt, upset, troubled, confused, insecure, bored, happy, or starved for endorphins.

On that night, when I got into my Hummer, I decided to take a Xanax to calm me down from all the Diet Cokes and ephedrine. I didn't want to act loud, amped up, and animated when I got home. That would be a dead giveaway. While driving home, I swished Listerine around until my whole mouth turned numb. I stopped at a gas station to get bottled water and a twelve pack of beer to drink after Michelle fell asleep.

I finally arrived home. My eyes felt as if they were popping out of my head, and I was parched. When I walked inside, I saw Michelle waiting on the couch. I tried like hell to appear normal. "Hi, baby. How are you feeling? I brought you a steak, asparagus, mashed potatoes, and a delicious chocolate cake." *God, I hope she doesn't smell the booze or notice anything in the way I'm acting.*

"Thanks. How was dinner?" She seemed not to suspect a thing.

"You know—same old, same old. Good steak, though." In fact, I'd barely touched my meal.

"Your Poppa wants you to call him after the shot. Gaga isn't doing so hot."

My grandmother, Charlotte Jablin, otherwise known as Gaga, had recently undergone exploratory surgery for appendicitis and bowel troubles. After a month in the hospital, her health was deteriorating. We were all shaken by it. She was small in stature yet huge in heart. All of five feet three inches, she had dark-olive skin and jet-black hair. She almost always pulled back her locks in a fashionable, vibrantly colored headband and wore matching stylish glasses. Although never flashy, she had pizzazz. She always looked glamorous. Her integrity defined her. My Gaga was voted Boca Raton's most dedicated altruist for her volunteer work regarding Alzheimer's disease. She gave and gave and gave, but she never sought fame or publicity. One of my greatest teachers, she taught me many things. Her main lesson to me was "Do unto others, care about people, and don't ever judge anyone by financial status."

I could always count on Gaga, and she spoke to me like an equal and with honesty and compassion. Around Gaga, my heart sang. She had this amazing gift in that she saw only the good in people. I'm not kidding. You could bring up Hitler, and she'd tell you, "It must have been something in his childhood. His inner self would never want to do that to people. It was all his ego." She was one of my best friends—I could tell her anything.

Her illness had been eating me alive. I visited her in the hospital daily. My grandfather, who I called Poppa, had upgraded her to a private room and lived there with her. Poppa, Morton Jablin, was also called the Captain, because he was a captain in the U.S. Navy during World War II and a captain of industry. A strikingly handsome man with ice blue eyes, he kept his white hair closely cropped and sported a powerful mustache—a duplicate of Paul Newman's as Fast Eddie Felson in the movie *The Color of Money*. (I tend to see life and people as if I'm in a movie. I connect them to lines of dialogue, facial expressions, or theme music, sometimes seemingly out of nowhere. It's how I roll.) Always impeccably dressed, he wore a shirt and tie every single day of his life. He always taught me, "If you dress appropriately, you could meet the pope or president."

Michelle's news scared me and sobered me up. The Xanax began to kick in, relaxing my jitters. "What's wrong?"

"She was having a bad night, and he wanted to talk with you. I feel so guilty that I'm not allowed to go over there."

The IVF doctors and nurses had told us that Michelle should stay away from hospitals because of the germs and the possibility of her catching an infection that would affect the medications she was taking.

I slowly walked over to the fridge to get an ice pack from the freezer and the fertility shots, Lupron and Gonal F. The news of Poppa calling from the hospital and the tremendous amount of focus it took me to prepare the shots helped to shift my attention off being buzzed. Michelle had caught me a few times in the past, but I'd sworn that I stopped when we started IVF.

I walked over to the couch and looked at her. Guilt sank in. *Adam, what's wrong with you! Your wife's going through hell with these shots, your Gaga is sick in the hospital, and you're drinking this much? Start acting like a man!* Tears started to form in my eyes, and I sat down next to Michelle.

I had a sudden urge to be honest and yet not too honest. *Adam, tell her you had a drink.* My mouth caught up with my brain. "Baby, I had a drink tonight. I know I shouldn't have. Just . . . everything with Gaga, the hospital, IVF, the doctor appointments and . . ."

"Honey, I'm proud of your honesty. Did you really have just one? Let me smell your breath."

"Won't do you any good. I wasn't planning on telling you, so I used mouthwash and chewed gum right before I came inside. I'm not drunk."

"You promise? You're all right to give me this shot?"

I had been good with the drinking "lately." The IVF process had relit a fire in me. We wanted a baby. We wanted to become a family. Lucidity spread through my body. I believed that having a child would finally put an end to my drinking and drug use. The precision of the IVF process granted me purpose, clarity, and daily goals. *Wow. Until tonight, I think I hadn't had a drink in about twelve days. I can't imagine what having a child will do for me. If Michelle only knew about all the pills I'm taking, though. But right now I have to deal with life somehow. I just won't drink anymore—not after tonight.*

"Thanks, honey. Trust me. I'm fine." *Yes! She believes me.*

I administered the shot like a pro. I felt like a man for having told at least part of the truth. After the shot, I looked in my daily planner, where I recorded my drinking episodes.

I tracked the days I drank and popped pills like I tracked my workout regimen, figuring that self-knowledge would help me to break the cycle and quit. In case anybody ever looked in the planner, I used a code—"A" for alcohol, "P" for pills, and "A/P" for both. I highlighted those days so they jumped out when I glanced at my calendar. Tonight was my first drinking episode this month. *Excellent! The master plan begins. She goes to bed, and I continue "relaxing."*

Michelle climbed the stairs to go to bed, and I called my grandfather. "Hey, Poppa. How's it going?" I had seen him just six hours earlier.

"Not so good, Addy, not so good." I heard the disappointment and worry in his voice. "The doctor will be here at 3 PM tomorrow to go over the next steps. Can you make it?"

"Of course. Is she okay? Can I talk to her?"

"She's sleeping, buddy. She's nervous. Very, very nervous."

"Don't worry. I'll be there. And, as always, if you need anything—anything at all—Poppa, just call me. I'll be there."

"Thanks, Addy. I love you, kid."

"I love you, too."

Six Amstel Lights, two Patron margaritas, and a couple glasses of pinot grigio later, I prepared for bed. *It's only 10:30 PM If I get seven hours of sleep, I'll wake up on time, feeling fresh. I can sweat it all out in morning cardio and then be as good as gold.* It was the perfect justification I needed for popping another Xanax and an Ambien to sleep.

A CALL TO ACTION

- Do you have constant conversations with yourself internally similar to the ones I had when I was drinking and drugging? Break out a journal or notes in a smart phone and document what you're thinking and feeling.
- Do you have any emotional triggers? Parents, spouses, work, friends, food, etc.? Write them down.

CHAPTER 2

DAZED AND CONFUSED

AT 5:30 AM, MY ALARM CLOCK BLARED. I was groggy. My eyelids were too heavy to open. The constant, high-pitched sound felt like a fire alarm blaring right between my temples. Beeep! Beeep! Beeep! It took all my effort to reach out my arm and hit the snooze button. *Got it. Ahhh.* My arm hit the bed, and I winced in pain. *Oh, God! How much did I drink last night?* Severely dehydrated, I tried to lick my lips, but I couldn't. My mouth was dry and sticky, and my breath was stale and toxic. *Yuck! I need water. I need water!*

I slowly pushed myself up, feeling soreness in every muscle. I somehow managed to grab the water bottle next to the bed and guzzle it. *More. More. More.* After forty-five seconds, I stopped sucking down the water so I could get some air. Drool fell from my mouth and ran down my neck, landing on my upper chest. *Ugh. My head. Hello, hangover.*

I sat there for a couple minutes, remembering pieces of the previous night. I squinted and noticed the mess I had made trying to drink the water as if it were coming out of a funnel. I looked over at Michelle. *Still sleeping—thank God!* I hobbled to the bathroom. With each step, I felt as if Mike Tyson was punching me in the head. I looked in the mirror.

Oh . . . my . . . God!

My cheeks had swelled from the accumulation of alcohol and pills. There were large bags under my eyes. My head was puffy and rounded like a bowling ball. I had booze face. I was rinsing my head with cold water when it hit me. I had hidden away some Vicodin, a narcotic pain reliever, for this very situation.

There are three ways to take care of hangovers. One was to sleep off the toxins. For me, this was a no-no. Taking the day off work and sleeping in would mean I was weak—had no willpower—and would put my drinking before my career and family. That would mean I'd probably turn into an alcoholic. *Ha!* The second way was to soak up the toxins with a nice greasy meal, like eggs over easy, toast with butter, hash browns, or something from McDonald's. I hated this option and avoided it at all costs. Eating a meal like that would just add extra calories and fat that I'd need to burn off. It would make me feel like a pig. The third way to deal with a hangover was to sweat it out in the gym. That way I'd even earn extra points by doing penance for the previous night's behavior.

But it went deeper than that. Working out had become my mask, my cover, and my personal "How bad is my drinking?" test. The identities of fitness fanatic and alcoholic just

don't go together. I remembered years back when Arnold Schwarzenegger starred in the movie *End of Days*. He played a cop who became an alcoholic after his wife and child were murdered. Later, he had to fight Satan to save the world. *Yeah, of course he does. . . .* But here's the point: Nobody believed that Arnold's character was an alcoholic. When he held a bottle of Jack Daniel's in his hand and took a swig, you couldn't help but notice his huge, perfectly shaped biceps. It just wasn't believable. An alcoholic doesn't have a perfect body.

I popped the precious Vicodin with a couple Advil. I get up around 5:00 AM every day for my morning workout—usually cardio. That workout provides me with the endorphins I need to start my day. More importantly, it maintains my lean, chiseled look, an example of vanity at its finest. Other than Michelle and Gaga, my physical appearance was the one thing I truly cared about. Shame sunk in. I thought of Michelle and Gaga. I thought of what they were going through, and then I took another swig of coffee to wash down fifty milligrams of ephedrine. *I'll never do this again while my girls are suffering.*

Working out was the only thing I felt I had any control over. For most of my adult life, I had worked in the family business. I always had sensed that something was missing. I wasn't doing what I wanted to do or living up to my potential. But the family business provided me with an upscale lifestyle and perks. I ate at expensive restaurants, stayed at fine hotels, and made deals with important people. Every day, I tried to sell myself on how I was living the dream. But whose dream was it?

I never felt proud. I felt no sense of accomplishment, no satisfaction. I had become a robot: Wake up. Exercise. Shower.

Eat. Go to work early. Walk around the factory. Say hello to all the employees. Review the yarn inventory. Check the machine efficiencies. Check in with the quality control department. Check in with the shipping department. Look at new samples. Organize daily meetings with the design department and the plant foreman. Review new lace costings. Reply to e-mails. Return phone calls. Review scheduling priorities, including machines going offline or online, and capacity. Check with the mechanics about parts for the lace machines. Monitor whether customers are paying invoices on time. Touch base with yarn suppliers. Attend videoconference meetings. Go to gym to work out again. Drive home. Watch TV. Self-medicate or get rip-roaring drunk. Go to bed.

I simply lived in each moment and reacted to daily events. I constantly felt lost and suffocated. But I felt the exact opposite about my dedication to exercise. I was extremely proud of my physique, which gave me some self-worth and power. My daily workouts provided me with a sense of accomplishment. They were an outlet that made me not only look good but also feel good. I put all my eggs in that one basket. God forbid an egg would crack.

I believed that people judged me everywhere I turned. I thought they measured me based on my beautiful wife, my car, my house, and my career. To shut up all those critics, I had a concealed weapon—my muscles. With the body of an Adonis, I could change the look in their eyes. Nobody asked me, "So, Adam, what do you do?" Instead, they said, "Wow! How much do you work out?" or "How much can you bench?" or "What can I do to get rid of my belly?" or "What should I do to lose this fat?" When my drinking got out of control,

my body never betrayed that I had a problem; it just looked as if Mr. Muscles had another big night out.

When I saw the guy in the mirror that morning, my motivation to look lean soared. *Hello, Mr. Fat Face. You make me sick.* After sucking down my morning cocktail of pills and coffee, I grabbed my iPod and zoomed out the door.

At first, every workout rep killed my throbbing head. In excruciating pain, I swore off alcohol altogether. *I'm never drinking again.* Then the pills kicked in. My body started to grow numb, and the hangover began to subside. Thick, toxic sweat literally poured out of me. I imagined my body pushing and squeezing the liquor out through my pores. The stench of booze wafted from every bead of sweat that dripped off me. The voices in my mind grew faint. I became a robot programmed with one purpose: Get rid of the alcohol.

When I returned to my house after an hour of detoxing by working out, I felt like a new man. I planned the morning in my head: *first, an ice-cold shower to revitalize; second, dress for work; third, prepare Michelle's shots; fourth, check e-mail on my iPhone; fifth, give Michelle the first shot; sixth, walk Cookie,* our adorable eleven-year-old Pekingese. The cold shower provided a great jump start. I loved the feel of the sticky, poisonous sweat washing off my body. I flexed each muscle to make sure I was strong as ever. While drying off, I looked in the mirror and, happily, saw that the swelling of my face had gone down. *Yes!* I ferociously brushed my teeth and then rinsed my mouth with Listerine twice. I styled my hair with pomade, making sure it looked as if I had just come from a fashion shoot. I made my way to Michelle's makeup kit and borrowed her small concealer stick to hide the black circles under my eyes. A few dabs under my eyes, a little smearing, and *Voila! I'm back, baby!*

While I prepared Michelle's shots, I thought about how much she was going through daily in order to get pregnant. Then shame sank in. *Why, Adam? Why do you do this? Well, I feel pressured all the time, constantly rushing. Is that any excuse? No. I'm a worrywart—about Michelle, Gaga, business, finances, my body. If I could just get my damned anxiety under control.* I thought of Gaga lying in a hospital bed. Every day, they took blood from her, gave her shots, and who knows what else. She had a catheter and some other tube attached to her that pumped black guck out of her and into a huge tank behind her. I so badly wanted to cure her. I would give my right arm if we could nurse her back to health. *And you, Mr. Muscles, drink while your girls suffer.* The guilt and remorse made me sick. I felt a little jittery from the ephedrine and dehydration, so I decided to take a couple Xanax before administering the shot to Michelle. *This has to stop. I've been good for so long.*

I arrived at the office at 8:00 AM When I walked in, my secretary, Bev, said, "Good morning, Adam. Can you please call your dad back?" *Unbelievable! It's only eight o'clock!* I tried to smile at Bev. It wasn't her fault that I always felt one step behind my old man. I felt that I had to be as good as him, which was an impossible task.

"Good morning, Bev. Of course. Thanks." My head started thumping again.

I walked to my desk and glanced at my unread e-mails. I picked up the phone and hit the speed dial. "Good morning, Dad. How's it going?"

"Hey there, pal. It's going good. The city is cold, but your mother and I are having fun. I have a busy day, a lot of customers to see. Did you read those e-mails from Mark?"

His question made me feel inferior. "Of course. What's up?" I faked enthusiasm as I found Mark's e-mail and read it quickly. The pressure I put on myself overpowered me. I viewed every question from my father as a test. If I ever told him, "No" or "I don't know," I would feel as if I'd let him down. Regardless of the reality, I resented him for that.

"Good. Why don't you arrange a meeting in the design office and call me back to patch me in? Let's say ten minutes."

"You got it. Call you back in ten." My stomach hurt. I popped a Pepcid AC and a couple more Advil before calling our design office to make the arrangements.

The speed, intensity, and attention to detail of our lace business stressed me out. Recently, the economy had been tough, and the rest of the modern knitting mills in the United States had gone belly up. Our competition now was global, and they were selling for prices as cheap as dirt. We had to do it better, faster, more efficiently, and more cost-effectively. There was no room for error. I never had time to catch my breath. Being asked to answer thousands of questions each day and having a boss/father who operated at light speed made me loathe my job.

My father's brilliance and savvy cast a big shadow. He didn't just enjoy the business; he was the business. The man was a genius. He was a human computer who could remember every detail—thousands of lace patterns, style numbers, prices, dates, conversations, yarns, budgets, expenses, and manufacturing machinery—at will. That ability had made him a major success, and his larger-than-life presence was felt all around our workplace. I felt unnatural trying to live up to his stature and answering his every order like a military soldier under his command. My entire life had been about proving to him, my grandfather, and everyone else that I could succeed as those previous generations of Jablins had. The insecurity of not living up to their standards had become a burning motivation for me. It created an unhealthy competitiveness within me.

I needed a break. I sought solace from the pressure and my constant striving to be better than everyone else. I opened my desk drawer and looked down at the self-help and spiritual books I kept there: *The Art of Happiness* by His Holiness the Dalai Lama and Howard C. Cutler, MD; *Think and Grow Rich* by Napoleon Hill; *Unlimited Power* by Anthony Robbins; *The Way: Using the Wisdom of Kabbalah for Spiritual Transformation and Fulfillment* and *The Secret: Unlocking the Source of Joy and Fulfillment*, both by Michael Berg; *Talking to Heaven* by James Van Praagh; *Many Lives, Many Masters* by Brian L. Weiss, MD; *Tao Te Ching* by Lao Tzu; *Zen Lessons: The Art of Leadership* by Thomas Cleary; *The Autobiography of Malcolm X* as told to Alex Haley; *The Message* by Eugene H. Peterson; *The 72 Names of God: Technology for the Soul* by Yehuda Berg; *The Power of Now* by Eckhart Tolle; and countless others. I had an even larger collection at home. I was a spiritual junkie.

At my job, I felt that I wasn't doing what I had been put on Earth to do. A lace manufacturer? I was always searching for more. *What's the meaning of my life? Why am I here? Why don't I feel fulfilled?* Anyone who knew me probably would tell you I was the nicest guy they knew. I always tried to see the humor

in life. I loved laughing, and I loved making others happy. I knew I was supposed to be doing something more with my life, but what? I searched, read, explored, investigated, and rummaged around every book I could find. Nothing popped out and said, "Here's the answer, Adam! You're not meant to be a lace man. You're meant to be . . ." The more I looked, the more confused I became. I couldn't find my own definition of God. I liked bits and pieces of many religions and beliefs, but none of them made complete sense to me.

I picked up *The Way: Using the Wisdom of Kabbalah for Spiritual Transformation and Fulfillment* by Michael Berg. It contained a great story, which I had read over and over, about a scholar named Rabbi Naftali Yehuda and how he had chosen his life. In the story, he wonders what would have happened to him if he hadn't focused on his studies and become a scholar. He summed up by saying that he probably would still be a nice guy, take care of his family the best he knew how, and even pray and study a little bit. "I would have lived a good, simple life. And after so many years I would die and stand before the Creator and the Creator would say, 'Well, Rabbi Naftali.'" And he would think to himself, Rabbi? I'm no rabbi; I am a good and undemanding man. What does he mean by rabbi? The Creator then would ask where all his students were. He wouldn't know what to say. "Students? Is He crazy? Where would I get students? I'm a simple guy. I'm a nice guy, but what do I know about teaching?" The Rabbi explained that the Creator would be disappointed in him because he would not have reached his potential. A person who has lived a good life hasn't necessarily accomplished what he or she was put here to do. Every time I read that story, a chill ran through my veins and the hole in my heart begged for purpose.

I had five minutes until the meeting. I looked around my office, uncertain. *What am I supposed to do with my life?* I looked at the photos on my desk, first the one of Michelle in her wedding dress on our wedding day, smiling from ear to ear. I glanced at the next photo, the one of Gaga and me dancing and laughing on a family cruise. Sunlight hit the photo right next to it. In a silver, mirrored frame stood my father and me. We were having a great time on a family trip while I was in college. Dad, seated, was dressed to kill, in his snazzy, tailored, gray tweed sport coat with fitted, black T-shirt underneath; his thick, silver hair was styled perfectly to look messy like a model in a magazine. People often stopped him, thinking he was Ralph Lauren. I stood behind my father, looking pretty snazzy myself. My hands were on his shoulders as if I were giving him a massage. You couldn't help but notice how much we looked alike. "Man, I miss those days," I said out loud to the photo. Remembering those times made me hate the family business even more.

My head throbbed, and beads of sweat formed on my forehead. My raw emotions integrated with my intoxication from the pills I'd taken earlier in the morning. I felt physically sick and tired. My worries continued to dance in my brain. I bent over and opened my black leather computer case. In a small, concealed compartment I had hidden a bunch of pills. I grabbed a couple Xanax and a couple Percocet, popped them all into my mouth, and sucked them down with a gulp of coffee.

As I headed to the meeting, my feelings continued to swirl in my gut like a tornado.

I bumped into our head mechanic, Steve. "Adam, everything okay?"

"Oh, yeah. Of course. Just in a rush. You know how it is."

Steve knew what was going on with Michelle and me doing IVF and Gaga being sick. He gave me a double take. "You sure?"

"Of course, Steve. But thanks for caring, buddy."

I rushed to the restroom. I turned on the sink, splashed my face with ice-cold water, and repeated in my head, *Real men don't cry. Real men don't cry. Real men don't cry.* I thought of my father's favorite cowboy line: "I didn't cry when Old Yeller died." Dad never showed his emotions. He was a rough, tough cowboy—a throwback to a time when men were men. Next to him, I felt weak and feminine. I hated my emotions. *Suck it up, Adam. What's the matter with you?* I tightened my stomach muscles and punched myself in the gut with the side of my fist. *Toughen up, Adam. Real men don't cry.*

I sucked it up. I sat through a forty-five-minute meeting with the design team, management team, and my father, who participated via video conference from Manhattan. I tried to focus on a specific customer's lace request but then suddenly found myself worrying about Gaga, whether the IVF would work, or whether I could do this job for the rest of my life.

I was afraid of the future. Would Gaga die? Would the IVF fail? Would the pressure of having a child further financially tie me down to my job? I grew more and more irritable as impressions and memories jumped into my head. I couldn't control them. The one I hated the most wouldn't leave me alone—the memory of the day I had committed myself to the family business.

I was fifteen. I'd just gotten home from school that afternoon, and I was excited for my mother to drive me to the gym. When I walked into the house, I saw that my father was home from work early. Dad usually came home late, around dinnertime. *What's wrong? Did I do something wrong? Am I in trouble?* The last time I had seen my parents in such a deep discussion, they had told me we were moving from New Jersey to Florida. I wondered what terrible news they were about to tell me this time, and I hesitated to enter the living room.

My parents looked up, and my mother rushed over to me. "Hi, Addy," she said. She was smiling strangely. "How was your day, baby?"

"I'm good, Mom. You?" I looked at my father, who looked as if his mind were somewhere else. "Umm. Hi, Dad. Why are you home so early? Am I in trouble?" The little hairs on the back of my neck stood out. Dad looked my way, and Mom jumped in again.

"No, Addy. It's nothing like that. Something very big has happened, and your dad and I would like to talk to you."

I could hear the housekeeper about to walk in, and I could see the gardener out back through the windows.

"Let's go to our room for some privacy," Mom said.

Something big? The small walk through the dining room, past my father's office, and to my parents' bedroom felt as if it lasted an eternity. *What's going on? Are we moving again?*

I sat down on my parents' bed, and they stood in front of me. My father still looked uneasy. My mother was uncomfortably jittery, but she spoke first. "Adam, we have a very big decision to make. Your dad was just offered *a lot* of money

to sell the business." My mind took over. *Awesome! Way to go, Dad! Now we'll have more time to hang out together!* I smiled broadly and I looked at my father in awe.

He smirked at me. I could tell that he was contemplating the future. He looked at me and said, "Unless *you* want it."

Time stopped. "Unless *I* want it?" The vision of us palling around with each other vanished from my mind. "What do you mean, unless *I* want it?"

My mother sat down next to me on the bed. "Do you want to go into the family business?"

I was shocked. Generally, in those days, my head entertained three subjects: girls, working out, and sports. I didn't know what I wanted to do for the rest of my life. Because of the business and my father's success, we lived in a beautiful five-bedroom home with a swimming pool in the backyard and valuable artwork in every room. Every time a new pair of Air Jordan sneakers came out, I got them on the first day they were available. My father's business had brought us to green, wealthy Boca Raton, Florida, where the sun shone every day and the beach was five minutes away from our house. We ate in fancier restaurants than we ever had in Tenafly, New Jersey.

That's when the confusing thoughts started whispering in my ear. *I would make Mom and Dad so proud of me right now if I said yes. I bet this would be one of our best family moments, and it's all up to me. Right here, right now.* I looked at my mother and then my father. "Yes. Of course. I'll go into the family business and work with Dad." I'll never forget that day.

Now, here I was fifteen years later, answering e-mails and feeling like hell from the drinking and the pills. *Stupid hangovers!* I looked at my watch. It was 11:15 AM *Nice. Almost time to work out.* I stopped thinking about my headache and went to the company kitchen to make a drink called N.O.-XPLODE, a preworkout shake guaranteed to give a boost. The manufacturer warned not to mix it with anything other than water and to avoid using it if you suffer from anxiety—which I did—depression, dehydration, or exposure to excessive heat. *Hah!* I sucked it down as fast as possible. It was time to work out. Nothing could stop me. No hangover, no emotions, nothing.

As I drove to the gym, I suddenly felt the rush of the caffeine from the N.O.-XPLODE shake. U2's "Elevation" blared from the Hummer's speakers as I thought about the body part I'd focus on that day—back. My psyche transformed into that of a soldier going into battle—beast mode. Everyone noticed my passion for fitness, and many people asked me how I kept such a hardcore, steady pace, how I could turn off my work day as if I had a button to control it.

This was my life; turning off work to work out had become routine to me. My switch from troubled businessman to unbreakable bodybuilder was an easy one. The Hummer was my telephone booth; during the drive to the gym I changed from Clark Kent into Superman.

I arrived at the gym and said my usual hellos. I pulled out the sheet of paper where I'd written my routine. I walked over to the lat pulldown machine and studied my list—*Front pulldowns. Deadlifts. One-arm rows. Bent-over rows. T-bar rows in corner. Seated rows. Dumbbell incline rows. Standing cable rows. Machine rows.* I warmed up by doing front pulldowns and focusing on the mind-muscle connection.

I worked out intensely, no matter what. Anytime I felt ill, exhausted, or hungover, I'd play mental tricks on myself. I'd think of the U.S. soldiers over in Iraq. The young kid who'd been up for three days straight, on his feet, under fire, fighting for his life. *I bet he'd like to just have to work out with a hangover.* I imagined myself a gladiator, a warrior going into battle. I never made excuses—not ever.

After an hour of pushing, pulling, breaking down, and sculpting my body, I was finished. But I hated leaving the gym. I loved the way the weights felt in my hands. I never wore gloves, and I had the calluses to prove it. Each and every exercise, set, repetition, bead of sweat, and groan of pain released the nervousness inside me. I never left the gym with a single drop of energy remaining in my tank. When my muscles were fully exhausted and my body was beaten and depleted, I felt at peace.

After showering, I returned to the office for part two of my day. I was facing seven phone calls, twelve e-mails, a trip to the hospital where Gaga was, an IVF procedure at the fertility clinic a half hour away from the hospital and, finally, administering Michelle's second fertility shot of the day. I was looking forward to seeing Gaga, hearing what her doctor had to say, and learning about Michelle's progress. The business side of things . . . not so much.

I enjoyed putting together a team and taking part in deals that enabled everyone to make a profit and be happy. I didn't like transactions that focused on shaving off some pennies for me and some pennies for others, but the pie was only so big. The way the garment industry or, as insiders call it, the schmatta (Yiddish for rags) business works felt like negotiating at a flea market. It rubbed my personality the wrong way, and I felt frustrated in conversations and negotiations.

Most of my customers who supplied finished lace (bras, panties, and so forth) worked in the garment district in Manhattan. They wore suits and schlepped fabric samples behind them in carry-on, wheeled suitcases. I enjoyed getting to know them as individuals. I asked about their families and their lives. That way, if one of them yelled at my art designer, I could respond from a perspective of knowing them as people rather than just seeing them as the jerks they often were in business.

But the schmatta business was a royal pain in the ass. The customers constantly badgered us with questions such as "When can I have it?" "How big does the order have to be?" "What can we do to make it cheaper?" Haggle, haggle, haggle. "Are you crazy? I can get it for half that price from China." "Thirty-day terms? What am I made of? Money?" "How do you expect me to hold that much inventory? What am I? Sears?" "I can't afford that. You're talking to a guy who has kids to feed." The Far East provided cheap labor, dirt cheap prices, and tough competition. Our market segment was customers who needed small minimum order quantities (MOQs), top quality, and timeliness! Compared to thirty years earlier, when my grandfather had held civilized conversations with his customers, the industry had become focused on price, price, price—and nothing else.

My father and I often butted heads about our customers. I wanted to befriend our customers and have relationships similar to the ones my grandfather had in the good old days. But my father could see right through these people. They

were constantly trying to pull one over on us. They'd use as a weapon the personal relationship I'd fostered. "Oh, come on, Adam. I can't afford that. What can you do for a good friend like me?" "You know the kinds of headaches I'm dealing with. I need a better deal." And they didn't want just a good deal. They wanted a deal that would make us bleed.

A victim mentality ran throughout the industry. When customers saw how successful our company was, they assumed that our success was at their expense rather than due to our skills. As a result, they often tried to push through agreements that didn't make sense for us financially. And they didn't want to give an inch.

My father stood firm. Nobody was going to intimidate or outwork the Cowboy. When customers came in wanting to use our lace to create brand-new products, he would work with them to create compromises convenient for everyone. But when customers came in with the intention of getting more than their fair share, he would cut them off. Don't try to take an extra inch from him, or he'll chop off your hands. Rule #1: Don't mess with Robert C. Jablin.

Although I handled myself similarly in negotiations, doing so didn't feel good to me. I wasn't being true to myself. I wanted to be able to speak from my heart. My whole being craved a kinder, gentler, more honest, more loving world than the schmatta business.

In business meetings, customers whined about how we, the manufacturer, didn't understand their troubles. In my early days, many of them had tried to pull me to their side, inviting me to visit dye houses so I could understand their headaches. They had hoped to pit me, the new guy, against my father.

But that was one thing I'd never do. "Don't ever take sides with anyone against the family." You must have heard those words from Marlon Brando in *The Godfather.* In my opinion, the number one asset I offered the business and my father was my loyalty, my heart. I backed my father 110 percent. If anybody said a word about him, rudely disagreed with him, or upset him, they had to deal with me. My father had to calm me down more than a few times, but he was proud of me. He knew that I was the most loving, sweet guy around, especially in *that* industry. I wasn't sure whether the family business was for me, but I knew that I wanted to spend time with my father. I hated that I needed to deal with one to get the other.

As I fielded phone calls, this conflict took over my mind. I wanted my father and me to have our old relationship. All he wanted was his son to take over the business. The two desires wrestled inside my gut. *Time for another Xanax and Percocet.*

When I left work that day, I relaxed a bit. Visiting Gaga at the hospital and doing the IVF with Michelle made me feel like a man. I took pride in being there for my family. I enjoyed being there with them, holding their hands, and giving them my love and support. It gave me that fulfillment I'd been searching for. Yet that somehow upset me. *Am I enjoying my girls needing medical help?* No. I enjoyed being needed, counted on, and wanted. The confusion depressed me. I popped another Xanax and Percocet.

THREE DAYS LATER, at my request, my doctor prescribed Zoloft for my anxiety. In the beginning, it helped me a lot. For the rest of the IVF treatment, I didn't touch a drink and I eased off the pills. Then life got crazy.

On May 6, 2005, my Gaga died. We were in the emergency room, and to this day I don't know what went wrong. I remember watching the numbers on the machines go crazy and asking Poppa whether that was normal. All Gaga wanted was a sip of apple juice.

But the doctors and nurses told us, "No liquids." We didn't know what to do. Gaga began burning up, and we put wet rags on her. I was so afraid. I screamed for a doctor, and a nurse ran down the jam-packed hallway. Poppa finally gave Gaga some apple juice. "The hell with this place," he said.

We were both holding her, and she looked at me. "I'm scared," she said. My heart broke.

I felt helpless. *What's going on? Help! Help! Please! This is my Gaga!* "Don't be scared, Gaga. We're right here. The doctors are on their way. Poppa and I are right here."

Two doctors and two nurses ran in. They tried to push Poppa and me out of the way, but we were rocks. We wouldn't budge. There was plenty of room for all of us, and they knew that.

My last memories in that room are vague. I think I heard someone say, "I can't find a vein." Gaga's body turned ice-cold, and that godforsaken beep blared across the room.

Afraid of living in a coma, Gaga had signed a legal document not to be revitalized. When the doctors asked Poppa whether they should bring her back anyway, he told them no. I'll never forget that moment. I knew that every bit of his soul must have shouted, *Yes! Bring my babe back! Yes!* But my Poppa wouldn't do that. I've never seen a tougher display of love in my whole life. I looked at him in utter shock and disbelief. He looked at me and said, "She's gone, kid." We fell into each other's arms.

Later that month, we found out that Michelle had become pregnant. My emotions were all over the place. I felt thrilled that I finally would be a father but devastated that Gaga would never meet her first great-grandchild. Only one thing would quiet my brain—alcohol. I bought a bottle of tequila, a bottle of vodka, and a case of beer.

Then our house had a leak, which forced Michelle and me out for months. We had to completely demolish the upstairs floor in case of fungus. We moved in with my in-laws, whom I adore. Unfortunately, at the time, Michelle was as big as a house and constantly uncomfortable. Just before we had planned to move back home, relax, and work on preparing the baby's room, the hurricanes (including Hurricane Katrina) came. They kept us out of our house for another three weeks. I dealt with the pregnancy, relocations, lack of electricity and air conditioning, lack of communication via cell phone and Internet, negotiations with insurance agencies, managing the family business's storm-related shutdowns, coordination of construction crews at our house, attorney calls, and the loss of Gaga. Not surprisingly, the drinking and drugging came back in full force.

I mixed the alcohol and pills with an antidepressant. I thought two things over and over again—*This all will be over when the baby is born* and *I want my Gaga back.* It took more and more cocktails and pills to quiet my mind.

SLOAN SLOANE JABLIN was born at 12:28 AM on December 9, 2005. I hung posters, with a pink Superman

S that read, "Welcome, Sloan Jablin," all over the hospital. I couldn't remember ever having experienced such a high. *I'm a daddy!* The drive home from the hospital was magical. Michelle and I felt as if the whole world had changed. We seemed to see all of the world's beautiful colors for the first time. It seemed as if the roads were empty and we saw only green traffic lights. We drove into our neighborhood in awe.

"Wow. I don't remember it looking so beautiful here," I said.

"Neither do I," Michelle said. "Adam, we're a family."

My heart sang. I thought that, finally, I'd left the crazy days behind. I had a child now. My daughter, Sloan. Supergirl. I looked at Michelle and couldn't believe what she'd gone through to get to this day. I looked in the back seat, and there sat this tiny thing, my baby! I swore to myself that my crazy days were officially over. I looked over at Michelle and smiled. "Thank you, baby. Thank you for everything."

After I'd pulled the Hummer into our garage, I turned around and looked at my daughter. "Hey, baby. You're home."

A CALL TO ACTION

- Have you ever felt that the life you're currently living is for someone else's happiness? This is something to really think about. Think deeply. We only live once.
- Do you buy a lot of self-help and spiritual books? Purchasing these books are signs thatyou are stretching for a greater wisdom and clarity. These books are your research that there is something bigger at play in the Game of Life.

CHAPTER 3

SICK AND TIRED

I JOLTED UP, startled by the noise on the baby monitor. *Is that her?* I thought I heard Sloan crying, but I waited a few seconds. "Waaa. Waaa. Waa." *Yeah, it's her.* Exhaustion hit me, and I shook my head to wake up. I somehow managed to quickly swing my legs out of bed, because I wanted to let Michelle sleep. I staggered through the pitch dark and across the hallway to the baby's room. As I quietly opened the door, the crying grew louder.

"There, there, baby girl. Daddy's here." I slowly picked up Sloan, gently kissed her little cheek, and walked to the changing table. I opened her diaper and . . . *Yes, no poop!* I changed the wet diaper, reswaddled her, and then, holding her, lightly tiptoed my way to the pink rocking chair next to her crib. I slowly sat down. "Shhh. Everything's okay. Shhhh. Daddy loves you." I rocked back and forth and softly sang to her. "Do you wanna sing the grammy-love-you song? Do you wanna sing the grammy-love-you song? Do you wanna sing the grammy-love-you song, 'cause I love you so much." Shortly, she fell back asleep, and then I went downstairs, to the garage, to slam down a few quick beers.

Overnight, our lives changed dramatically. They now revolved around our precious baby girl. We bought bottles, diapers, baby wipes, a changing table, hand sanitizers, playpens, baby monitors, and so on. I fell head over heels in love with my daughter, but I was hanging on by a thread. I thought that going through IVF and losing Gaga had been tough, but adjusting to parenthood challenged me on a whole other level. I had envisioned snuggling, vacation at Disney World, and ice cream. I learned the hard way that child rearing meant sleepless nights, dirty diapers, and constant worry. Parenthood was the most wonderful—but most difficult—job on the planet.

Michelle and I baby-proofed our home from top to bottom, including latches, cabinets, and toilets. Parenting added new phobias, such as sudden infant death syndrome (SIDS), and we were on high alert for fevers, rashes, colds, flus, infections, constipation, and diarrhea. We thoroughly researched and purchased the perfect baby mattress, crib, car seats, and strollers. We loaded up on medications, ointments, powders, and creams. We found baby formulas and pacifiers. We were constantly going to doctor appointments and reading seemingly millions of books about raising a child. Did I mention sleep deprivation? There's a reason the government uses it as torture! My entire life had been reshaped. I wanted to be a hands-on dad and give Michelle some well-deserved rest. The exhaustion, anxiety, and responsibility rattled me, and I knew only one way to calm my nerves.

I woke up again, at 5:30 AM, completely exhausted. I drank my coffee, with amphetamines and fat burners, while preparing the baby formula for Sloan's 6 AM feeding. Then I took some more pills, to even myself out, and went off to work. At work, I called the house several times to check on Sloan. At lunchtime, I took more pills and supplements and then headed to the gym. I worked out, hard, and then popped even more pills and supplements. Afterward, I had a meeting about yarn inventory, a conference call with a customer, and a visit from suppliers. At 5:30 PM, I drove home to spend time with Michelle and Sloan. I fed and bathed Sloan. And then I snuck into the garage, drank some beers, and popped some pills before running upstairs to use mouthwash to disguise my breath. I tried to get some rest before Sloan's 11 PM feeding. At 10:30 PM, I prepared another bottle and took a few pills. Michelle and I fed Sloan in our bed, and then I put Sloan back in her crib. I desperately tried to get some sleep. At 2:45 PM, my alarm went off, waking me up for the 3 AM feeding. After the feeding, I drank some hard alcohol to get back to sleep.

At 5:30 AM, I woke up and repeated my actions of the previous day. I drank coffee with extra stimulants . . . went to work . . . self-medicated, exercised, took more pills . . . worked some more . . . snuck a few drinks . . . and went home. I spent time with Michelle and Sloan, popping pills and slamming drinks behind Michelle's back whenever I got the chance. I woke up for night feedings and to rock Sloan back to sleep. My daily routine basically consisted of pills, baby, pills, work, pills, exercise, pills, work, baby, alcohol and pills, baby, pills, baby, alcohol.

WEEKS OF BOOZING AND drug use followed. My body and soul deteriorated from the around-the-clock intoxication. On what should have been a beautiful romantic day with Michelle, I got smashed, and it all went straight to hell.

Michelle's parents had offered to babysit Sloan for the day so that Michelle and I could enjoy some time alone with each other. Michelle suggested we try a cute, rustic bistro in West Palm Beach.

The last few weeks she'd been smelling alcohol on my breath even more than usual. When she confronted me, I lied to her, trying to conceal my drinking, which only made things worse. Michelle said that she hoped that the date would help us to reconnect.

But I immediately thought, *Adult time!* That, of course, required a bottle of wine. I ordered a bottle of Santa Margherita pinot grigio. Earlier that morning, I'd taken my usual pep pills, Vicodin, and Percocet, with caffeine. After my daily workout, I'd popped a few Xanax like Tic Tacs, to help calm me down before our date.

I drank the wine at my usual fast pace, and it rapidly mixed with the medications in my system. It hit me.

Hard!

My shoulders caved inward. My voice got low, and my speech slowed. I moved my arms slowly and clumsily as I struggled to keep my eyes open. I became comfortably numb.

Michelle sat stiffly, her shoulders inching up toward her ears. Every one of her movements showed her internal tension. She tried to act calm, but even in my condition I sensed her anger. Her look penetrated me. Each time she spoke, I shook my head quickly, trying to wake myself up. *I'm nodding off.*

Wake up, Adam. Pay attention. Her voice sounded fuzzy, as if we had a bad connection on cell phones. I couldn't concentrate. I tried to speak, but my words came out slurred and quiet. Michelle had seen me wasted plenty of times, but my eyes slowly opening and closing concerned her even more than my usual behavior.

"What's wrong?" Her voice cracked. Usually when I was wasted, she'd say, "How much did you drink?" She scrunched her eyebrows and squinted.

"Nothing, honey. Just tired."

She's on to me! My damned, beloved body was turning on me. *I'd better pep up before this gets ugly.* I raised my hand up to get the server's attention. "Miss, can I please get a Diet Coke?"

When she brought the soda to me, I drank it down fast.

"Thirsty, sweetie?" the server asked.

"Always. Can I get another? And an espresso?" She took a step or two backward. Michelle looked at me, her eyes wide and jaw hanging.

"Another Diet Coke and an espresso coming up." I sensed that the server thought me insane. I looked at Michelle and tried to act normal.

"An espresso?" she asked when the server had left.

"Didn't sleep well last night, baby, and I killed myself in the gym."

"Uh-huh."

I slammed back the next Diet Coke at the same lightning speed as I had the first. Trying to make polite table conversation, I asked Michelle, "What looks good to you?"

I made an effort to sip my wine like a gentleman, but I was obsessed about getting the espresso into me so that I'd seem coherent. I tried to cover my distraction with more polite conversation, asking what color to paint Sloan's bathroom and how Michelle liked the new kitchen cabinets.

The effects of the caffeine crept up on me. My body temperature rose, and my heart palpitated. Beads of sweat formed on my forehead and I wiped them away. "Honey, excuse me. I need to use the men's room."

I rushed into the restroom and locked the door behind me. Panicking, I looked in my small, upper-right-hand pocket, where I usually kept my stash of uppers and downers. I took a couple more Xanax and then splashed cold water on my face. I looked in the mirror. *Just act normal, Adam. Drink water. No more wine. No more caffeine. Try to have a nice date with your wife.*

I was on a roller coaster from hell. I had taken something to pep me up and then something to calm me down. Up and down.

By this point, I knew I'd screwed up, so I made excuses to Michelle when I returned to the table. "I'm pushing too hard, baby. I need to relax. I'll cut back on my workouts. You know, I'm getting less sleep now that we have Sloan."

After we left the restaurant, I pretended that all was normal. We struggled to go along with our "romantic" day, but the negative vibes between us continued. While we visited boutiques and art galleries along the avenue, I sulked about how my life had turned out. The oppressive July heat and humidity mirrored my inner discomfort.

I wanted to fill the void in my heart, to make my pain go away. I wanted to feel—not just look—secure and confident. My thoughts were manic and incoherent. *This weekend: Get*

wasted. Monday: Get back to the grind. Monday afternoon: Work out my chest and triceps. . . . Man, I miss Gaga.

The drinking, drugging, exercising, marriage, and even fatherhood weren't fulfilling me. I craved more.

When we arrived home, we both knew what a disaster the day had been. There had been no romance, no bonding, and no sense of partnership. *Another day flushed down the toilet by Adam. This is my life now.* But I didn't care. I felt thirsty!

"Honey, I'm going to take Cookie for a walk." I planned to visit the extra refrigerator in the garage, which was full of Amstel Light, Heineken, Bud Light, and Diet Coke. "Cookie, come here, baby." Cookie raced toward me, wagging her tail and barking happily. "You want to go outside, girl?" Cookie did that adorable little trick of going up on her hind legs and using her front paws to beg. "That's a yes!"

Cookie and I walked through the laundry room and entered the garage, where I raced to the fridge. I surveyed my beer collection. *Hi, boys!* I grabbed two Amstel Lights and pounded them both in less than forty-five seconds—a trick I'd learned in my freshman year at Arizona State University. *Ahhh, that's more like it.* I grabbed another three bottles, one for the walk out, one for the walk back, and one for somewhere in the middle.

If I get caught smelling like alcohol when I walk into the house, I'll just tell her I sipped a cold one while I walked the dog. I thought my white lie clever, since it held a grain of truth. *What's the difference between three and one?*

I almost wanted Michelle to say something. I justified my drinking by how I always adjusted my schedule to accommodate her and answered her constant questions. "What time will you be home?" "Can you pick up baby food on your way home?" "Honey, can you. . . ?" I deserved a break. *C'mon. It's Saturday. No work. July heat and humidity. We already had wine together today. Who can argue with that? Maybe she won't even notice, since I already smelled of alcohol from the wine. But if she does notice, it's her problem. If she didn't make so many demands on me, I wouldn't need to drink so much!*

When I walked back home, two empty beer bottles were sticking out of my pockets and one nearly finished bottle was in my hand. Michelle was standing in front of the garage, waiting. My two previous beers were lying behind her, at the edge of the garage. I could see the disgust on her face.

"You had to drink?" Her jaw dropped. "You had to slam one, two . . ." She saw the two empty bottles in my pockets and the bottle in my hand. "Five? Whoa! Five beers? Adam, we've only been home for fifteen minutes! What the hell is going on?"

All my built-up pressures and resentments toward her and the world came to a head. I could no longer sit back and take it. My excuses and denials mounted as I screamed, "What the hell is it with you? Am I not a good husband? Am I not a good father? Compare me with any of your friends' husbands." The rage inside me took over. "Any of them! You ride my ass constantly. I'm sick of it. I take care of myself. I work out, and I look good. I make plenty of money. We have everything we need. What more do you want? I'm sick of this!"

Why can't I do what I want? I like to drink. All our friends like to drink. My family enjoys drinking. I can't go through this same old nonsense anymore. She has to take me or leave me. I drink! This is who I am.

Unleashing my fury felt good. I felt as if I'd broken out of prison. "It's not me. It's you. It's everyone! What the hell does everyone want from me? Everyone's always asking me to do a million things, and I, Superman, say yes and take care of every one of them. This is fucking *it*. If they want me to be this super guy, I deserve to be able to have a few drinks and pills every now and then. How am I supposed to deal with all this?"

Shock and disappointment were written on her face. She cried. She probably wondered whether the guy lashing out at her even was related to the happy, easygoing, loving guy she'd married.

I carried on like a mad man. "Maybe it's better if I leave. You obviously don't like me, and I'm not so thrilled with you, either!" In the past, whenever anyone asked me what was the best thing that ever happened to me, I always answered that it was Michelle. I had fallen in love with her at first sight. She always wanted the best for me, and vice versa. She loved me with all her heart. Until we met, I had never imagined that the romantic love I'd seen in movies existed in real life. In her, I had found my soul mate.

Now, Michelle looked at me in hurt and disbelief. "Adam, what's wrong? This isn't you!"

Torn from the inside out, I wanted to quit. Yet, at the same time, I somehow felt that she was testing my manhood. Giving in or admitting that I was wrong would mean I had failed the test—and if that happened, I'd have to take a hard look at my drinking.

I got in my car and slammed the door.

I'm not taking this shit anymore. I called my mother on my cell phone and ranted about the fight and Michelle's impossible demands. I probably scared her with my rambling. "I'll leave. We'll share custody. Let her find somebody better. I can't wait!"

That horrible fit turned into five very dark days. I slept in the guest room and refused to talk to Michelle. Each day, I woke up, fed Sloan, and then left. I continued drinking and drugging alone in my office and my car, day and night. In the evenings, when I returned home, I walked right by Michelle as if she weren't there. I made Sloan's bottle, fed her, changed her diaper, and then went straight to the guest room. I felt dead inside. Nothing seemed real.

On Wednesday morning, when I got home from working out, my mother-in-law was sitting at the dining room table, her hands on Michelle's hands and Michelle's head on her shoulder. My mother-in-law asked me, "What's wrong with you, Adam?"

It was the wrong time for her to ask me that. I screamed, "What's wrong with me? What's wrong with all of you? What do you expect from one person? Wait, let me guess. You want me to do more, too? Please, give me another favor to do. The guy who bends over backward for everyone is the one with the problem, right? Where are my cape and red boots?" I went upstairs to the guest room and slammed the door.

That afternoon, while I was at work, I experienced a brief moment of clarity. *Wait! What the hell am I doing? Why am I acting like this? What am I hoping to achieve? What do I want?* I sat in my office, in disbelief. I felt as if I were a stranger entering someone else's nightmare. *How did this all start?* I couldn't recall what had set me off.

I picked up the phone and hit the speed dial.

"Hello?" Michelle's voice sounded sad.

"Hey. It's me."

Silence.

"I'm, I'm . . . I'm sorry."

"We'll talk when you get home." She sounded exhausted.

I called my mother-in-law. "Hi, Mama." I apologized to her.

"Adam, I love you no matter what. You're like my own child. But something is wrong with you."

Somehow, I'd thought apologizing to them would put me in the clear. I knew that my marriage was in critical condition, but I thought we could brush away this incident. When I got home, I apologized to Michelle again. She just sat there and listened.

"Baby, I'm so sorry. But don't you think maybe you're a little hard on me sometimes? Just a little?" I still had all those justifications and excuses for my behavior.

"Adam, now's not the time for this. . . . I'm worried about your drinking."

Everyone drinks on the weekends. Why can't she loosen up? If she could just take it easy on me, my life would be better.

THE NEXT MORNING, unbeknown to me, Michelle spoke to Michael Walsh, an interventionist. In the afternoon, my mother accompanied her to check out two nearby alcohol and drug treatment centers Michael had recommended. Michelle told me about this all much later, when I was able to appreciate what they had done for me.

"Michelle, Mrs. Jablin, this is where you want Adam to be," Ben Harrison said. Ben was the director of the men's unit at the Hanley Center, a premiere alcohol and drug rehab center in West Palm Beach. It offered a broad range of programs and the most advanced research into the disease of addiction.

Earlier in the day, Michelle and my mother had visited another rehab center, but they knew it wasn't for me. It had looked seedy and unclean, and hadn't had a gym.

The Hanley Center was completely different. Surrounded by striking Moorish architecture, sculptural fountains, beautiful flowers, doves, pelicans, and exotic butterflies, it offered the patients a sense of peace. The professional offices, clean rooms, and amazing staff put Michelle and my mother at ease.

My mother stopped dead in her tracks and looked Ben in the eye. "Ben, I appreciate everything you've done for us today. I feel comfortable imagining Adam in this environment. There's just one thing—the gym. Does Hanley have a gym? He's a bit of a lunatic when it comes to fitness."

Ben grinned. "One of those? Is he coming off steroids?"

"No," Michelle said. "That's the one thing he won't touch. He'll pop any pill in the world and drink anyone under the table, but no steroids—ever. He's all natural in terms of exercise."

"Okay, guys. Just checking. We've had a few of those in here. They're pretty crazy—too much testosterone."

Michelle and my mother followed Ben to the wellness center. Ben possessed a natural charm. Dressed to kill in black Prada pants and a light-blue, tailored shirt, he looked as if he'd just jumped out of the pages of *GQ*. He wore a silver necklace of a triangle inside a circle, the symbol for recovery. The equilateral triangle represented the three-part answer—unity, service, and recovery—to a three-part disease—physical, mental, and spiritual. Michelle and my mother said that

they had liked Ben the moment they met him, because his sincerity had shone through. They had liked him enough that they had trusted him with my life.

The next day, unaware of their plot, I went home from work early. I still don't remember why. I do remember that I felt more exhausted than I ever had. At that point, I could have fallen asleep in front-row seats at the Super Bowl.

Michelle took a hard look at me when I stepped into our house. "Are you all right?"

I nodded.

"Why don't we lie down?"

We went upstairs to our bedroom, and I collapsed on the bed.

"I'm so sorry about this past week, honey. I don't know what got into me. I love you so much. I'm going to make this right. I'll see a therapist again, slow down, and stop trying to do everything for everyone. I feel so bad. I know where I've gone wrong. I'm going to change."

I apologized over and over for what I had put her through, and I swore that this time would be different. I could almost hear her thoughts: *I've heard this a million times before.* She tried to comfort me and get me to relax. I lay my head in her lap, replaying the week's events in my mind. I fell asleep. It was 3:45 PM.

According to what I was told later, while I was sleeping Michelle quietly and cautiously went to the guest bedroom and called Michael Walsh. He was with the rest of my family, finalizing preparations for my intervention. With Michelle on speakerphone, they all discussed the plan. To reassure everyone that my disease had gotten bad enough to warrant rehab, he asked each person to share a story in which my extreme behavior had terrified him or her.

Michelle went first. "Let me tell you all about my missing Xanax when we visited Mom and Dad in Aspen." She explained how, a few months earlier when we had traveled to Colorado to visit my parents, I had taken all of her Xanax and blamed the missing pills on the pharmacy not filling her prescription with the proper amount. That medication had been prescribed for her to help with her fear of flying. When she had called Dr. Leslie Levine, our family internist, and explained that she needed more Xanax because some of the pills had gone missing "suspiciously," the doctor had told Michelle that she was extremely worried about me and, due to my many requests for refills, believed that I had taken the pills.

My best pal, Lew, who also was my sister's husband, shared that when we went to Las Vegas for his bachelor party I got so drunk on the plane that I fell on my face in the middle of the aisle. "And the main night that Adam had secretly planned and worked so hard on for me . . . He didn't go. He drank so much during the day, at the pool in the Vegas sun, that he got too drunk to make it out."

My in-laws mentioned the bottle caps in their garbage from beer they hadn't drunk, and their worry about missing prescription medications, from Librax for my mother-in-law's irritable bowel syndrome to oxycodone for my father-in-law's chronic back pain. My brother-in-law and sister-in-law talked about how I had been drunk, reeking of alcohol, around their boys.

Reluctantly, my mother explained that I always asked for her prescription medications, which made her feel uneasy

and awkward. And, going against the Cowboy code of not talking and instead gritting it out, even my father participated in the discussion, recounting times he'd found me in his garage pounding beers by myself while the rest of the family enjoyed one another's company in the living room. The stories went on and on. Everyone agreed that I had a problem, but my mother and father still wondered whether it was bad enough to require rehab or was just stress.

Michelle needed to close the deal. Michelle had seen it all. She had witnessed the moments after the party, when everyone else had gone home: my streaks of meanness, bizarre silliness, and hangovers from hell. She had found pills hidden under the mattress in the guest room, beer bottle caps behind the TV and inside the medicine cabinets, and empty tequila bottles behind the trees in the backyard. Once, she had heard a clang when she had thrown out a peach pit. *Jesus, don't let this be what I think it is,* she had thought. When she had lifted the sauce-covered paper, plastic wrap, and aluminum foil in the top of the garbage, she saw the empty Patron bottle underneath.

She had honored our marriage and kept our problems within our house. Now all that protection could backfire on her, because no one else knew just how bad my drinking, drug use, exercising, and secrecy had become. Michelle also realized that the situation would only get worse, not better. She thought that she'd caught my problem relatively early.

"Michelle, does Adam really need rehab?" my father asked.

"Yes! This is my marriage. My family. This has to stop." She broke down.

Michael spoke up. "Look, everyone. Adam has a disease, not a lack of willpower. It's not that he doesn't love all of you. It's not that he doesn't *want* to stop. He *can't* stop. The disease has taken over. You can review all the information we discussed about the disease of alcoholism and addiction. You can also find out more on our website. Adam has an allergy to drugs and alcohol and, once he puts the slightest bit in himself, it's dangerous, especially with a baby. That will never change—unless he gets help."

Michael had been on the other side of an intervention, too. His friends and family had identified his disease early. He felt extremely lucky, and so he dedicated his life to helping others. He wanted me to have the same chance. "Can Adam continue to live like this? Think of Sloan. Is this the kind of home you want her to grow up in? Is this what you want her to see in her daddy?"

Michelle cried, "No."

Michael sighed deeply and looked around the room. "Is this how you want Adam? Miserable? He'll only end up in one of three places." He paused. "Jail, an institution like a mental hospital, or . . . the grave." Michelle had seen me slowly deteriorate and had vowed not to allow me to continue to kill myself.

Later that evening, I woke up in a panic. I still had on my work clothes. *What's going on? What the hell happened?* I felt nervous. I looked at the clock. It was 1:45 AM. *What time did I fall asleep?* Fear set in. I looked at Michelle, who seemed to be sleeping. I walked to Sloan's room and stood there watching her for ten or fifteen minutes. *What's wrong with me? I have to stop all the damned pills and booze. But how? Please, God! Help me!*

I felt something weird that night. Call it a sixth sense. I had a feeling that something big, something serious, was

going to happen. I couldn't put my finger on what, though. I hated the feeling. It gave me the creeps. *It's all in my head. I need to quiet my mind.* I'd hidden bottles of Xanax and Ambien in the Hummer. I jumped out of bed and crept downstairs. I turned off the house alarm and ran outside to grab my fix.

Michelle told me later that the beep from turning off the house alarm startled her. Anxious about the next day's intervention, she hadn't fully fallen asleep. Tomorrow at this time, she'd be alone in the house *if* all went well. I would be checked into the Hanley Center for a month. She kept asking herself, *Am I doing the right thing?*

When she heard the house alarm, her stomach tied itself in knots. She got out of bed and looked out the window to see if I had snuck outside. She saw me standing beside the Hummer, popping pills into my mouth and washing them down with a bottle of beer. She watched me hide the pill bottles back in the car and run back into the house. She had her answer. *Yes. I'm doing the right thing.*

A CALL TO ACTION

- Do you feel like you're living the same day over, and over again? Is life repetitive?
- Are you currently concealing any negative habits? Share this with a friend and loved one. Control it, before it controls you.

CHAPTER 4

INTERVENTION

THE NEXT MORNING, I woke up confused, regretful, and ashamed. Anxiety kicked in, and thoughts raced through my head. *What's wrong with me? Why can't I stop? Why did I have to make such a mess of things?* Between passing out in the afternoon and then going back to bed after taking the Xanax and Ambien in the middle of the night, I'd been in a chemically-induced sleep for fifteen hours, more than I had in years. *God, I need this to end.* I knew in my heart that the alcohol and drugs were destroying me, and I made a new commitment to myself to turn over a new leaf. *I'll take fewer pills, cut back on the supplements, and drink less. I'll do it all in moderation.* I chugged coffee and popped some ephedrine, and then I followed my daily routine of feeding Sloan, doing some cardio outside my house, and heading off to work.

After walking around the factory and reviewing the morning's quality control reports and the daily production spreadsheets, I sat at my desk . . . depressed. I felt dead inside.

I looked around my office, at all the Superman posters and memorabilia. I stared at the statue on my desk, of Clark Kent ripping open his shirt to show the famous S, as I replayed my behavior of the past week. I had screamed at Michelle about everything I try to do, and she had looked at me like I just didn't get it. I felt trapped by this image of myself. *I wanted to be this super guy, but I'm a failure.* My thoughts grew darker and darker until Bev, my secretary, paged me.

"Good morning, Adam."

"Good morning, Bev."

"I have your dad on line one."

Of course you do. "I'll take it. Thank you."

I pushed the button for line one. "Hi, Dad! How are you?" I sounded almost chipper.

"Hey there, pal. I'm good. Listen, I'm going to take the day off today. Your uncle Peter is in town. I want to show him my new horse, and we're going to hang out. Can you cover all my calls?"

"Of course. No problem."

"Thanks. Love you, pal."

"I love you, too."

Much later, my father explained the truth about his absence: His heart had been broken. As he had thought about my intervention, which would take place at his house later that day, he had known that he couldn't put on an act around me all day. He would tell me, "I just couldn't, son. I love you too damn much."

For the rest of the morning, I took care of all our business calls, e-mails, and meetings, checked the yarn inventory, and reviewed the schedules. During my lunch hour, I hit the gym

hard, trying to sweat out toxins and make sure I looked as perfect as possible.

Later that day, I got the call from Michelle.

"Hi, honey. What's up?" I tried to pretend that the past few days hadn't taken place.

"Can you meet me at your folks' after work? They want to see the baby. Maybe we'll join them for dinner."

"Sure. Sounds great."

On my way to my parents' house, I popped two Xanax. I wanted to be relaxed in front of them after such a horrific week. I knew that if I became emotionally uncomfortable, my eyes would wander toward their bar. *Better to keep calm.* My thoughts jumped around. *I can't believe Michelle is comfortable seeing my parents after our fight . . . Well, I guess they want to see Sloan. Gaga would have eaten her up. . . . I wonder how Poppa's doing. . . . What weight training should I do tomorrow? I'm so over all the booze and pills. . . . I want to be the best father ever.*

After parking in front of my parents' house, I sat there and took a deep breath. That eerie feeling from the night before, as if I had been blindfolded and placed in an obstacle course, scared and disoriented, came back. I had a mild panic attack. But I took another deep breath. *C'mon, Adam. Relax. It's all in your head.*

I got out of the car and walked to the front door. I rang the doorbell as knots tightened in my stomach. *What the hell is wrong with me?* Time seemed to stand still, as if I'd been waiting outside for hours.

But only ten seconds later, Marta, my parents' housekeeper, opened the door. She stood there, smiling, all four feet eleven inches of her. "Come on in, honey," she said in her Honduran accent.

I didn't think anything of it, because she had answered the door plenty of times. But then she grabbed my hand, and the vibes felt weird. *Why is she holding my hand? Something is up.* I stepped in and gave her a hug and kiss.

"Hi, Marta. How are you? Are Michelle and the baby here?"

"Yes, in the living room." She moved her grip to my upper arm and led me down the hallway to the living room as if I'd never been there before and was lost. *Why is she holding my arm? What's going on?* As we walked down the hallway, my stomach was full of butterflies. I felt as if I was walking on a treadmill—walking and walking yet unable to reach the living room only ten feet away.

My mother greeted me in the hallway. She looked gorgeous, as she always does. She'd modeled in Israel before moving to the United States. She had come here on a vacation to raise her spirits, because her father, Moshe Mashiah, had passed away. A few days into her vacation, she had met my father. It had been love at first sight. On their first date, they had needed a Hebrew–English dictionary to communicate. (They still have that very dictionary.) They could barely hold a conversation, yet they spoke the language of love. My mother stayed on in the United States, and my Dad proposed one month after that first date. They were married three months later.

I realized that my mother was biting her lip. Then I saw that a strange man who I'd never met was following her.

A nervous wreck, my mother tried to introduce us. "Hi, baby. This is . . . umm . . . well, this . . . uhh." As she stumbled

over her words, I put on a smile and looked the man in the eyes.

"Hi, Adam. I'm Michael Walsh," he said in a Boston accent. He reached out his right hand. "I'm an interventionist." He spoke slowly.

"Hello, Michael." I extended my right arm to shake his hand. "I'm Adam Jablin." *What's an interventionist?* I wondered.

The weird thing is that I liked Michael right away. There was something in the way he carried himself. He was a strong man, but he was calm and compassionate. He didn't seem threatening. About five feet eleven inches tall, he reminded me of Kevin Costner. I could see that he took care of himself. He looked like a retired athlete. He appeared to be just a bit older than me—late thirties or early forties, I guessed.

He continued, "Everyone is here today because they love you. This family *really* loves you, Adam. Please listen to what they have to say. I'll be here for you if you need me." His statement was short and sweet, but what confused me was that last line, "I'll be here for you if you need me." Michael seemed to be there for my family, not for me. But I nodded, pretending that I understood. Somehow, I guess Michael's statement had helped. I did feel safe.

I walked into the living room and saw some of my family sitting on the couches. Frightened, I looked at everyone and tried to grin casually. I felt a chill in the air.

They were sitting on two couches that faced each other with a coffee table in between. The setting was intimate, and everyone could see one another. Scott, my brother-in-law, sat at the far left end of one couch. On his right sat Tori, his wife and Michelle's sister. On the opposite couch, Michelle waited impatiently. Each couch had an extra spot—probably one for my mother and one for Michael Walsh, since they had greeted me in the hallway. I looked around at everyone's faces. You could have heard a pin drop.

Scott was one of my favorite people in the world. We considered each other brothers. Voted the favorite morning meteorologist in South Florida, on NBC 5's news broadcast, Scott was a local celebrity. Each weekday, when Al Roker said, "And now here's what's going on in your neck of the woods," it cut to Scott. He played a major role in everyone's lives in South Florida after the hurricanes. Every time I saw him on TV, I was filled with pride. He's well built by genetics, with wide shoulders and a broad back—He's *GQ* handsome. But at that moment he seemed ill at ease, and concern was written on his face.

Tori was holding Scott's hand in her left hand and a piece of paper in her right hand. She was another of my all-time favorite people. Tori and I shared the same sense of humor, and she was the big sister I'd never had. Honesty and directness were her specialties. Michelle and she looked almost identical. I had a little game in which every time we saw each other, I had to tell her how hot she was. It was play flirting. But hey, it was true. She was a beautiful brunette with dark-brown eyes and olive skin. She was about five feet two inches tall and had a knockout figure. When Tori walked by, guys spilled their drinks. In this moment, however, she looked sad and nervous, and I wondered what that piece of paper was about.

I turned to Michelle. When our eyes met, it was as if everyone else in the room vanished. We'd weathered five

years of ups and downs. I always knew that the only thing that got in our way was my extreme lifestyle. Always having to have one more drink, one more pill, one more workout, one more coffee, one more everything, I pushed life to the limits.

Today, she wore a simple, white T-shirt and blue jeans. She looked tired, like Bill Murray in Groundhog Day after he'd repeated the same hellish day dozens of times. She didn't look nervous like the others, though. She looked determined. She was a woman protecting herself, a woman who'd had enough. She patted the seat, gesturing me to sit down next to her.

I walked toward her slowly. With each step, I became more scared of how whatever this was would play out.

When I said, "Hi, honey," my voice cracked.

Michelle again tapped the spot next to her on the couch, signaling for me to sit there. I did.

She grabbed my hand. "Baby, we had to do this for you. This is as serious as it can get. Please listen. Listen to every word. You're sick—very sick—but. . . ." She seemed to consider her words. "I still want to be married to you. Just, please listen."

I felt cornered. I looked at Michelle and then down at the floor. I was ready to listen. I wanted my nightmare to be over.

Everyone except my mother stayed seated; she paced. I could feel the intensity of the emotions in the room. My family seemed scared of how I'd react to this intervention. I was certainly afraid of the unknown. I had no idea what to expect. We were all waiting for it to unfold.

As I sat in silence, a weird sensation came over me. A rush of well-being took over my body and kicked the nervousness and panic out of my soul. It was much more calming than any effect from a drink or sedative. A clear, still voice in my head told me, *Everything's going to be okay.* I became conscious of love that everyone in the room had for me. I could see them in their purity. I realized their true value—not as the labels of wife, mother, and so on, but on a much deeper level—their core, their hearts, and their love. I felt as if I was inside my body yet simultaneously watching from above, like another dimension. All the pieces of my life came together in that one second. Flashbacks of all the stages of my life rushed through my mind. My five senses pulsed, and I grew more and more alert.

"Adam."

I turned my head toward Michael Walsh.

"Do you know what this is?"

I knew that lately I hadn't been myself and that my entire family was worried sick about me, but I didn't know how this meeting would go. I shrugged.

"Adam, everyone in this room is here because they love you. They are very worried about you." He paused. "I've asked each member of your family to prepare a letter. What they have to say is important, and it's critical that you listen."

"Okay." I nodded. Although still serene, I was growing eager to hear what my family had to say. Michelle gripped my hand, both of our palms sweaty. Michael maintained direct eye contact with me. His eyes softened, and his body language shifted from a protective stance to a relaxed stance.

"Adam, if you have any questions or need to say anything, please let me know." I felt as if a coach had told me what to

be prepared for, slapped me on the back, and then sent me into the game.

My mother went first. Shaky, she walked toward me and sat on an ottoman in front of me. She grabbed my free hand and cradled it tightly in both of hers. My heart broke. From the corner of my eye, I saw Scott. Teary, he nodded his head. I interpreted that as him signaling to me, *You can do this, Adam.* That simple nod comforted me.

Michelle squeezed my other hand in reassurance. Although I knew that everyone loved me, I could feel her love as the strongest and most courageous. It was the love of a leader willing to go to any length in desperate times. I looked at her and noticed on her lap what must be a letter—a letter I'd be most anxious to hear.

My mother didn't have a letter prepared. She said that she just hadn't been able to write down the words; just thinking about what she wanted to say had hurt too much. She thought I'd be angry and upset with her for hosting the intervention. As my mother, she felt responsible for my situation. *A mother's love!*

"Addy," she said in her Israeli accent. "Addy, do not be mad at me, baby. I love you with all my heart. You are the best. Lately, honey, when we talk, you seem so confused . . . angry . . . not yourself." She took a deep breath and started to cry. "You and I, we are sensitive people. We are not strong like Daddy. Anything can hurt us. We care about others more than we care about ourselves. You seem so lost, baby. I just want you to get better. You try to do everything for everyone. You cannot. You cannot make everyone happy! You are not

Superman! And now you have Sloan. . . . Please accept this help we are offering you today. I love you."

I squeezed my mother's hand and shook my head. "Mom, please. I'm not angry with you at all. I'm relieved, in a way. Please don't cry. Everything will be all right." I wanted to make this easier on her. "I love you, Mom."

Michael nodded at Scott, who looked at me and then down at his letter.

"Bro, I love you. It's killing me to do this right now. You're the best brother I ever could have asked for. We have a special bond and special sayings. My sons, the boys . . . you're their uncle or, as they say, shmuncle. They love you *sooo* much. I see how hard you always try, bro, how you always want everyone to get along and be happy." He paused and looked up at me. Sadness crept over his face. "But I know you've lied to me. I know you haven't been honest with me all the time. I've smelled alcohol on your breath when you've come over to our house. This isn't my first rodeo. I have a brother with a substance-abuse problem. I know when you've been drinking or you're high on something. I know about your extreme working out. I know and have known more than you think. I love you, bro, and I want you to get help."

He knows. He knows I sneak drinks and pills. And he's known the whole time. Oh, man! I've let him down. The hurt sank in. All the damned lying and . . . everyone knew. It killed me hearing the pain in their voices, seeing the tears in their eyes, knowing I'd caused heartache.

Tori, Michelle's sister, spoke next. "Adam, I love you very much. I admire how you take care of your family. I love your childlike sense of humor and your carefree spirit." She dabbed

at her eyes. "But I've never seen you upset, and that concerns me." She took a breath and started to cry, and then the truth came out. "Adam, you're sick. Not long ago, you apologized for driving with my child, your nephew, in your car after you'd been drinking." The memory came back and hit me like a tidal wave. *I did! Oh, my God. What's wrong with me?*

"I've seen you getting worse. Much more hungover and tired on our family days together. Or the opposite, with off-the-wall energy that scares me. I love you so much, Adam. I'm asking you to please get help."

My head sank. I couldn't believe I'd caused this. I felt so ashamed.

When it was finally Michelle's turn, chills shivered down my spine. My heart started to beat faster, and I got goose bumps all over my arms. I knew she'd been the driving force behind this intervention. I knew I'd hurt her. I focused especially hard on listening to her. She took her hands gently off mine, opened her letter, and looked down at it.

I was waiting for her to point her finger at me, reprimand me, and tell me what a bad person and husband I was. Instead, she spoke about how we had fallen for each other and how I made her laugh. Wiping tears from her eyes, she said, "I'm so grateful that you're such a family man and a loyal person." My pride melted away. She had disarmed me. Only then did she describe my drinking, drugging, and lies.

"Adam, remember when you came home drunk and told me some crazy story that your employees bought you a bottle of tequila and a piñata? It never happened. You were drinking alone in your office. No piñata. Or when I was eight months pregnant with Sloan, and I caught you drinking vodka from a water bottle? You wouldn't tell me the truth. You swore it wasn't alcohol. I almost took a swig of it with our baby in my stomach." I recoiled in humiliation.

Something was happening inside me. I felt a change, a surrender of some sort. Michelle was simply stating the facts of what had happened and the effects of my behavior. She wasn't beating me. "The times when I was driving home from an evening out and you were passed out snoring in the car? Or all the pills and empty bottles I've found over the years. . . ." Feelings of guilt and shame washed over me. But they were followed by a deep sense of inspiration and motivation to change. *I've caused your suffering. I've lied constantly. I've put you through hell.* I was mortified.

"Sloan, Adam. I have to protect our baby girl. She's the most important, and she deserves better."

When she had finished, the room became silent.

Loving, honest, and direct, her words had been felt in every cell of my body. I looked at her. I was defeated. "I'm sorry, baby. I'm so sorry."

"Adam, right now I'm not asking you to apologize. I'm asking you to get help. Get help now, or we're through."

That sunk in—quickly. I wanted my wife. I wanted my daughter. I nodded. I understood. I was disgraced, but I was also relieved. I had made it through the letters. I looked at Michael.

"Your family loves you, Adam, with all their hearts. And because of their love and concern, they contacted me." Michael readjusted himself on the couch. He leaned forward, elbows and forearms on his lap and hands clenched. "Adam, I share your story. I worked for Anheuser-Busch. I moved up

the success chain very quickly. I worked hard, and I partied even harder. As time went on, I realized I didn't like my job. I drank more and more. I tried to make everyone happy: my bosses, coworkers, customers. You know." *Yeah, I understood completely.* "I tried to make my father proud. All that stuff. When your family told me your story, I just couldn't believe it. I've done a lot of these interventions, but I had yet to hear my own story. Nobody has lived quite the same life as mine. You, Adam . . . you and I are the same. " He told me about how he'd become an empty shell. His family and friends had performed an intervention on him. "It was the best thing that ever happened to me," he said. He sat completely upright, and a huge smile burst onto his face. "Adam, your family has reserved a bed for you in the same rehab center I went to—the Hanley Center. I can say proudly that it was the best experience of my life."

My jaw dropped. "Rehab?" I thought of all the celebrities who I'd heard had entered rehab. *I'm one of those people?*

"It consists of a ten-day evaluation followed by an additional eighteen days, if necessary."

Ten days plus eighteen days is . . . twenty-eight days. Twenty-eight days? No way! I can't be away from my family and responsibilities for twenty-eight days!

"Michael, look. . . . I'd do twenty-eight days, but I can't. I have a daughter, a seven-month-old baby. I have a career. My family. I've never been away from them for longer than a week. Who will take care of everything? Ten days, sure, I can do that. But twenty-eight days? There's just no way, man."

Michael looked me in the eyes. He pushed himself forward on the couch, inching closer to me. His voice remained steady. "Adam, is twenty-eight days too long to save the rest of your life? It's nothing, a drop in the bucket. Michelle, with the support of the family, will take care of Sloan. Your dad will watch the business. Everything will be fine."

What? Everything will be fine? How can that be? This was a lot to take in. The shock and worry returned . . . quickly. I spoke faster. My palms got sweaty, and I fidgeted in my seat. I couldn't process all that Michael had thrown at me, but I did trust him. *How could I just vanish from my life for that long?* I didn't know how to comprehend that I could be away for twenty-eight days. I swallowed hard, uncomfortable and overwhelmed. *A cocktail would be good right now.* I didn't want to imagine myself in this situation, so I focused my thoughts on everyone else.

"What will we tell everyone? My friends? Where will you say I am?"

Michelle jumped in. "Adam, I'll tell them you had to go away on business. You had to leave and take care of the New Hampshire plant. Nobody will know."

Not bad. "Okay. What about work?"

"Your dad will tell them you and I needed a little time with the baby. You never take time off, and we never go away."

Hmm? I guess they'll go for that. We did just have the baby. And she's right—I never take vacation. I rubbed my upper lip and chin with one hand as if stroking an invisible goatee. I thought for a moment. "What's the place like? Do they have a gym?"

The room burst into laughter. I realized that everyone must have been waiting for that question.

"Your mom and I visited it. It's beautiful, and it has a gym," Michelle said.

Michael jumped in. "Adam, the grounds are immaculate, serene, relaxing. Hanley is secluded and near the beach. The property was created to provide peace and comfort for people going through recovery. There are butterflies everywhere. They have a pool, a big field, a volleyball court, and a beautiful running track around a pond. Four times around is a mile. I remember that one. There's a basketball court, too." He smiled. I was loosening up, and he probably could tell that, since he'd been in my shoes before. He continued reeling me in. "I understand you eat a strict diet. You'll love the healthy menu they have. You can get anything plain, and they'll stock the fridge in your unit with fresh fruits and vegetables."

"Tuna fish?" I asked. "You know, for the protein? Can I get canned tuna throughout the day?"

More laughter from the others.

"All the tuna you can eat," Michael said.

I sat in deep thought, looking down at my lap, for a couple more moments. *Can I really do this? Twenty-eight days—a whole month. Everyone will be suspicious.*

"Look, guys, I can do the ten days. I'm sure they'll tell me I'm fine!" I looked at Michelle. "A month away from you?" Away from Sloan! Twenty-eight days away from my little girl? No. I'd miss you guys too much." I sat back, looked down again, and shook my head again and again, thinking about the time away from them.

I truly believed that the people at the rehab center would determine I was totally normal. *I'm really not that bad. In ten days they'll see that. They'll realize that everybody else's nonsense is what stresses me out. Who wouldn't be stressed if they had my life? Everyone just needs to leave me alone a little more and do things for themselves. If anything, I just need to find a way to say no to people and speak my truth. I can't keep trying to play Superman all the time.* I needed a new way to cope and, yes, clean up my act a little bit. To drink a normal amount. *I'm just excessive.*

Michelle later told me that my family and Michael had anticipated my fear about the twenty-eight-days. They had agreed beforehand to do whatever it took to get me to check into the Hanley Center. If they had to offer a ten-day trial period, they would. They'd do anything to get me to go.

"This is really what you guys think is best?" I slowly looked around the room. Each person nodded. I looked one last time at Michelle and then glanced at Michael. "Okay, I'm in. When do I go?"

Scott pumped his fist, and everyone else sighed in relief.

Michael said with a smile, "Now. Your bags are packed, and there's a bed waiting for you." Michelle nodded.

Are you freakin' kidding me? My voice rose. "Excuse me? Now? Right now?"

Michael nodded.

I looked around in shock. The negative voice in my head took over again. "I need to say good-bye to Cookie."

Michelle assured me that she'd be fine and that dogs had no concept of time.

Frightened, I grabbed Michelle's hands. The idea of going into rehab had just became a hell of a lot more real to me. *They really think I'm sick?* I looked at Michael. "Does this mean I can never drink again?"

Michael said, "We'll see. Let's do the ten-day evaluation and take it from there."

Hey. Maybe I can drink again. Let's see what they say. I tightened my fists and bit my lower lip. "Okay. Let's go." Michelle called my dad; her parents; and my best pal, Lew into the house. Even Sloan was there, being held by my father-in-law, Allan. I'd had no idea they were waiting in the backyard the whole time.

My brother-in-law pulled me aside. "Bro, you have the biggest balls of anyone I know. Everyone else thought this would go down differently. They thought you might run out or fight. Not me. I told everyone last night, 'My bro will take it like a man. My bro will do what's right.'"

His words meant the world to me. To hear somebody I looked up to believe in me like that inspired me to try. That moment became one of my driving motivations during my time in treatment.

I said my good-byes to everyone. In typical "hero" fashion, I tried to make it easy on them. They said they were proud of me and told me to just get better. I'll never forget what my mother-in-law said: "You know, Adam, when we met Michael, I couldn't stop thinking how good you would be at his job. You're so amazing with people. You may do this kind of work one day. My money is on you, Adam. I know you can beat this thing."

I took Sloan to another room. I stared at her, completely in love. As soon as we were alone, I promised her, "I'm going to get better, baby. I'm doing this for you and Mommy. You will never ever see me all messed up again!" In that moment, I was focused on doing it for them, not for me. *I'm not worth it, but they are.*

I walked to the door and beckoned for Michelle to join us. I wanted us to be a family together for a few minutes. *What have I done? How is Michelle going to do this all by herself? Man, Adam, what's wrong with you?*

Michelle read my mind. "Adam, we'll be fine. We can't be a family if you don't get better. It won't work unless you get help."

I understood. My drinking, drugging, lying, overworking, dieting, supplementing, and excessive working out in the gym would be behind me soon. I felt relief, as if my family had removed the weight of the world from my shoulders. We slowly walked back to the living room, where the family was waiting for us. Their spirits seemed high. The nightmare was finally over. I felt like Ray Liotta in the movie *Goodfellas*. "Okay, now take me to jail."

I got in the car with my parents and Michelle. We headed north, to the Hanley Center in West Palm Beach. Ashamed and scared, I couldn't make conversation. We tried to joke, but the moment was too real. I felt a huge amount of guilt. When we arrived, we received the tour. We walked into the men's unit. I stared at paintings of people having fun and holding signs that said SOBER PARADE. *Sober parade? What is this place? I can't believe this is happening to me!*

We walked around the beautiful grounds, to the gym, which they hoped would calm me. I found it hard to take in anything, despite the tranquil surroundings. I made one observation: The place reminded me of summer camp.

I triple checked that I would be able to eat healthy there. They hadn't lied about that. In fact, the menu blew my mind. The fitness menu even reported the protein, fat, carbohydrates,

and calories of every item. I slowly checked off my mental list of necessities: gym, protein, raw vegetables, and fresh fruit. We walked over to the detox unit to check me in.

"Name, sir?"

"Adam Jablin."

"Ah, yes, Mr. Adam Jablin. We've been expecting you."

A CALL TO ACTION

- I rationalized my alcoholism and addictions. We see that clear as day in this chapter during my intervention. What are some of your excuses not to change certain behaviors?
- Did you ever feel like me in Chapter 4—scared and full of anxiety? It's therapeutic to write these feelings down on a piece of paper. Get that journal out again and write down all those things that are making you troubled.

CHAPTER 5

DETOX

AFTER MY FAMILY HAD LEFT, a pretty woman in her early thirties who had long, blond hair, blue eyes, and an endearing smile arrived to greet me in the waiting room. She wore a streamlined, black, feminine business suit and conducted herself professionally, from her upright posture to her gracious mannerisms. "Hi Adam, my name is Jennifer. I'm your case manager here at the Hanley Center."

We shook hands in silence. I tried to smile, but I was frozen.

"Let's get you settled. Please follow me to your room in the detox unit."

I plodded wearily behind her with my head bowed in shame. As we walked down the fluorescent-lighted hallway, I noticed that she was cradling in her left arm a thick, light-blue binder labeled with my name in big, bold, black ink and a bar-coded patient number. I felt like a criminal being booked into prison and escorted to my cell.

When we reached a giant wooden door, Jennifer turned around. "This is the detox center." She explained that Kat, the head nurse on the night shift, was expecting us, and then she slowly opened the door.

"Hello, y'all!" Kat, a tall black woman with red, curly hair that went all the way down her back and red glasses that matched her hair, pranced toward us in her blue nurse's uniform. "Well, this must be Adam," she continued in a Southern drawl. Her happiness irked me, and I felt like a beaten man.

Jennifer and Kat quickly began speaking in a recovery-and-addiction language that was completely foreign to me, and I tuned them out. I studied my surroundings. The bland, beige room was dully lighted. There were two couches and a 50-inch TV in the center of the room. Beyond the TV, the nurses' station was separated into two sections; one side contained a desk where two nurses watched blood-pressure monitors. Four nurses worked at the pharmacy on the other side, which was loaded with boxes, compartments, dispensers, bottles, tubes, syringes, jars filled with liquids, pills of every shape, size, and color, and ointments and creams. It looked as if they'd squeezed the supplies from a whole hospital into a 20 × 20 ft. room. Each nurse stood by a computer in a position of readiness.

I looked back at Jennifer and Kat, who were staring at me patiently, apparently waiting for me to respond.

"Do you understand?" Kat asked me.

"I'm sorry, ma'am. Did you ask me something?"

"Ma'am? Good manners. I like that. Did you catch what I said about your bag?"

In a frenzy, I tried to get my bearings. "Oh, my God. I'm sorry. I have a lot on my mind. I just said good-bye to my wife and daughter. An hour ago, I was in an intervention." I shook my head. "I'm terribly sorry. What did you say?"

"Don't apologize, darlin'," Kat said in her sweet Southern tone. "It's all going to be okay. I met your wife and daughter. That's one beautiful family you got there, and they love you very much. You're in the right place." The thought of my family being okay with me being in the detox center depressed me.

"I know you're fearful, but this is a life-changing experience. You have a sweet heart, darlin'. People here scream at us, or much worse." I had no idea what she was talking about. I was trying to focus, but I was a nervous wreck.

Kat continued, "I was just saying that we'll be inspecting your bag while you and Jennifer fill out your patient information and admissions paperwork in your room."

That didn't make sense to me. I wasn't in an airport, and I didn't own any weapons. "Check my bag? For what? I didn't even pack it. My wife packed it while I was at work."

"For drugs and alcohol, darlin'. Don't take it personally. It's mandatory."

"Drugs and alcohol? Isn't the whole idea of coming to this place to get away from that? Why would anyone check into rehab and bring drugs and alcohol?"

Kat's gaze was sharp and intense. "You'd be surprised. We've had people trying to sneak in every drug you can imagine. Mouthwash and colognes are no-nos, too."

"Why?"

"People try to drink them."

"What? You have to be joking!" *Sickos.* I'd hidden alcohol in secret places and drunk warm booze straight out of the bottle and beer before it had been refrigerated, but—mouthwash and cologne? Hearing that unnerved me, and I thought that Michael Walsh and my loved ones had made a mistake in sending me here. *I'm not that bad!*

"I like you, Adam," Kat said. "You're innocent and naïve. Your family caught you early. You should thank your lucky stars."

I felt like a five-year-old about to go on an enormous, terrifying roller coaster. *Get me off this ride! I want to go home!*

Kat pointed toward her left. "Adam, you see that room over there, number twelve? That will be your private room just for tonight. Tomorrow we'll take you down to the men's unit. You'll be living in a community of people who are going through exactly what you are."

My eyes widened, and I bit my lip.

"Don't worry, darlin'," she said. "It's much better down there."

I reached down to pick up my bag, but Kat quickly reminded me, "Adam, please leave your bag here for inspection, and fill out the forms on the desk in your room."

"Um, okay. No problem."

I entered the bedroom, feeling dizzy and lost. The 12 × 10 ft. white-walled room held one cot, a desk covered in books, and a small bathroom. It reminded me of Gaga's room in the hospital. I looked up at the ceiling in desperation.

Jennifer and I diligently reviewed all the paperwork and filled out the ones for admissions, financial arrangements, liability release, and insurance. I skimmed the seven-page

document titled "Patient Expectations." I looked over a sample schedule for the week, in which every hour of the day was accounted for: 6:30 AM meditation, 7:10 AM breakfast, 8:30 AM study time, 9:15 AM lecture, 10:15 AM therapy, 11:35 AM lunch, 12:15 PM study time, 1:30 PM lecture, 2:20 PM wellness, 3:30 PM first-step group, 5:00 PM dinner, 5:45 PM leisure education, 7:00 PM lecture, 8:00 PM high-low, and 8:30–10:00 PM outside AA meeting. *Whoa!*

I looked over the dress code: "Shoes and shirts must be worn at all times outside your bedroom; no short shorts, mesh shirts, or tank tops; bathing suits must be on and fastened in the pool area; undergarments must be worn at all times; clothing cannot advertise alcohol, drugs, or sex or be disrespectful to others." The room inspection sheet followed. "All rooms are to be inspected each morning at 9:00 AM by the peer leadership group. The inspection sheet is to be returned to the supervisor by 9:10 AM." *This place doesn't mess around. It's like the military.* I skimmed the checklist: bed neatly made, desk and living area clean, towels hung, new towels available in the linen closet, and sheets put inside the pillowcase and placed at the foot of the bed each Friday morning so that they can be replaced. *What the hell have I gotten myself into?*

There were pages and pages of materials and rules. I flipped to the page that was titled, in big, black, underlined, bold font, "Center for Men Recovery Unit's Expectations." I read the first line: "Finish the nineteen-page Assessment Guide provided to you by CMR CD TECH before attending activities." The next line said, "Patients are expected to participate in all scheduled activities. Catnaps are not permitted during the therapeutic day, even during personal time.

Attend all minigroups as assigned." That was followed by "All patients MUST share their story, including their history of use and abuse of chemicals, within the first ten days of treatment." *My story?* The list of expectations went on and on. The last thing to catch my eye was "Peer leaders serve as liaisons to the staff. Peer leaders are elected by the staff randomly every seven to twenty-one days, to provide unity and harmonious action."

I shook my head in disbelief. *What happened to me? How did I let things get this far?* I looked at a stack of books on the desk: *Alcoholics Anonymous, Twelve Steps and Twelve Traditions, Twenty-Four Hours a Day, Narcotics Anonymous, It Works: How and Why.* My stomach turned. *Am I an alcoholic?*

Knock, knock, knock. I turned around and saw Kat and a sharply dressed man standing in the doorway.

"Hi, Adam. Me again," Kat said. "I have a special visitor for you. He stayed late tonight just to meet you. This is Ben Harrison."

Ben walked through the door. He took one look at me and then stuck out his hand.

"Hi, Adam. I'm in charge of the men's unit. I helped your wife, Michelle, and your mother get you in here. And I met your gorgeous daughter." He then looked at Jennifer. "Hi, Jen." Something about his Boston accent and chill vibe helped me to feel somewhat human again. I smiled, and we shook hands.

"You met Michelle? You saw Sloan and my mother?"

"Yeah, man. Yesterday. They love you so much. We're gonna get you better here. I promised them I'd take care of you. They have a special way about them, and they got right to my heart. You're a lucky man."

I smiled, but I was still full of shame. "I know."

"What are you doing there?" He pointed at the desktop.

I shrugged, feeling overwhelmed. "Just filling out the paperwork and reviewing all this material."

"Nah. Come with me, man. Let me bring you down to the men's unit to meet the guys. And don't let that stuff fool you. You read that by yourself, you're gonna think you entered the army." He chuckled. "Jen, can I borrow Adam?"

Jennifer agreed and then patted me on the back, reassuring me that I was in the right place. "Adam, I'm three years sober, and there's nothing wrong with admitting you need help."

That floored me. Jennifer seemed so polished, and businesslike. I couldn't believe she was an alcoholic or addict. She was nothing like the people I'd seen in the movies *New Jack City* and *Leaving Las Vegas.*

She continued ". . . and there is no better place to get help than the Hanley Center."

When I stood up, Kat interjected. "Adam, before I let you go off with Ben, we need to know what you're coming off of."

"Coming off of?"

"Yes, what's in your system right now and what's your drug of choice."

I sat back down. *Drug of choice? Well, for a good time, I love to drink. Before I go to the gym, I like a strong stimulant like ephedrine with coffee. Lately, I've enjoyed working out on Percocet and Vicodin so that I can't feel my injuries. I love Xanax to chill me out, Ambien to sleep, and Zoloft for anxiety. What do I tell them? Do fitness supplements count?* "It depends on the time of day," I said.

Ben, Jennifer. and Kat laughed hysterically. I didn't see the humor in what I'd said, but they laughed on and on. "Ha ha ha! Adam, you're too much. Kat, we've got a good one here. Matters what time of the day it is. Oh, man. I'm gonna love you!"

I smiled, unsure what to say. Kat asked, "Adam, when was the last time you took a drink?"

I thought about drinking the beer at 1:45 AM last night to get back to sleep. "Yesterday," I said.

"And a drug?"

Wanting to appear healthier than I was, I considered not being honest. But I shook my head and decided to let it all out of the bag. "I took a Xanax today and a few yesterday. I'm on Zoloft. I take a thermogenic energy supplement before I work out. I popped some painkillers—Vicodins and Percocets."

"How many?"

"Honestly, I have no clue. Too many."

"Okay. That's all we need for now. Thank you, Adam. Ben, he's all yours."

Ben and I walked down the hallway, exited the medical facility, and then slowly followed the beautifully lighted outdoor path. I heard people laughing and the sound of running water from the fountains in the background. The grounds looked well groomed. I closed my eyes and sighed, deeply relieved to be out of the detox center. We passed the cafeteria that was attached to the psychiatric building on our right and a beautiful garden on the left. A little farther along, we passed the chronic pain, experiential therapy, and other recovery buildings. I was impressed with how serene and

clean the campus was. Then we passed the women's unit. A group of girls muttered and giggled as they followed me with their eyes. Behind us, a young girl's voice called out, "Hey there, hot stuff!"

Ben looked at me and spoke casually but sternly. "Adam, don't respond. There is absolutely no fraternizing. I don't care what age the woman is. We have a zero-tolerance policy."

"Don't worry. I'm in love with Michelle."

"I'm not worried about you. I'm worried about them interfering with your program." *Program?* Ben gave the girls a dirty look. "Your body is going to be the talk of the women's unit."

"Ben, I have absolutely no clue what you're talking about." *Fraternizing? My program?*

We continued our walk, and he gave me great advice. "Adam, if you want this to work, if you want this to really take, you need to keep an open mind and to be willing to try. We'll teach you how to be sober. Both Hanley and the twelve-step programs are spiritually based."

That one line eased my mind. I thought about my enormous collection of self-help, religious, and new age books in my office and my home.

"We also offer acupuncture, massages, physical therapy, aqua therapy, and a slew of wellness activities, so you'll be comfortable here." Ben winked as he flexed his bicep. When we reach the next building, Ben said, "Ah, we're here—the Center for Men's Recovery."

We walked inside. The men's unit's lounge was buzzing. The guys appeared to be having a blast. I noticed a few guys painting and making collages. Two men were sitting on a couch in the far corner, jamming on guitars, while several others were having a conversation. Five or six men were watching ESPN on a flat-screen TV that was mounted on the far wall. Everyone was dressed casually and comfortably, in shorts, T-shirts, and flip-flops. A feeling of tranquility filled the air.

Ben shouted, "Boys, listen up! This is Adam. He's gonna spend tonight in detox, but he'll be down here first thing in the morning. Can I get someone to be his buddy?"

A young guy wearing flip-flops, khaki shorts, and a white Florida Gators T-shirt popped up from his chair and smiled at me. His face was lean, and he had tightly cropped, light-brown hair. "I will."

"Thanks, Grant. That's perfect, because tomorrow Adam will be your roommate."

Grant winked at me. Then all the guys stopped what they were doing to introduce themselves. One by one, they met me with a handshake or fist bump. There were about twenty-five guys in all.

An announcement sounded from the loudspeaker: "High-low in five minutes! Come one; come all!"

I walked over to Grant. "Thanks for putting your hand up."

"Don't mention it. You'll be doing the same soon. We work as a team here. We're all here for the same thing, more or less. What's your drug of choice?"

"You're the second person to ask me that today. I still don't know how to answer. I love to drink, and I take prescription meds and supplements."

He looked me up and down. "Steroids?"

"No, never. Funny, huh? If it makes me feel good and have fun, I'm all for it, but I won't touch anything for performance enhancement, like steroids or growth hormones."

"I hear ya. That's not so weird. You'll hear weird things in here. Mine's alcohol and cocaine."

"I take it this is normal conversation here?"

"Yeah. After a couple days, everyone will know your story. Don't sweat it. You should stick around here for high-low."

"Anything to keep me away from detox."

Grant laughed. "Detox sucks. Don't worry, though. Tonight is nothing like the rest of your stay."

"What's high-low?"

"We gather around and share our highs and lows of the day. A high can be something like you got a call from your lady. A low can be you hated group."

"Group?"

Grant smiled and patted my back. "Don't worry, man. You'll get the hang of it. Just follow us. We're like bees working in a beehive. This place keeps you busy, and everything flows." I was certain that he and everyone else could tell that I wanted to jump out of my skin.

We all gathered around, and Bruce, the peer leader for the week, stood in front holding a clipboard. Bruce was a young kid, probably about twenty-two years old. He was small in stature, with a thin, well-defined body. His arms were covered in tattoos: tribal bands, a yin-yang symbol, and one in Chinese lettering that I would later learn said, "I am, therefore I am." His dark hair hung down to his shoulders. He had a yogi–surfer look. Around his neck, he wore the peer leader necklace—a rope with a walrus tooth on it.

"Okay, guys. Let's get this going, starting with the new guy," Bruce glanced at me. "So, Muscles." It was a nickname I'd received before. "What was your high of the day?" He raised one eyebrow. I felt as if a spotlight was shining on me. Everyone in the room, who I had met only three minutes earlier, was staring at me.

"I guess my high is that my family loves me enough to have an intervention for me and send me to rehab."

Everyone chuckled.

"And the low?" Bruce asked.

"That my family loves me enough to have an intervention for me and send me to rehab."

More laughter. I looked around. They weren't laughing at my expense. They seemed to know exactly how I felt. I listened to everyone's high and low, but I couldn't escape my own anxiety. Thoughts of Michelle and Sloan flashed in my head. I couldn't concentrate.

After high-low, Grant and another patient, Tony, walked me back to detox. Tony was about six feet five inches tall, weighed in at about two hundred and forty pounds, and looked to be about my father's age. He wore a black Hell's Angels T-shirt and a fancy platinum Rolex with diamonds. He put his arm around my shoulder. "Listen here, Muscles. This place is a blast. Ya'll learn to like it here. I've been here forty days, and I'm signing up for more."

My eyes jumped out of their sockets, and I stopped in my tracks. "Forty days? Why? Guys, I plan on only being here for ten."

They laughed. "Ten? Ya kidding? Nobody comes in for ten!" Tony said.

Grant shook his head in disbelief.

Tony continued, "Look, kid, don't tell anyone I told ya so, but that's some line of BS they sold ya to get ya in here. Don't worry about it! This ain't like prison. Trust me!"

I looked at Grant.

He nodded slightly and stared into my eyes. I got the message—Tony knew what he was talking about.

"Prison?" I asked.

"Yeah, prison." Tony looked serious. "I did eight years in the pen."

"You mind me asking for what, Tony?" My head was spinning.

"Nah, I don't mind. I worked for the Gambino family under Gotti. Not his son, mind you, the original. I wouldn't rat. That's all I'll say about it."

I liked Tony. He had what I respected most in other people and in myself: loyalty. "No kidding?"

"Yeah. Ya'll hear my story. I made a clean break with them and found my second family." He pointed to his shirt.

"You're with the Hell's Angels?" *Where have they put me?*

"Yeah, kid. We'll share stories. I'll make sure I tell ya mine on ya day eleven." He chuckled. "We'll go fishing or something." His sarcasm sent my heart down to my stomach.

When I returned to my temporary room, back in detox, I felt dirty and uncomfortable. I looked at my open suitcase on the bed. I took out my toiletry bag and headed to the shower. Under the warm stream of water I thought about the fight I'd had with Michelle a week earlier. My angry feelings from then felt vague and removed from this reality; I couldn't recall why I'd gotten so upset. Then I replayed the intervention and my family's letters asking me to get help. I cried, trying not to make a sound, but this was no regular cry. Every bit of shame and guilt rose in my chest and throat and came out as anguish and pain. I hit my stomach, but that didn't do any good. "God, I know you know I've been looking for you a long time. I could really use your help right now. Please." I sat in the shower for another five minutes until my emotions had subsided somewhat, then I added, "And tell Gaga I love her."

I found my favorite sweats in the suitcase Michelle had packed for me. As I put on the sweatpants and sweatshirt, more tears came out. I couldn't control my crying, and I no longer cared. If there was ever a good time to cry, that was it.

"Knock, knock!" Despite Kat's cheery voice, I was alarmed. *What now?*

With bloodshot eyes and tears rolling down my face, I turned around and opened the door. I tried to speak, but I couldn't. I squinted hard, and two big, hot tears fell. I nodded my head in shame, forced a fake smile, and sat on the bed.

Kat entered the room and then sat down next to me on the bed and put her arm around my shoulders. "Adam, darlin', I know this is tough. Your family wants what's best for you. They want you to get better. You should hear how they talked about you. I actually thought you might be Superman."

I shook my head as more tears rolled down my face. "I can't believe how I've let them down. I can't believe Michelle would still be with me. What are they going to do without me to take care of them? What if a hurricane comes? I've left my family all alone while I'm in rehab! What kind of man am I?"

"Adam, look at me, darlin'."

I looked up.

"You're a real man. Do you know how many men are out there active in their addictions? You know how many of them just don't care? You're facing your demons head on, like a man, Adam, like a man. Now, if you don't want to do it for yourself, do it for your amazing wife and your beautiful baby girl."

"I will. I will get better." I didn't realize at the time that I was admitting I was sick.

Kat stood up, handed me a tissue, and pulled a needle out of her pocket. "Okay, Adam. Do it for them. Now, just to cheer you up, I need to take some blood from you," she said with a huge, bright, sarcastic smile.

After the blood work, I sat in the chair by the desk. I looked up and grabbed *Alcoholics Anonymous.* I skimmed through the foreword as I thought, *A book written by a bunch of drunks.* Then I read the title of the first section of the book: "The Doctor's Opinion." *Hmm . . . a doctor I can trust.* As I read, a light switch came on in my head. Every word I read resonated. The doctor described men and women who were highly successful in other areas of their lives but who, when it came to alcohol "in any form," had no control whatsoever. "The action of alcohol on these chronic alcoholics is a manifestation of an allergy" and "the phenomenon of craving is limited to this class and never occurs in the average temperate drinker."

I had never thought about my strong cravings as allergic reactions. Eager to learn more from the doctor, I continued to read. "These allergic types can never safely use alcohol in any form at all; and once having formed the habit and found they cannot break it, once having lost their self-confidence, their reliance upon things human, their problems pile up on them and become astonishingly difficult to solve." *Whoa.* I thought about my recent difficulties—my drinking and popping pills like a madman while trying to accommodate everyone else. Every word from the doctor popped off the page. "The Doctor's Opinion" described my behavior to a T, which scared me to death.

I took out my photos of Michelle and Sloan. The tears quietly came back. I had to face it: *Alcohol and pills are my kryptonite.* I felt beaten and weak. My Superman ego was terminally ill. My mind raced with images of the intervention, detox, nurses, blood work, the men's unit, high-low, strangers, patient paperwork, and books about alcoholism. Getting a good night's sleep would be impossible.

What had happened to me? What seemed like a moment earlier, I'd been in my office. *Now I'm in rehab?* When I placed the family photos next to the bed, I saw a business card lying near my suitcase: MICHAEL WALSH, INTERVENTIONS, CONSULTING & MONITORING. Just a few hours earlier, Michael had said, "Adam, if you need anything, anything at all, call me. I'm the only one on the outside who knows firsthand what you'll be experiencing. I'm here for you 24/7." I closed my hand around the business card and wished I could call him to take me back home.

A CALL TO ACTION

- The rehab schedule at The Hanley Center kept us patients very busy. It focused on us getting healthy and task completion. Are there any small tasks you can complete today? Simple ones like making your bed or saying a prayer!
- In treatment, I learned the emotional game/technique called High-Low. I use this process in my life and my coaching to this day. Seeing that the day has both its high and low points can be a great introduction to finding middle ground and balance. What's your High-Low today?

CHAPTER 6

UNHEALTHY SPIRITUALITY

KAT ENTERED MY ROOM at 5:00 AM I hadn't slept a wink, and we immediately made eye contact. "More blood work," she announced.

"Is something wrong?" Jitters ran through my body. "What came back on my other test?"

"Relax, darlin'. Nothing's wrong. This is just a formality. We haven't received the results from the first test yet." She cleansed my arm and then took out a needle. I felt the brief pinch. After bandaging the tiny wound, Kat said, "Here, take these." She handed me two pills—one to detox me from alcohol and the other to detox me from the narcotics. "You'll take these for the next four days. During that time, stay out of the sun, and don't push your body."

"Can I work out lightly?" I asked frantically.

"Very lightly."

"Perfect." To me a light workout meant exercising with the same intensity but lightening the weight and increasing the number of repetitions. *Hey, I can do that for four days.*

"Darlin', whenever you want, you can head down to the men's unit. You've been cleared." Carrying a vial of my blood, Kat left the room.

By 5:30 AM, I had packed my belongings and walked to the men's unit. When I entered the lounge, I ran into a couple guys hitting the coffee machine. "Whoa! Look at the arms on this guy," I overheard one say to the other. I was wearing a sleeveless black T-shirt with the Michael Jordan Jumpman logo on the front.

"Morning, guys. Don't worry, these are an illusion," I said, looking down at my right bicep. "I'm sorry. It's been a crazy time, and I don't remember your names." The shorter, younger guy took a step forward as he stirred his coffee. He looked familiar, but I couldn't place how I knew him. About five feet six inches tall, he had brown, messy, rock 'n' roll hair, and his twenty-one-year-old baby face sported a shaggy beard. Colorful tattoos covered every inch of his visible skin, and his ears had plugs—quarter-sized earrings that nestled inside the lobes.

"Welcome, Muscles! I'm Jeremy," he said, putting his coffee down to shake my hand. I noticed a tattoo, on his inner forearm, of a guitar labeled "Stalker". I recognized the band's logo.

"Jeremy, I'm Adam." We shook hands. I squinted and pointed at his tattoo. "Bro, are you the lead singer of Stalker?"

"Yeah, man! You're only the second person to recognize me in here." He smiled.

"I love your music. I listen to *Entourage* when I'm running, and I weight train to *Into the Light*. I love the energy!"

"Thanks. While we're here, maybe you could show me a thing or two in the gym?" He pointed to his bony arms while looking at my muscled ones. "Put some meat on these bones!"

"My pleasure."

The second guy extended his hand. "Hi, Adam. Jack. I'll be one of your roommates, along with Grant and Seth." Jack was the spitting image of the actor Gary Busey. He was six feet two inches, and he had bright, blondish-white hair. He wore casual Life Is Good beachwear. From his laidback tone, I knew instantly that he'd be easy to get along with.

"Hi, Jack. Pleasure to meet you. Where exactly is our room? I'd like to put my stuff away."

He turned around and pointed down the hallway. "We're in the swamp, 'cause it has room for four people. . . . It's right around the corner, second on the left. I'd wait, though. Grant is still sleeping, and Seth . . . well, Seth never wakes up. Tell you what: After morning meditation, I'll walk you over there."

"Thanks."

"What are you in for, Muscles?" Jeremy asked.

I felt like the new inmate on the cellblock. "Alcohol and pills." The reply felt strangely comfortable leaving my mouth. "What are you guys in for?"

"Heroin and OxyContin. I love that stuff," Jeremy said sadly, looking down at the floor.

Jack replied matter-of-factly. "Mostly crack for me. I can drink with the best of them, but deep down I'm a crackhead."

Hearing the names of these hardcore narcotics made me feel better about myself. It confirmed that I'd be at Hanley for only ten days. *Heroin and crack! I definitely agree with the twenty-eight-day plan for those. Me, I'm a guy who drinks too much and pops too many pills. Yeah, I experimented a little in college and into my twenties. But hey, who hasn't? How long can I possibly be in here? Maybe I have a drinking problem, maybe I'm even an alcoholic, but I'm sure they can teach me how to drink more normal amounts. Those drugs—crack, heroin, and OxyContin—those are the ones that'll kill you.*

A few minutes went by, and eight guys showed up for morning meditation. I noticed Grant getting coffee, and I walked up to him. Something about him made me feel safe. "Morning, buddy," I said. "Where is everyone? I read last night that meditation and activities are mandatory."

Grant took a giant gulp of his coffee. "Well, Hanley is flexible, and if you want to recover you're in the right place. But, lots of slackers here. If you want to get better, do everything the staff suggests. You'll see the same guys here this morning come to all the meetings. These are the ones on the right track."

Morty, a squat, heavyset man in his forties, wearing a baggy Hawaiian shirt, long, loose shorts, and flip-flops, bopped toward us. He looked as if he'd had ten cups of coffee and a happy pill. "Hi there, friend. I'm Morty," he shouted in a twangy Southern accent. "What's shakin', bacon?" He put his hands around one of my biceps. I recognized him from last night, when he'd been wearing a loud Aloha shirt of a different color. He had yelled, "Welcome to Happy Land," when I walked into the men's unit. I would learn that Morty was a high-powered, successful attorney from Tennessee

and one of the sweetest men I had ever met. . . . And he was proudly gay.

"Hey, Morty. I'm Adam. I remember you from last night . . . just as cheerful. I think you were painting then." I looked down at his hand on my left arm and smiled.

"Did you see what I painted?" He pointed at the wall across from us. "That's my little poodle, Cha-ching, and next to him is my private wardrobe that the real world never sees."

Next to the painted dog was a bunch of brightly colored dresses. I closed my eyes, chuckled, and nodded in approval.

"And that's me, in the center, wearing the beautiful pink dress, *sober* and shopping." He looked me in the eyes and patted my back. "Oh, yeah, Hot Bod, I'm gay."

I put my arm around him. "Good to know, Morty. If you weren't, I'd be a little worried about you!" We had a good laugh at that.

My head started tripping. *Where the hell am I? Famous rock stars? Guys from the mob? Men in dresses?* That was when Bruce, the peer leader, trotted in, looking exhausted, and I heard Tony's deep, scratchy voice over the loudspeaker. "Okay, guys. Morning meditation starts in five minutes. Get up, ya lazy alcoholics and addicts. Don't make me come and drag ya butts out of bed. Meditation starts in five minutes. Repeat. Meditation in five!"

I poured myself a cup of coffee and sat on one of the three couches that were pushed together in a U shape. I took a sip and thought about Michelle and Sloan. Michelle had left me at the Hanley Center only eleven hours earlier. But I felt as if I hadn't seen them in weeks.

Everyone took his seat on the couches. They were all carrying things to read: books, pieces of paper, and magazines.

Bruce began. "Good morning, guys. My name is Bruce, and I'm an alcoholic and addict."

The gang replied in unison, "Good morning, Bruce."

He continued. "Can we please have a moment of silence followed by the Serenity Prayer?" Everyone lowered his head, closed his eyes, and sighed deeply. Ten seconds later, Bruce started, "God . . ."

Everyone except me joined in. ". . . grant me the serenity to accept the things I cannot change, the courage to change the things I can, and the wisdom to know the difference."

"Good morning again, gentlemen. I'm still Bruce and still an alcoholic and addict."

"Hi, Bruce," they all responded.

"This morning, I've chosen to read out of *Twenty-Four Hours a Day*." He flipped through the pages of the book for a couple seconds and took a sip of his coffee. "Today, July 15th. AA thought for the day: 'After we had sobered up through the AA program, we gradually began to get a peace of mind and serenity which we never thought were possible.'"

As Bruce continued to read, I studied my chaotic surroundings. Hand-colored polystyrene manikin masks lined the top of each wall. Underneath them, loud, crazy paintings like Morty's—done by other patients—hung randomly. There were two huge blackboards on opposite sides of the room. One showed the daily schedule by category; next to each activity was a dash followed by names. The other blackboard had a list of topics, such as gratitude, willingness, and acceptance.

Next to the second blackboard hung a huge poster of thirty different cartoon faces. Under each face was written a corresponding emotion: exhausted, confused, sad, confident, guilty, embarrassed, and so on. The other wall held an even bigger poster, which read, "Here are the steps we took, which are suggested as a program of recovery." I read down the list:

1. Admitted we were powerless over alcohol and our addiction—that our lives had become unmanageable.

I flashed back to when my father and I had gone on a business trip to Thailand. It was 5:30 AM, and we'd been entertaining customers all night. I remembered ordering another glass of wine before heading back to our room and then saying to my father, "The first step is admitting it. Cheers to you, good man."

2. Came to believe that a Power greater than ourselves could restore us to sanity.
3. Made a decision to turn our will and our lives over to the care of God ***as we understood him***.
4. Made a searching and fearless inventory of ourselves.
5. Admitted to God, to ourselves, and to another human being the exact nature of our wrongs.
6. Became entirely ready to have God remove all these defects of character.
7. Humbly asked Him to remove our shortcomings.
8. Made a list of all persons we had harmed and became willing to make amends to them all.

9. Made direct amends to such people wherever possible, except when to do so would injure them or others.
10. Continued to take personal inventory and when we were wrong promptly admitted it.
11. Sought, through prayer and meditation, to improve our conscious contact with God ***as we understood Him,*** praying only for knowledge of His will for us and the power to carry that out.
12. Having had a spiritual awakening as the result of these steps, we tried to carry this message to alcoholics and to practice these principles in all our affairs.

Oh, boy.

"Thank you, Bruce," everyone said. I quickly looked away from the twelve-steps poster. Bruce and the group all looked at Grant, who was seated at Bruce's right.

"Good morning. I'm Grant, and I'm an alcoholic and addict."

"Good morning, Grant," we all answered. *I think I have the hang of this now.*

"Today I'm going to read from the *Tao Te Ching*." *Ah, that I recognize.* I craved spirituality with every ounce of my soul. I swore to myself that if God would just point to what He wanted me to do, like building an ark, I'd jump to work and be His humble servant. The *Tao* refers to God as "the named and nameless" and "All That Is." I had read verses from the *Tao* hundreds of times. While Grant read, I thought about

all the spiritual teachings I'd read and wondered which one would help me the most in the rehab center.

"Being at one with the Tao is eternal. And though the body dies, the Tao will never pass away." Grant closed the book and his eyes, signaling that he was done.

"Thank you, Grant," the group said.

Uh-oh. My turn. Everyone looked at me and smiled. Time froze. "Um, I don't have anything to read."

Bruce casually said, "That's okay. Just introduce yourself, and say, 'I pass.'"

Introduce myself? How? Do I say it? Do I admit that I'm an alcoholic and addict? "Good morning, guys. My name is Adam . . . and . . . I'm . . . an . . ." The next two seconds felt like an eternity. A huge gorilla was sitting on my back, pounding his chest. The weight of the world was pressing down on my shoulders. I started again, my voice booming in my ears like thunder. "I'm . . . an . . . alcoholic . . . and addict." I felt the words echo off the walls and boomerang, hitting me in the face.

All the guys spontaneously stood up and clapped. They roared, "Hi, Adam!"

"Hi, guys. I pass."

By the time they all sat down again, that huge gorilla had vanished from my back. So had the weight of the world. I had finally discovered what I was, why I couldn't act normal. I was always wanting more, lying, hiding, frightened, and going to great lengths to get my fix. Once and for all, I acknowledged that I was different from other people. I couldn't drink alcohol or take drugs like a normal person. I would find out later that I had become "pickled," as they say in treatment. Once a cucumber pickles, it stays a pickle. It can never go back.

Yet, I had mixed feelings. *Yes, now I know what I am, and it all makes sense, but do I like what I am? I'm no fun. No more partying, no more going to bars, no more taking speed before working out. When Sloan gets married, I won't be able to have a glass of champagne. When I take Michelle to Europe, we won't be able to have a glass of wine together. What will I order? A Shirley Temple?* A deep sadness and loss sank into my heart. I looked at the guys around me and wondered whether I was actually like them. I swore that I must be different somehow. *At least I'm in the beginning stages. I'm not as bad as these hardcore alcoholics and addicts.*

After meditation, Jack showed me to our room. I took the available bed, the one next to the window.

Directly across from me, Seth lay in bed, sleeping. Seth, a nineteen-year-old crack addict, was about six feet six inches and extremely skinny. Recounting this now, after having heard his story while I was at Hanley, I can't help thinking about how, before Seth had found crack, he had been an amazing athlete. He had been one of the top-scouted wide receivers in South Florida and heavily recruited for basketball, too. But he had fallen in love with crack cocaine and flushed all his dreams down the toilet. This was his fourth rehab visit this year, his second at Hanley.

The way Seth had found his way back to treatment this fourth time blew my mind. Poor kid had a heart attack. The story went like this: Seth and his girlfriend were smoking crack, and they didn't sleep for three days. Out of nowhere, the cops pulled up to his apartment building. Naked from

just having had sex and scared out of his mind, he bailed on his girlfriend and jumped out the back window. The cops chased him by foot and patrol car as he ran in and out of alleys, streets, and people's yards. Just when he thought he'd lost them, he heard the helicopter. He bolted, lightning fast from his sports background but even faster from the intense high of smoking crack cocaine. Finally, the cops surrounded him. His last memory of the incident was all the cops screaming violently and the megaphone blaring, "It's all over. We have you surrounded. Lie down on the ground, with your hands behind your head, or we'll be forced to shoot." Exhausted and frightened, Seth passed out.

That's Seth's memory. But Seth's parents told the staff at the Hanley Center what really happened. Seth and his girlfriend were smoking crack at his apartment for seventy-two hours. One of those days, unable to take anymore, his girlfriend went home. The last evening, right after taking a shower, Seth took a hit off his crack pipe and became extremely paranoid. He imagined that cops were outside his apartment. He jumped out of the back window, still naked after the shower, and ran through the streets, like a lunatic thinking cops were chasing him. His heart finally gave out in the middle of an old woman's backyard. She just happened to look outside, and she had the hell scared out of her when she saw a naked man lying in her garden. The cops and ambulances got to him and saved his life, thank God. I learned later that aggressive, paranoid hallucinations are common for people on crack.

As I started unpacking, Grant walked in, holding up a piece of paper. "Adam, I have your schedule. As your assigned buddy, want me to look it over with you really quick before we go to breakfast?"

"That would be great." I pushed aside the pillow on my unmade bed, and we both sat down.

Grant pointed at the top of the page. "Your name will always be on the top, right-hand corner, last name first. Okay?"

I nodded.

"So, we're here," he said, pointing at the top, left-hand corner of the page. "At 7:10 to 7:40 AM, we eat breakfast. This is when you get your meds. Afterward, we have a free hour for wellness."

"Wellness?"

"Yeah, man, wellness: extra time for exercise, homework, or doing something for yourself."

Exercise—yippee! My face lit up like a Christmas tree.

Grant arched an eyebrow. "I walk in the morning. Want to join me?"

"I'd love to. Morning cardio."

He cracked up. "Yeah, man. Morning cardio—whatever that means. Doesn't take much to make you happy, huh?"

I squinted one eye. "Wise ass."

He looked at my schedule again. "At 9:15 AM, we have our first lecture of the day. You're in for a treat. Today is John Dyben, the chaplain on the men's unit. He works in spiritual care."

I loved hearing that word—spiritual. It made me feel safe and optimistic. Finally, I could put all my reading to good use.

"Next, at 10:30 AM, we have group. You asked me about that last night. The men's unit is divided into two groups.

It's pretty much a big therapy session. It gets intense—deep and heated. Lunch is after that. The food here is awesome. Delicious cookies and cakes. But it looks to me like you watch what you eat."

"I'm pretty strict."

"Okay, then. Let's move on. Shall we?"

I enjoyed his flippant humor and felt at ease around him.

"Now, you, Adam, have a pretty swamped first day here at Camp Hanley. From 12:15 to 12:45 PM, you'll meet with your counselor." His voice went up an octave. "Oh, man, you got Brent B.! You're a lucky guy. Brent's not my counselor, but he ran my group yesterday. Really knows his stuff. He looks like Brad Pitt. Cool cat. Okay, man. Next on tap is . . ."

The second those words came out of his mouth we made eye contact. And then we both chuckled at his slip.

"Let me rephrase that." He cleared his throat. "Your next appointment is with Dr. J Wirth at 1:30 PM in the psychology wing of the cafeteria building. Have fun with that one." Grant rolled his eyes and sighed. "He's going to give you a 360-question test with the craziest questions."

"Like what?" I raised my eyebrows.

"Like . . . would you rather be a florist or a dentist? If you were watching a bank robbery, would you root for the bad guys to get away or for the police to capture them?"

"Weird."

"I'm getting my results today. I'll let you know how they turn out."

"You do that," I said, patting him on the back. We both laughed. Camaraderie was building.

"3:30 PM, wellness activities. A bunch of us play volleyball in the pool. You should join us. It's a blast."

"Grant, I'll be in the gym, weight training," I said firmly.

"Right, right. What was I thinking?" He made a fist and pounded on my chest. "Damn, man. You're solid."

I smiled.

"So, after your training, dinner at 5:00 PM From 5:45 to 6:45, someone shares his story. That's called leisure education. From 7:00 to 7:45, we meet for another lecture. After the lecture, we process and go through high-low, which you experienced last night. Usually, we attend an outside AA or NA meeting after that. Last night, after you went back up to detox, we went to AA. But tonight . . ." Grant looked up from my schedule, made a fist, and pumped his arm up and down. "Saturday night: pizza and a movie. Yes!"

I didn't share his excitement. "When can I call Michelle? I need to speak to my wife. I don't see time in the schedule to call loved ones."

"Whoa, man. Calm down. We get two phone calls a day. Use them at your leisure. We have four private phone rooms in the men's unit."

"Two calls? That's it? I need more! I have a six-month-old daughter, bro."

"Don't kill the messenger. Ask Ben if you can use the phone more. I'm sure it'll be okay. We're here to get better, get sober." He looked at my fists, the veins sticking out on my forearms, and my shaky legs. "Calm down, Rambo."

"Sorry, I—I—" My anger broke out for the first time. I wanted what I wanted.

"I understand."

We headed to the cafeteria, for my first meal at Hanley. I put up my guard instantly, ready for the food to be filled with sugar, butter, oil, and fat. I picked up my tray and followed Grant like a puppy, studying my choices. I grabbed a bowl full of beautifully ripe mixed berries, a Fuji apple, and a banana. My shoulder blades lowered a bit. Grant looked back at me and smiled as he grabbed a chocolate muffin. As we got closer to the end of the line, my stomach knotted. Hash browns and eggs over easy with bacon or sausage. *Dammit, I knew it! But I can't live on just fruit. I need to talk to somebody. I'm going home today!* Just a couple more steps, and I found my "bread and butter": two heated aluminum chafing dishes labeled with big signs in front of them that read FIT MENU. I looked inside the first one: scrambled egg whites. *Yes!* I peeked inside the second one: oatmeal. *It* was *a dream come true.*

"Sir, what can I get you today?" the woman behind the counter asked. Here it comes, my big question. The pass-or-fail test.

"Ma'am, do the egg whites or oatmeal have any butter in them?" Everyone in the line stopped and looked at me. I stood tall, waiting to hear the verdict. She turned her head to the side and looked at me as if I had three heads. But she took a half step backward and called out, "Does anyone know if the egg whites or oatmeal have butter in them?" The whole line waited patiently for the answer, watching the Wild West showdown. Who would flinch first? Who would draw quicker? I heard the famous theme song from *The Good, the Bad and the Ugly* movie playing in my head. *Doo-doo-doo-doo . . . waa, waa, waa.* I felt like Clint Eastwood as I scratched my rough beard and squinted my eyes tightly. Then we all heard, shouted back from the kitchen, "No. Everything on the fit menu is cooked in PAM. The oatmeal is made with water. No milk. No butter."

My smile shone from ear to ear. "I'll have the egg whites and oatmeal, please," I said, like a child ordering a banana split with sprinkles.

Grant and the woman behind the counter shook their heads at the same time.

"What's your name, dear?" she asked.

"Adam. What's yours?"

"Charlotte."

"Charlotte. I love that name! That was my Gaga's . . . um . . . I mean, my grandmother's name. Thank you, Charlotte. I apologize for the little scene."

"No, dear. Don't you be sorry at all. I like a man that takes care of himself. Pleasure to meet you, Adam."

"The pleasure is all mine, Charlotte." I grabbed her hand and kissed it. *I guess I'll be able to eat in rehab after all.*

After breakfast, I went back to my room and finished unpacking. I noticed a stack of photos Michelle had tucked in the bottom of my suitcase. Underneath the photos was a card. I looked through the photos, and my heart pounded in my chest. The one on top showed Sloan, Michelle, and me on the day of Sloan's birth. *I'm a daddy. Scratch that—I'm a daddy in rehab.* Guilt. Shame. I flipped through the photos. I found one of my father holding Sloan. A tear formed, and the butterflies in my stomach started again. *Hey there, Daddy.* I found photos of my nephews; my in-laws; my mom and Gaga, and my best pals, Lew and Nino from college.

The next photo jumped out at me. It was of my Uncle David and me standing shoulder-to-shoulder and each posing like Superman, with our fists on our hips. Uncle David and I had a unique bond. I was born on his birthday, May 19th, and we acted the same and sounded the same. I was his clone . . . but with muscles. The family joke was that my mother must have gone into the wrong bedroom one night.

When I spent time with Uncle David, I felt like I was on top of the world. I wanted to be just like him—a kid in a grown-up body. Like a child, Uncle David had a special sparkle in his eyes—it was his imagination. Actually, his company was named, appropriately, Imagination Productions. He is a director and producer in Hollywood. That always fascinated me. He believed in himself, and he didn't enter the family business. I admired him for that. But more than that, he made me feel special and loved. Around Uncle David, I felt as if I could walk on water.

He introduced me to Superman on my first day on the planet—our shared birthday. But he was more than a superhero to me. He was also a role model. I wanted to be a hero, too. Looking at the photo of us, I realized for the first time that, while my uncle only pretended to be Superman, I thought I should try to *be* the larger-than-life superhero. Big difference.

I put down the stack of photos and opened the card. Michelle had enclosed a photo of Sloan and me that had been taken at Sloan's naming ceremony a couple months earlier. I was holding her in my arms. The only part of me visible in the photo was my eyes. The rest of the photo was filled with Sloan looking directly at the camera. Our eyes were identical.

I stared at the photo in shock. *Mini me! She is me. I am her.* I looked down and read the card.

Get better, Daddy.
I love you!
Sloan

A tear rolled down my face. *I will try with all my heart, baby. I will try.*

AT 9:15 AM, I FOLLOWED the other guys to my first lecture. John Dyben stood at the front of the room. He was about five feet ten inches tall, and he looked ten years younger than his reportedly thirty-plus years. He wore his brown hair short and cropped. He'd added a touch of pizzazz to his counselor's uniform by wearing a colorful Save the Children tie. Having rolled up his sleeves, he looked casual and relaxed.

I took a seat and read the blackboard behind him. "John Dyben. What is spirituality?" *This is going to be a treat.*

"Good morning, everyone. My name is John Dyben. I'm the chaplain for the men's unit. Today, I want to talk about spirituality, specifically, healthy spirituality. Anybody know where the word *spirituality* comes from?"

I raised my hand.

"Yes, the muscle man," John said.

The crowd chuckled.

"It comes from the Latin word *spiritus*, which means breath of life." All eyes in the room focused on me.

"Wow! You're the first person to answer that one in my entire career. What's your name?"

"Adam, sir," I said.

"Sir? We're not in the military, Adam." He smiled, looked down at his hand holding a marker and then back at me. "Adam . . . the first man."

We nodded at each other. For me, it felt as if everyone else in the room had disappeared.

"As our good man Adam said, *spirituality* means breath of life or way of life." He wrote that on the board. "Now, we can have healthy spirituality or unhealthy spirituality. Spirituality is like having muscles." He grinned and pointed the marker at me. "If I tell Adam I want more muscles, you know what he should answer? 'John, you have all the muscles you need. You don't need more of them. What's important is how healthy they are.' Gang, it's the same with spirituality. You don't need more of it. God gave you all the spirituality you need. But how healthy is your spirituality?"

John turned to the blackboard and wrote the words LOOK, SPEAK, and ACT. "We can break this down into how I look, how I speak, and how I act." He turned to face us again. "A person with healthy spirituality looks *aware,* speaks from *connectedness,* and acts in *celebration* of being alive. Unhealthy spirituality creates the exact opposite behavior: people who act unaware and disconnected and denigrate life."

I was drawn to John just as Neo is to Morpheus in *The Matrix*. He was connecting the dots for me.

John continued, "Let's look at spirituality as food. We need food to live, right? When we wake up, the first thing that happens to us is we get hungry. When we get hungry, what do we do? We search for food. We go to the kitchen, and we see what there is to eat. We *discover* the food." John wrote the word DISCOVER on the blackboard. "Next is our *response*."

He wrote the word RESPONSE. "We pick the food we want to eat. And if we don't eat, what happens?" He paused.

Someone said, "We starve."

"Right. We get hunger pangs. Many of us don't want to deal with those pangs, so we smoke a cigarette, drink coffee, or take a diet pill."

John seemed to know my life story. When I dieted so that my muscles would look more defined, I cut back on food and loaded up on caffeine and fat burners, even though I knew doing that was unhealthy. But that behavior was a metaphor for my spirituality. I ran myself into the ground by saying yes to everyone and trying to make myself look perfect on the outside. I didn't heed the pangs by saying no or allowing myself time to just be. *Wow!*

"If you keep masking your hunger pangs with stuff, and then someone tells you to stop, you'll yell, 'No!' Because it would hurt too much to stop and feel. You guys have masked your hunger for too long. You need to develop a life that *deals* with hunger pangs, not covers them up." *Yes. That's me. I'm always covering up by saying yes to people, always trying to make everyone happy, so they stay off my back. I never express how I truly feel about anything.*

"Sometimes, guys, we don't want to connect with other people or even with ourselves. We need to choose to *connect* to other people. The twelve steps provide a way for you to make that connection. Healthy spirituality is a journey of becoming." John paused for a moment and looked at us one by one, making eye contact with each person. "That is why we are here. To help you become who you really are. God bless all you guys, and have a great day."

Everyone applauded.

I yelled, "Woo hoo!" John's speech had moved me. I had felt something inside myself awaken, and I wanted more.

As the others filed out of the room, I ran over to John. "Wow! Your lecture was amazing. A flash went off inside my head when you explained we have all the spirituality we need, we just need to make it stronger. I've read countless books, always seeking but never finding."

John beamed at me. "Thanks, Adam. Your participation impressed me. Have you been in the program before?"

"Program? What program? Oh, the twelve steps? No. I've just always been looking, trying to find out why I'm here, what's the meaning in my life."

"You may find it in the weirdest of places." He winked at me.

"This is exactly what I need! Can I make an appointment with you?"

John patted my back. "You just did."

A CALL TO ACTION

- Can you think of a time when you told the truth about something, maybe for the very first time? Like when I first admitted I was an alcoholic and addict. What did it feel like? Did you feel a little nauseated, maybe, or were you sweating or anxious? Now see if you can remember a time when you were caught in a lie. What did that feel like, for contrast?
- What would Healthy Spirituality look like in your life?

CHAPTER 7

DENIAL

IT WAS 10:25 AM I'd arrived early for group therapy in the lounge.

"Hey, man. I'm Matt. I'm in here for heroin. . . . Oh, and I'm clinically bipolar. If you ever need protein powder or a preworkout drink, I snuck some bottles into my room." His voice was harsh and raspy.

I shook my head. "No, thanks. I want to follow the rules. That was one of my issues—supplements. I want to give this my all."

"What, you're addicted to protein powder?"

My guard went up. I took a step backward and squinted angrily but tried to ignore the condescension in his voice.

"Whatever, man. You ever want some, come to me, any time." With a devilish look in his eyes, he patted my back and walked away.

My first impression of Matt: scumbag. His greasy, black hair and oily skin made him look as if he hadn't showered in days. He reminded me of the typical drugged-out, dirtbag villain in the movies. I didn't like him—not one bit.

I looked past him, around the circle, to see the other nine guys—including Grant, Jack, Tony, Morty, and Jeremy—file in for group therapy.

Ben led the session. He passed a clipboard to Jeremy and asked him to read the rules aloud.

Jeremy looked down at the clipboard and cleared his throat. "Okay, here we go. . . . Please show respect to other men by arriving at group on time. What a man says in group stays in group. This is vital for creating a safe group. Please respect the man sharing; no side conversations, cross talk, interruptions, or distractions. Please stay until group ends. If you need to leave early, let the other men know before the group begins. Risk being open and honest. This is our recovery! Recovery starts by honestly sharing our thoughts and feelings with other men. When giving feedback, be kind. When receiving feedback, stay open; think about this other man's ideas. Please, no food, drinks, or gum. Remember, as men, we all share the same disease: chemical dependency. Every man is asked to share, because we all are important parts of the group. Each man is encouraged to process his feelings without fixing or solving other men's problems. This may be hard for us as men, because we are taught to fix things. The common concern of this men's group is that we help one another recover from the disease of chemical dependency." He put the clipboard down on his lap and sighed. "Whew!"

Ben took the clipboard back from him. "Thank you, Jeremy. Gentlemen, we have a new addition to our group. Has everyone met Adam?"

The men nodded and made eye contact with me.

"Adam, you want to tell the group why you're here?"

"Hi, guys. Yesterday, my family performed an intervention on me." I took a deep breath. "I'm here because I've gotten out of control. Last week, I had a huge fight with my wife and threatened to leave her and my six-month-old daughter due to my drinking and popping pills." My hands trembled. Admitting this out loud hurt.

"What pills?" Someone asked.

"A long and distinguished list of pills. . . ."

There were a few chuckles.

"Okay. . . . Zoloft, for anxiety. Lots of Xanax on top of it, any time I felt edgy. I pop ephedrine—fat burners—before I work out, twice a day, along with high amounts of caffeine. Painkillers: Vicodin, Darvocet, Percocet, and oxycodone. I don't feel my injuries that way." I saw a few nods and even heard an "Ahh." I scratched my temple and looked somewhere imaginary, off in the distance, as I remembered all the tablets and capsules. "I've taken Adderall, Ritalin, Dexedrine, and other amphetamines. At night, I pop an Ambien or three to fall asleep. I also love to drink. Alcohol is my first love."

"What's your favorite drink?" Morty asked.

"Ice-cold beer and good tequila. But I've gotten wasted on just about anything, from a 1964 Birtani Amarone to zinfandel out of a box, the best tequilas to cactus piss, twenty-dollar bottles of beer, and Keystone Light, Ketel One, Belvedere, Johnny Walker. I have no prejudice when it comes to alcohol. I like to have fun."

Ben raised an eyebrow. "Thank you, Adam, for your honesty. Let's try to steer away from what we enjoy in our addictions."

I shamefully hung my head.

Ben continued, "At yesterday's group, we shared our fears about recovery. Where did we leave off? Jeremy? Okay, what's your biggest fear?"

"That's easy. Going back on tour with the band. The lifestyle . . . it's hard to be the only one sober. Alcohol and drugs are everywhere. I can get my hands on pills or a bag any time I want. None of my bandmates will understand. . . ." He closed his eyes and dropped his head into his hands.

I felt for him. He would be returning to a world that offered little to no support for his sobriety.

"I just don't know how I can do it." Jeremy made a fist with his right hand and used it to hit his open left hand as if he were breaking in a baseball glove. "I hate this disease. Why can't I just be normal?"

Would Jeremy have to quit Stalker to stay sober? What else could he do for work? I raised my hand.

"Adam, you have a question?" Ben asked.

"For Jeremy, if that's okay?" I didn't want to get Hanley's equivalent of solitary confinement.

"Of course. That's what group is all about: sharing." Ben motioned his hands to indicate that I should proceed.

"Jeremy, have you played with the band straight before? Or were you always high?"

He looked at me, smiled, and sighed deeply. "Muscles, I wish you'd been here for my story. I've played in all conditions, but now Oxys and Roxys are the only thing I think

about. I may be jamming and performing at my best, but my mind is on my next fix. When I play, it's like there're two of me. One: the guy performing and hitting the strings. And two: this voice in my head, counting down the minutes to get high again."

I knew that voice, too. Jeremy reminded me of myself when I was with my family, truly wanting to be in their company and yet, at the same time, desperately wanting to drink. It was hell.

After a few more people had taken their turns, it was my turn. Ben readjusted himself in his chair so that he could look me in the eyes.

"Adam, day one in treatment, your first group: your biggest fear about the recovery process. Let's have it."

I squirmed in my seat. My biggest fear? Twenty-four hours earlier, being in rehab would have been near the top of the list. But my heart took over, and the answer came out easier than I'd expected.

"My biggest fear is losing Michelle and Sloan."

I bit my lower lip and tensed up. I could feel the group's compassion at my honesty. A couple guys raised their hands and offered words of support, but I couldn't hear them through my brain fog. Losing Michelle? Losing Sloan? Heartache set in.

At the end of the session, we huddled together in a group hug, arm over arm, forming a circle.

"Let's close group with the Serenity Prayer," Ben said.

We bowed our heads.

I had enjoyed the prayer from the moment I had heard it that morning.

"God, grant me the serenity to accept the things I cannot change, the courage to change the things I can, and the wisdom to know the difference."

At the end, everyone yelled, "Unity!" When they all left for lunch, I sat back down in my chair. I could lose my family. Reality hit me, and I stayed there for a minute. I couldn't relax. I couldn't keep my mind off my family. *What did they have to go through to get me in here? What would Michelle have to go through during the next ten days, by herself with a six-month-old baby? What kind of man am I to have let all this happen?*

Lunch surprised me again—grilled salmon, without butter, and mixed vegetables. They offered three flavors of Crystal Light—orange, lemonade, and fruit punch—which was like a fitness freak's ice cream parlor. I gossiped with the guys and asked them a million questions about rehab. Everyone gave me the same message: "I was just as scared as you. It gets better, a lot like camp. Just relax."

I arrived at my assigned counselor's office at 12:10 PM, five minutes early. Growing up, I'd learned from my grandfather and father to be punctual. And that habit had become even more ingrained in the business world. "Always be five minutes early, Addy. Show them you mean business and you value their time. Never ever keep them waiting for you." I wanted everyone to know that I was all business in this place, always prepared.

I knocked on Brent's door.

"Come in!" Brent's voice sounded friendly.

I opened the door and saw that he looked exactly like everyone had told me: Brad Pitt's character, Rusty, in the *Ocean's Eleven* movies. He was dressed in a sharp, royal-blue,

Armani button-down, the top button unbuttoned, and a casually loose tie.

"Hey! Adam, right?" He stood up from his chair. "I'm Brent, your counselor. How are you today?"

We shook hands.

"I'm doing, Brent, I'm doing. Been a crazy few hours."

He pointed to a leather recliner about three feet from him. I sat down and took in my surroundings.

Brent's office didn't possess much glam. It had white walls and a plain wooden bookshelf loaded with textbooks about addiction and recovery. Behind Brent, his desk held a computer with a flat-screen monitor, a couple files, and a phone. A window took up most of the wall. Through his window, I could see a fountain surrounded by the beauty of well-groomed plants and trees.

Brent smiled, leaned back in his office chair, and crossed his legs. "Tell me a little about that, would you?"

I told him the story of my intervention—who had been there and how much their letters had affected me. We discussed my night in detox, meeting the guys, and the questions about my drug of choice. I rambled on and on.

". . . And today has been an absolute roller coaster. This morning, I said the words 'I'm an alcoholic and an addict,' for the first time. I've enjoyed the food so far. I can get everything healthy."

Brent laughed and made a most muscular pose like a five-year-old kid pretending to be the Hulk.

I smiled but kept going. "I feel completely ashamed of myself and guilty as hell. This morning's lecture with John Dyben felt like seeing Tony Robbins. I'm here for only a ten-day evaluation, but everyone hints I'll be here longer. Oh, and I've only met one person who rubs me the wrong way. So, I'd say I'm just doing." *Whew!*

Brent clapped his hands and grinned. He seemed to sympathize with my bafflement. "Adam, before we start, I need you to know something. I've been there. I've actually been right there." He pointed to my chair. "I was once a patient here. I, too, am an alcoholic and an addict."

I took a deep breath and rubbed my stubble from my cheeks down to my chin. Somehow, Brent sharing his disease with me made it more real for me. Seeing a guy who had his act together explaining that he, too, had felt like this gave me hope.

He continued. "I understand you're here for a ten-day evaluation, so let's keep it at that. The more honest and open you are to your recovery, the faster we can get you out of here."

My face lit up in anticipation. "That's great news, Brent. I have a young daughter and a beautiful wife. I need to get home."

"Then we better make sure you go home the very best father and husband you can be."

Brent raised his arms and clasped his hands behind his head as if he were lounging in the sun. His drawn-out words matched his stretched-out arms. "You admitted, on day one, that you're an alcoholic and addict. That's pretty big, Adam. You mind telling me how you came to that decision?"

I wanted to show him that I was calm and controlled, yet my mind wouldn't stop racing. I couldn't find the answers to his question quickly enough to make me feel secure. I felt ridiculous. Like Alvy "Max" Singer, Woody Allen's neurotic

character in the movie *Annie Hall*, I was trying to intellectualize that I'd been through all of this therapy stuff before and it was no big deal. My voice grew loud, and I felt uncomfortable and edgy. "Umm . . . well, I'm in rehab, so my family believes I have a problem of some sort. I don't know if I'm as bad as the other guys here, though. And I don't really know what all this means."

"Tell me about that. What do you think *all* this means?"

"Well, I'm confused. I mean, I know I drink way too much. But an alcoholic? It seems so . . . so severe. So pathetic and final. I mean, well . . ."

"You mean what?" Brent waited patiently.

I rubbed my hands together and cleared my throat. "Well, does this mean I can't have a glass of champagne at my daughter's wedding?"

"Adam, how old is your daughter?"

"Six months."

"Ha!" Brent clapped his hands together loudly. "Adam, only an alcoholic would worry if he could drink at his six-month-old daughter's wedding!"

That hit me right between the eyes.

Brent chuckled a bit more and then said, "Is that it, Adam?"

"No. Last night I read 'The Doctor's Opinion' in the book *Alcoholics Anonymous*."

Brent's face lit up. "And?"

"And . . . I think there's a lot of me in there. I connected with having an allergy to booze. One drink, and I'm off to the races." For some reason, when I said that, I felt completely at ease, not fake. "When I drink, I like to have a good time, and I don't know how or when to stop. Anyone would tell you that."

"Would you say that you're powerless over alcohol, once it's in your body?"

"Yeah, I would."

"Amazing! Not many people come into my office on day one and admit they have a problem or even come close to picking up the Big Book."

"The Big Book?"

"The book *Alcoholics Anonymous.* It's like our Bible."

My counselor had just made me feel good about admitting I had a problem. *Weird.*

"Would you say that your life has somehow become unmanageable?" He raised one eyebrow like John Belushi's Bluto in *Animal House*, hands in the air as if questioning, and gave me a big smile.

"Not sure about that, Brent. I have a good job, and I make a decent living. I have a roof over my head and food on the table. I'm married with a child. I take good care of my body physically. Tough to say it's unmanageable."

Brent stared at me for a few seconds. "Adam . . ." His tone was stern.

"Yes."

"You're in rehab. Let that sink in."

I'm.

In.

Rehab.

Oh, my lord.

Brent asked again, gently. "Adam, would you say that your life has somehow become unmanageable?"

I felt frail. I confessed, "Yes."

"Your first day, and you've completed step one. You've admitted you're powerless over alcohol—that your life has become unmanageable. You should be proud. I'm very proud of you, and I'm looking forward to being your counselor during your stay here. Now, what's the one thing you think you need to do here at Hanley in order to get better?"

That one was easy for me, but it also would let Brent know how my sick brain worked. "The one thing I need to do here to get better is work out! I can't go through rehab without weight training. I need to be able to exercise to get through this."

Brent pushed up on his chair. In seconds, his body language shifted from proud to uncomfortable and disturbed. *Uh-oh. What the hell did I say wrong?* Brent narrowed his eyes. "Did you say the one thing you need here at Hanley, in your time of treatment, is to work out?"

I got defensive. My guard—the big, muscular me protecting the little, chubby kid who hated being teased and made fun of—showed up. "That's right, Brent. I need to be able to train. Without the gym, I'm useless. I don't even know who I am if I can't." I spoke firmly, letting him know that this wasn't negotiable. No workouts, no rehab.

"I encourage you to exercise, but we need to take a deeper look at what it means in your life. You *have* to work out? Okay. I think this is a good place for us to stop for today."

1:30 PM I SAT PATIENTLY in Dr. J Wirth's office as he searched inside his desk for the Minnesota Multiphasic Personality Inventory (MMPI) test. The MMPI is one of the most widely used personality tests in the mental health field. Composed of 370 items, it is designed to help identify personal, social, and behavioral problems. It is used in many substance abuse programs.

As Dr. J fished out the test, he made casual conversation about fitness. "So, you work out a lot, Adam. That's obvious. I just started getting into the gym a bit myself. I go on fitness websites, like bodybuilding.com, looking for the perfect meal plan or supplement. Tell me, do you take any supplements?"

Do I take any supplements? Hello? "Too many—fat burners, ephedrine, protein shakes and puddings, preworkout cocktails, postworkout drinks, vitamins, you name it. It's actually one of the things that got me in here."

"Really? Supplements can be addictive?"

"Well, I abuse them. But that's not all I abuse. I drink a lot of booze and pop a lot of pills."

"Why would you take a fat burner or ephedrine if you need Xanax to calm down?"

"Good question. I feel like I need the speed to work out intensely and stay cut, but the supplements make me jittery or wired . . . so I take a sedative. I've been mixing it all for a while. It's weird. Honestly, if I were writing out a workout or diet for anyone, I'd tell them that most supplements are a scam and you don't need them to get results. I'd admit to them that the majority of stuff in bodybuilding magazines is synthetic crap. But I love that crap."

While we spoke, I sized up Dr. J. He looked about thirty years old, had short, brown hair and a good build, and was about six foot three inches tall. He was wearing a light-blue button-down, a yellow tie, khaki pants. He had an easygoing

nature about him that made me feel comfortable opening up to him.

He handed the MMPI test to me. "Maybe, while you're here, you can teach me how to eat right."

"Sure." I smiled at him having asked me for help.

"Okay, Adam. You have an hour and a half to finish this. Don't worry or overanalyze the questions. Some may seem silly. In two days, we'll go over your test scores and get to know each other a little better."

"Sounds good."

I went to the office next door and sat down at a random desk.

I like cheese pizza. A) True, B) False.

A) True.

I prefer horror movies to action movies. A) True, B) False.

B) False.

My mother did not love me. A) True, B) False.

B) False.

Is this a joke? What can the results from this test actually diagnose? I continued, for the next hour, to answer what I thought to be meaningless questions. When I finally finished, I looked at my watch—3:20 PM I looked at my schedule and saw that from 3:30 to 4:30 I had time for wellness activities. *Hallelujah! I need a good workout.*

I returned the test to Dr. J, in his office, and then walked from the men's unit to the wellness and recreation center, sipping a cup of coffee on the way. I usually had no problem at all getting into workout mode, but this time I felt off. Since the intervention, I'd been on the wildest ride of my life. I thought of last night's high-low session. High: "that my family loves me enough to check me into rehab." Low: "that my family loves me enough to check me into rehab." Memories of the intervention flashed in my head. Michelle holding my hand and saying, "You're sick, Adam. Right now, I'm not asking you to apologize. I'm asking you to get help. Get help now, or we're through." "Get help now," she'd said. *I am sick. I'm an alcoholic and an addict? Oh, my God! I am!* My guard came up again, and denial crept in. *Well, I'm not as bad as these guys.*

The outdoor pool was next to the gym. Some of the guys, including Grant, were already in there, splashing around and having fun. Morty yelled over to me while scratching his hairy belly. "Muscles! Why don't you jump your sexy bod in here and play some volleyball with us?"

But I wasn't in a joking mood, and I had to get my mind focused on working out. I smiled, waved, and walked right by the pool.

When I entered the gym, I saw that dirtbag, Matt, doing dumbbell curls. There was nobody else in the facility. Just him and me. I thought back to the body part I had trained yesterday, preintervention—arms—which meant that today was back. I walked to the lat pulldown machine and warmed up on it. The weights felt heavier than usual, and I remembered Kat saying, "Don't push your body too hard." I lightened the weight from my usual and banged out twenty-five repetitions. *Yeah, less weight but more reps should do it!*

Quickly, the sweat poured off me. When I positioned my body for the next exercise—bent-over rows—I felt dizzy. I ignored it. I grabbed lighter weights than I would normally use and cranked out the reps. My head ached, and my chest

tightened. *What's going on?* I continued to ignore my body's warning signs.

Matt followed me with his eyes. He studied me and how I weight trained. He came over to ask me a question, and I shot him a glare like the Terminator. Just as he was about to speak, I picked up the weights and started my next set. His staring at me fueled my dislike of him. I cranked out forty reps.

"Wow. You do really high reps, huh?"

"No, not usually. Kat, the nurse at the detox unit, told me to train lightly, because I'm on detox meds."

"Detoxing from protein supplements, right?" *Sarcasm again. I can't stand this guy.*

"Matt. Your name is Matt, right?"

He nodded.

My eyes narrowed, and I lowered the tone of my voice. "Matt, I don't like to talk when I train."

I picked up the weights again, breathing heavily, as if he weren't even there. Blood rushed to my muscles. I looked twice my size, and I knew it. I could feel the fear I was creating in Matt, and I liked it. I may be a nice guy, but don't mess with me. He lowered his head and went back to his station. My intensity was greater than usual because of the quicker pace and less rest between sets. My head throbbed, and my heart felt as if it would explode any second. I quickly placed the pads of my pointer and middle fingers just below my wrist to check my pulse. Too fast. I decided to rest in a lounge chair by the pool to lower my heart rate.

When I opened the door, Grant saw me and shouted, "Hey, Adam, come on in and play with us."

I waved my hand but shook my head.

Jeremy yelled, "You girlyman," in an Arnold Schwarzenegger voice and splashed water at me.

But with my rapid heart rate, I was in such a panic that I couldn't even gather enough energy to talk. I forced a smile and collapsed on a lounge chair. I tried to act normal, but I was frightened for my life. *Something is seriously wrong!* My headache got worse, and I saw stars. I took off my shirt, laid it over my eyes, and stretched out on the chair, in the sun, completely forgetting Kat's warning to stay out of the sun.

"Whoa. Nice body!" some girl shouted. *Don't say thank you. Don't engage. No fraternization.*

I closed my eyes and tried to calm down. *It's not as bad as you think. You've been worse. Everything must be catching up with you.* All of a sudden, the volleyball hit me lightly in the stomach.

"Adam, you mind grabbing that?" Morty asked.

I leaned over to get the ball, listening to them laughing and arguing about whether the shot had landed in bounds.

"In!" Tony shouted. He laughed.

"Out!" Jeremy yelled back.

I sat up and threw the ball to Morty.

He caught it and then said, "Who gives a shit? There's no score in alcoholic, cracked-out volleyball."

That sent me over the edge. *Alcoholic, cracked-out volleyball? What the hell am I doing here? I'm different than these guys. They're here having fun. My wife and child are at home while their man is sick, in rehab. This is all wrong.* My head pounded even harder. The chest pains became unbearable, and my shoulders caved in.

Grant walked over to me. The pool water was dripping off him. "Adam, ya all right?"

"Something's wrong. I feel like I'm having a heart attack."

"You're probably just freaking out, but go to the nurses' station and get checked out. Ya want me to walk ya there?"

"No, thanks. I'll be all right."

When I got up to walk away, all the guys in the pool asked if I was okay. I liked their camaraderie. It reminded me of my childhood summers at Camp Wigwam up in Maine, when I was carefree and happy. *But I'm different.* Maybe making new friends could be a good thing for me here? I wrestled with my thoughts. *No. No. No! What's happening to me?* I felt as if I were beginning to split into two different people. I had never felt so lost in my entire life. *Where did my life go? What have I become?*

When I arrived at the nurses' station, the frenetic activity overwhelmed me even more. The little room seemed to have transformed into a full-scale hospital. One nurse yanked a syringe out of someone's arm, another grabbed pills from the pharmacy, and a third shouted orders to a fourth, behind the desk.

Kat walked up behind me and tapped my shoulder. I turned around.

"What's wrong, Adam?" she asked in a kind, surprisingly patient tone.

"I'm freaking out. I did a workout and feel really dizzy. My heart and head were pounding hard, but with everything on my mind I didn't want to stop."

"Darlin', you're bright red. Were you in the sun, too?"

"Oh, yeah, for a little bit. I forgot about that, Kat. I'm sorry. Please help me. Something isn't right."

Kat walked me over to a chair so that she could take my blood pressure. I sat down. As she wrapped the strap around my arm, she looked at me inquisitively. "Now, didn't I say to exercise only lightly?"

"I did. I lightened the weights up and did a lot more reps."

She shook her head and smirked. "Girls, listen up. I told Mr. Muscles here he can exercise lightly and . . ." She started to laugh, "Go on and tell them what you told me."

"I said I did. I lightened my weights up and did more reps."

The nurses giggled.

"What's so funny?"

Kat looked down at me. "Listen, darlin', lightly means a brisk walk, or throwing a Frisbee. Not going crazy in the gym. Now, can you not weight train for four days?"

I looked down at the floor. I was bummed. "Hell, no!" I looked back up at Kat, who was no longer listening to me. She looked panicked.

"What?"

"You sent your blood pressure through the roof—180 over 70!" She shouted to the pharmacy, "Get me a Vistaril!" Vistaril is a mild, safe sedative.

Another nurse brought me a pill and a small cup of water.

"Take it," Kat ordered me.

I did.

"Listen, Adam. We need you to calm down. You're on edge. You need to realize that you're here and your family wants you here. They're the ones who asked you to come here. Please focus on getting better. In just three days from now, you can exercise again, with no crazy side effects. Please, for that beautiful baby girl of yours, please try to relax and enjoy your journey."

A lightbulb went on in my brain, and my eyes lit up. *My journey.* My spiritual and self-help books always referred to life as a journey—a process of personal change and development. Not a dark, redundant existence of going to work, paying bills, doing chores, and accommodating people. With little effort, Kat had opened up a new doorway for me and changed my perception a bit. *Why am I fighting all this so hard? Why do I think myself so different from the other men?*

I gave Kat a kiss on the cheek and left the detox unit, in deep reflection.

I went from the nurses' station directly to dinner. When I walked into the cafeteria, Jeremy, Tony, and Bruce gathered around me.

"You all right, buddy? Grant told us what happened," Bruce said.

Their concern made me feel welcome.

"Yeah, guys. I'm doing fine now. I shouldn't have worked out on the detox meds, or been in the sun. The nurses and my counselor want me to calm down, but I can't seem to shut my mind off. I'm scared, and honestly I just don't know if this is for me. I really miss my wife and daughter."

Tony jumped in. "Adam, I want to talk to ya alone tonight, but right now ya have to remember they *want* ya in here. Capisce?"

"Yeah, I'm getting that." I felt heartbroken.

We jumped into the cafeteria line. When it was my turn, Morty interrupted, "May I please have the protein and steamed vegetables platter with a side of Brussels sprouts?"

Morty roared. Laughs and hooting from the other men followed.

But I didn't care. I was delighted again with the fit menu: grilled snapper with steamed broccoli and brown rice. It occurred to me that, eliminating the alcohol and drugs from my system, I could transform my body to be completely healthy. I could have a new physique built on lean proteins, vegetables, fruits, and whole grains rather than protein shakes, energy drinks, and fat burners. Like John Dyben had said about spirituality in his lecture, I could become healthy inside and out.

A CALL TO ACTION

- When we surrender to a higher power, it's freeing! We feel that life is a journey and not a destination. You don't need to see the entire trip—just be here now, in the moment. It's enough to ask yourself: Where am I right now?
- Surrender may feel like a big word and an even bigger concept. But, its simply going to the winning team. What little issues are you holding on to right now? Why don't you just let that go?

CHAPTER 8

AN ALCOHOLIC, ADDICTED, CODEPENDENT MUSCLEHEAD

"WHAT'S IT LIKE IN REHAB?" Michelle sounded exhausted. It had been twenty-four hours since I surrendered to go to Hanley. All the work, love, and courage it had taken Michelle to get me the help—on top of taking care of a six-month-old baby by herself—had taken a toll on her.

I told Michelle how Kat had woken me up at 5 AM for blood work. I described the fast pace of the day, from morning meditation to unpacking to breakfast to lecture to group therapy to lunch to Brent to the MMPI test to working out to freaking out and sending my blood pressure spiking to 180, and, finally, to dinner.

I surveyed the tiny, private phone room—a plain, beige, 3 × 3 ft. space occupied by one small, yellow phone, a white, plastic stool, and a box of baby wipes for cleaning the phone. I felt jailed.

"Honey, you want me here, right?"

"Adam, I don't *want* you there. I *want* you healthy. But . . . the way you're going, we're not going to make it. I mean, do you realize every single fight we have is over your drinking, lying, or extreme ways? Do you realize what you put me through this past week? Do you remember how you spoke to me? How you spoke to my mother? I want you to get better. Sloan needs safety and stability. But you're sick, so . . . yes, I want you there."

Again, I felt as if I were being ripped in two.

"I'm going to give it my all. Just . . . I don't know if I belong here, that's all. I mean, a lot of the guys in here are on hardcore drugs: crack, heroin. I feel so different."

"Adam, don't you go judging people. They're there for the same reason you are. Please, give this your all. Promise me."

I thought long and hard before making that vow.

"I promise."

"It killed me putting you in there, but I know in my heart it's the right thing. I know you can do this, just like you do everything else, like Super—"

"Don't say it." The last thing I wanted to hear was a compliment, especially one about my being Superman. The humiliation and remorse of having been caught and put into rehab made me feel more like Superman's villainous clone, Bizarro—backward and defective.

"All right. But I know you can do this. Everything you do, you put 200 percent effort into. That's just your way. Extreme."

"I'm sorry, Michelle. I'm ashamed you married an alcoholic and addict."

"I'm not. You're also a man who's strong enough to get help. You have the guts to admit you have a problem and take care of it. I'm proud of you."

"Proud of me? Leaving you and Sloan alone for ten days, nobody to take care of you, to help you?"

"Adam, it's time for you to take care of *you*. You almost left us forever, remember? I *need* you to take care of you," she said with earnest.

Take care of myself? I didn't even know who I was without taking care of responsibilities, doing favors, and running around a million miles a minute. I hated myself. Taking care of myself sounded like the most uncomfortable, painful, exhausting task.

"Honey, I have to run. It's someone's story in five minutes."

"Story?"

"I'll explain later. I love you."

"I love you, too."

I walked into the lounge and grabbed a seat next to Grant.

He smiled and patted my back. "I'm happy you're okay, man. Ya gave me a scare. Someone in your shape complaining about his heart?"

"The nurses told me not to work out on the detox medication, for the next few days, and to try to *relax*."

"Oh, man, you're on detox meds? I didn't know, or I would have warned ya. That stuff is strong. I came here with a month of sobriety. Didn't have to take the meds."

"You were already sober when you got here? What's up with that? Why are you here?"

"I'll tell ya more later, but I came here after two weeks in the hospital, followed by two weeks in jail. I was already detoxed by the time I got here."

"Hospital and jail? What the hell happened to you?" He looked like a poster boy for the Boy Scouts. Earlier in the day, I'd found out that he was a teacher of fifth-grade history. Grant's impeccable Southern manners made him seem like a clean-cut, do-good, outstanding American citizen. Something didn't fit. "You can't unleash that on me and not explain the story just a little."

Grant paused, made himself more comfortable in his seat, and folded his arms. "My last drunk, I blacked out. Supposedly, I started a fight with some girls at their house. They say they were forced to call the cops. After the officers handcuffed me, they beat me badly, puncturing my stomach and causing internal bleeding. At the station, they saw my condition and took me to the emergency room. I woke up in agony, handcuffed to a hospital bed, and with my terrified parents looking down at me. Two years ago, we lost my brother to an overdose of GHB. They were crying, broken, and ashamed, and two officers were sitting outside my room like I was on the most-wanted list. After I healed, I had to serve two weeks in jail. After rehab, I go to trial. I came here on a firm suggestion from our lawyer. My parents are laying out the cash for Hanley and the best attorney in Gainesville."

"What did you do? Why did the girls call the cops?"

"I don't know. I don't remember. I'm not a violent guy. I've only been in one fight my entire life—in elementary school.

I do remember the girls at the bar asking me to go back to their place. I think they slipped something in my drink, and then. . . . Wow . . . I don't know, man." He shook his head. "I just don't know. I *do* know that the only way I could ever get violent is if I had to protect myself. Maybe they wanted to hurt me? Don't ask me."

"I can't imagine you being violent. I'm sorry you were beaten bad enough to have to go to the hospital. And then to be forced to serve time? What a nightmare! Are you going to sue the police department?"

"My attorney suggests we don't, though he thinks they're guilty as hell of abusing me. They beat me with my hands already in handcuffs."

"Are you kidding?"

"We can talk about it more later. Maybe tomorrow morning on our walk?"

"Yeah, that sounds great. Walking lightly, I'm allowed to do. We're on."

We shook hands on it.

THAT NIGHT'S STORY WAS from Taylor, a young kid hailing from Boston University. He was about six feet three inches tall and around 235 pounds—muscular and athletic but not overly cut—and strikingly handsome. He was the starting safety for BU's football team. Right before his parents sent him to Hanley, he was arrested for his third DUI. He totaled his car and walked away without a scratch on himself. Taylor somehow managed to get out of his car and walk home, all while completely wasted. He woke up to two cops pounding on his front door.

Taylor sat in a big leather recliner, facing everyone. As he shared his story, I focused on him as if he were the only person in the room. I pictured every detail of his story. He shared his life history, from birth and childhood up through today. He'd been taking antidepressants since middle school, and sports was the only thing that made him happy and comfortable around other people. He drank his first beer at ten years old. I couldn't believe he could remember how old he had been when he first drank. But so could I—at a Super Bowl party when I was nine years old.

Taylor slowly linked specific events with alcohol and drugs and how his disease had progressed. He ended by saying, "My parents bailed me out of jail on one condition: I go to treatment. So, here I am at Hanley." We all applauded and stood up. We gathered around him and waited our turns to hug him and thank him for sharing. That was the first time I had ever heard someone tell his story.

I pulled out my schedule: 7:00 to 7:45 PM, lecture. I looked down at my watch. It was already 6:55 PM *They sure keep us on a tight timetable.* I bit my inner cheek, stretched my neck, and shrugged like a boxer warming up for a fight. *I've got to give this my all. I'm not losing my girls.*

The evening lecture usually featured a person who was from outside Hanley but also involved in recovery, often a past patient of Hanley sharing his or her experience, strength, and hope in addressing alcoholism and addiction. On this night, Sheryl, a divorced mother of two, walked up to the podium. She was about five feet seven inches tall, and she had long, blonde hair and fair skin. I would say she was about forty-five years old. She wore a black business suit and spoke with such a powerful voice that she barely needed a microphone. She shared that five years earlier she had been living in a crack house and had sold her baby for crack. Two weeks before this lecture, though, she took her company public, and it's worth a little over thirty million dollars. We all were riveted.

Sheryl began her story of how she'd gotten to this point in her life by talking about her upbringing. She explained how her father had worked constantly in order to pay the bills and how her mother, a religious nut, had scared her with her focus on the Bible and salvation. As a teenager, she had rebelled and run with the wrong crowd. They experimented with alcohol, pot, and cocaine. Soon, she tried crack cocaine. And she couldn't stop. Sheryl explained her uncontrollable cravings.

"I needed a fix so bad, so I sold her. I sold my baby girl." Tears flowed from Sheryl's eyes. "My last and most prized possession."

I understood. Sheryl had lost the power of choice. She couldn't turn off her brain's powerful desire for the chemicals. She couldn't "just say no" to her addiction. It consumed her and controlled her. I related to that.

As Sheryl shared more about her life, I started to identify with this broken woman who had sold her child for drugs. I began to connect the dots of my own story. It wasn't simply that I used alcohol and drugs to escape my problems. No, my story started with my childhood and the significant events that had shaped my personality. My story included my behavior patterns, my education, my career, my legal problems, and my current relationships.

Taylor's and Sheryl's stories showed me that I needed to think about who I truly was and how I had gotten to rehab. I wasn't just a heavy user—or even abuser—of alcohol and drugs. I had crossed some invisible line in my relationship with substances. I was a full-blown alcoholic and addict.

Sheryl ended her talk by explaining that her sobriety felt like wearing a warm cashmere sweater on a cold day. She felt comfortable and protected. She puts her sobriety first, before her daughter, who she eventually got back in "a miracle" of her program," and before her thriving business. She said that surrendering and accepting help was the best thing she ever did and that she wished the same for us.

SATURDAY NIGHT: pizza and a movie. No way would I be able to sit calmly and pay attention to a movie. I grabbed a pen and notepad and headed down to the pond. I walked down a beautiful, grassy mount toward the still, glassy water. I thought of the high-low session that had taken place an hour earlier.

"Adam . . ." Bruce had searched for me through the wall of guys milling around. "What's your high-low today?"

"My high was John Dyben's lecture this morning, about how spirituality is like having muscles." I had scratched my head and sighed. "My low is how much I miss my wife and daughter. I feel so guilty for being here." I had looked around the room and received nods of understanding. This second high-low session meant that I had completed a full twenty-four hours of rehab. I now had a sense of the structure of the nine days that lay before me: the activities, the learning, the insights, and the emotional ups and downs.

Now, sitting on a bench by the pond, memories danced around in my mind. I thought about all my time with Gaga, her always being there for me when I was a kid. All of a sudden, random drinking scenes popped into my head. I saw myself back at Arizona State University drinking by myself in my room in Manzanita Hall. Then I was sitting in jail in Tempe, Arizona, after the DUI I got during my senior year. I remembered the horrible anxiety and paranoia I'd felt when I'd tried to detox off Xanax just a year ago, at twenty-nine years old, and the fake calls I'd made to pharmacies, pretending to be my doctor. I'd even stolen my mother's stash when she wasn't home.

Suddenly, a deep, rusty voice called out, "Yo, Adam! Let's have that talk."

Big Tony was jogging toward me. He looked like Shrek, the ogre, running. When he finally reached me, huffing and puffing, he sat down beside me.

"Whew! Man, I'm getting old." He took a few seconds to catch his breath. "Adam, I want ya to listen to me, okay?"

I patted his shoulder but didn't turn around.

"First off, when anybody in here hears about my past, they get scared of me. But you . . . you were respectful. That's big, in my book."

He patted my back and rubbed his hand up and down.

I shook my head and continued to stare at the water, glassy-eyed.

"Ya here for a reason, kid—to get better. I saw that beautiful family of yours, ya know that?"

"You did? When?"

"When they came for the tour. They met a whole bunch of us. It was easy to figure out who ya were, 'cause the lady with an accent—"

"My mom?"

"That's your mom? She's one sexy lady."

I smiled. I'd been getting that my whole life.

"She described ya," he said. He grabbed my arm in his thick, huge hand. "And ya don't have to be a detective. Ya have a lot to live for. I wanted to talk to ya, because I lost my son to this awful disease." A tear welled up in his right eye. "Anthony Jr. What a kid. What a special boy. He would have been around ya age. I miss him so much."

"What happened?"

"He overdosed. I think about him almost every minute of every day." Tony paused, staring at the pond. "Look, just don't give up, okay? That's all I ask. I see ya, and I think of my son. Just don't give up on this place, kid."

Tony slapped my thigh, stood up, and then slowly walked away. I'd been adopted into the rehab familia.

I looked at the pond. I listened to the birdcalls, crickets, and the flapping fish as they jumped for insects. The sounds took me back to my childhood summers at Camp Wigwam up in Waterford, Maine. I looked down at the notepad and wrote

at the top of the page: ADAM JABLIN'S STORY. I scribbled down a few highlights and lowlights from my life.

THE NEXT MORNING, I woke up freezing after having tossed and turned all night. The Hanley Center keeps the inside of every building extremely cold, for hygienic purposes (i.e., bacteria growing from us sickos detoxing). As I rose slowly, I realized that every muscle had stiffened from the subzero temperature. I clasped my hands together and rubbed them and blew on them to warm them up. I looked at my watch: 5:00 AM. I decided that I had enough time to get out of bed and walk outside. In the pitch-dark room, I found my sneakers and headed out the door.

Blinking my eyes at the light in the hallway, I was like a jet-lagged traveler in a foreign airport. Everything felt alien to me. My sense of direction failed me as I looked around and wondered which hallway to take to get outside. I stumbled by the SOBER PARADE paintings in the lounge and found the coffee machine. I pressed the blue BREW button on the Keurig machine. Soon I was breathing deeply, inhaling the aroma of fresh, hot java. *Ahh!*

The outside air felt warm and pleasant on my skin. I made my way to the pond, taking in all the colors of the early morning Florida sunrise. A half-moon still was shining brightly. As I sipped my coffee, I noticed that an ocean breeze was blowing. *Outdoors in Mother Nature.* I sensed a natural order to life, which made me think deeply about what God or a higher power really is. *How can I get close to this Power?*

I took a seat on the same bench as I had the previous night. I thought about the bullet points I'd written down:

- *Growing up a fat kid in New Jersey*
- *Moving to Florida*
- *Losing weight*
- *Muscles*
- *High school*
- *Drinking*
- *Arizona State University*
- *Partying*
- *Family business*
- *Michelle*
- *Gaga*
- *Sloan*

I thought about what my life would be like as I moved forward sober. How would I think and behave? Would I turn into some monk or super-religious zealot? As I contemplated my future, I glanced down at the pond and saw a number of magnificent turtles. There were probably fifty, of all different sizes and shapes, with shells full of dynamic, colorful patterns. The day I had checked in, I had seen an older woman throwing pieces of bread into the water. Now, I wondered whether she'd been feeding these turtles. I realized that life goes on. The turtles had been here for many patients before me, and they would be here when I was gone. But who would I be?

John Dyben's lecture had carried me, and I couldn't wait to see him again. His lecture felt like a good Rocky Balboa speech, like the one he'd given his kid: "It's about how hard you can get hit and keep moving forward. How much you can take and keep moving forward."

Ding ding! I knew what I needed. I needed to strengthen my spiritual muscles. I wanted to do something spiritual at this serene moment, but I didn't know what or how. I supposed I could pray. I stared up at the sky, "Hey, God. Gaga? . . . Well . . . umm . . . it's me, Adam. You know that, of course. So, here I am . . . in rehab. Can you please help me get through this? Please?"

A gust of wind came through, and suddenly I felt a little lighter, a little more hopeful. I could almost hear Michelle's words from our phone call the previous night: "I want you to get better." I took another sip of coffee, and it hit me that today was visiting day. A smile grew on my face. *I'll see my family!*

When I walked back to the men's unit for morning meditation, I went to the table that held all of the patients' schedules and found the ones for Grant, Jack, and me. As their roommate, I figured it was the least I could do. Seth was still sleeping. I looked down at my schedule: 6:50 to 7:10 AM meditation, 7:10 to 7:40 AM breakfast, 9:15 to 10:00 AM wellness meeting with Cynthia and Robert, 10:15 to 11:30 AM personal time, 11:35 AM to 12:15 PM lunch, 1:00 to 4:00 PM visiting hours, 5:00 to 6:15 PM dinner and story time, 6:30 to 7:15 PM lecture and high-low, 8:00 PM outside twelve-step recovery meeting.

When Grant and Jack trotted in to get their coffee, I handed them their schedules.

Half yawning, Grant said, "Thanks, man."

Jack said, "Thanks, Muscles. What are you doing up already, man?"

"Couldn't sleep. Can't stop thinking about my wife and my daughter. You'll meet them today." I smiled.

Jack smirked. He raised his schedule like an attorney presenting evidence to the judge. "Muscles, you're codependent. Know that?"

I hated the sound of that word. "What do you mean? I rely on my wife too much?"

"Sort of. You think of others too much. Don't worry. I just learned this yesterday about my own relationships. We rely, or—no, excuse me—allow," he said, using his fingers to indicate quotation marks around the word *allow*, "others' behaviors and thoughts to consume us until we have no identity of our own. It's common in families of alcoholics and addicts. Let me ask you this: Does your wife try to control you?"

"Sometimes. How did you know?"

"Most wives do." He made a sinister cackle. "But wives of us alcoholics and addicts even more so. They try to stop our shenanigans. You need to do this for you, man, not for her. That's what they're going to teach you here. You haven't shut up about your wife and kid since you got here. You just got our schedules for us like you were making your daughter her bottle. We're not your responsibility, Adam. *You* are your responsibility. You're a codependent musclehead." He chuckled.

I thought about it. He was right. I hadn't shut up about Michelle and Sloan. I missed them terribly, and I just couldn't come to terms with the fact that Michelle wanted me in here. I began to chuckle with him.

"I'm an alcoholic, addicted, codependent musclehead!" I couldn't believe what had just came out of my mouth. I stopped for a second and tried to see myself from the perspective of these other guys. A weird, silly energy bubbled up from my gut and, for the first time in years, I laughed hysterically. I couldn't catch my breath. My face turned bright red, and my stomach cramped as if I'd done a full ab workout. *That's what I am—an alcoholic, addicted, codependent musclehead. Good Lord!*

My roaring was contagious. Soon, everyone in the lounge was laughing.

Jeremy walked in, half asleep, took one look at me, and smiled. "What's so funny this early in the morning?"

I tried to catch my breath. "I'm an alcoholic, addicted, codependent musclehead!"

Jeremy yawned and then said, "Congratulations, man."

AFTER MORNING MEDITATION and breakfast, I took Grant up on his offer of a walk. We got dressed in our room, which was nicknamed the swamp. He put on a comfortable pair of mesh Nike shorts, a broken-in University of Florida Gators T-shirt, and sneakers. I put on my black Under Armour sweatpants with a matching black Under Armour sleeveless shirt. I tossed my black baseball hat onto my head, attached my iPod to my arm, and draped the white earphones around my neck.

Grant took one look at me and jumped back. "Whoa! Adam, you look like you're out of a commercial." He pointed at my iPod. "I thought we could talk as we go and get to know each other. I could finish telling you the rest of my story."

It hit me that I wanted to do the same thing. My daily cardio had become such a routine that I was like a programmed robot.

"You're right. Would you believe I trained myself to be like this? Honestly, I didn't even think about it just now. I just put on my clothes, focused on exercising. Weird, huh?"

"Nah. It must take a tremendous amount of discipline to be as fit as you are. I respect that."

"It does, but I don't even think of it like that anymore. I just suit up and go. Strange." I took off the iPod and earphones, and we left our room.

As we walked, the conversation flowed. I shared feelings and emotions I'd never come to terms with, and he did the same. I admitted how lost I felt without Gaga, that her passing had made me obsess about death, spirit, and the afterlife. I hated that my best pal, Lew, had married my sister. Grant let me in on how scared he was about his upcoming trial. I told him how unfulfilled I was in my work life and how I wished I could be a personal trainer, a public speaker, or perhaps create my own business from scratch. He shared how much he missed his brother, who had passed away, and how he was terrified of going back to jail. The hour flew by, and I felt as if I had just met one of the greatest friends of my life.

I showered and got ready for a hot shave. Before applying the shaving cream, I looked in the mirror and slowly studied my face. My skin color looked healthier, more vibrant. The

whites of my eyes were shinier. I couldn't believe I could see a difference in my appearance already. *Was I really that messed up before?*

AT 9:15 AM, I met Cynthia, the head of the wellness center, and Robert, the head of fitness, in front of their office inside the gym. I felt at home in that gym.

"Adam, come on in," Cynthia said in her North Carolina accent. A tall, beautiful woman in her late thirties, Cynthia had an athletic build, brown, shoulder-length hair, and bold, brown eyes. "Looks like you know the weight room pretty well." She smiled and gestured for me to close the door behind me.

Robert sat at his desk, which was across from Cynthia's. Of course, he had an amazing physique—a good amount of muscle mass and good definition (I'd heard that he practiced yoga every day)—which I noticed instantly. His cleanly shaven head, ice-blue eyes, and square jawline reminded me of Mr. Clean. I felt a strange connection with Robert, since we were both fitness junkies. We both knew what it took to keep our bodies in prime condition, and that created mutual respect. Fitness enthusiasts were in an almost cult with one another.

"Hi, Adam. Please take a seat." Robert pointed to the chair between his and Cynthia's desks. His aura was calm and reassuring.

I sat.

Robert said, "I'm just going to sit in on your session with Cynthia. Is that okay?"

"Absolutely."

Cynthia said, "Looks like I can skip most of the preliminary conversation I have with our patients, about the importance of healthy eating habits and exercise."

I winked at her.

She smiled back at me and then looked down at a folder labeled ADAM JABLIN.

"I have some notes here saying that you're nervous, energetic, and extremely high-strung. Is that correct?"

"Yes, I tend to be a worrywart." *That's why I drink heavily and take Xanax to calm down, Ambien to sleep, and Zoloft daily.*

"I'd like to use this session to identify activities that can make you feel more relaxed here at Hanley, ones you can continue to use outside, in your real life." She looked at Robert and then back at me. "The weight training isn't exactly relaxing you, huh?"

"It doesn't help that I take amphetamines, fat burners, or speed supplements beforehand to train with maximum intensity."

"You take all that stuff while you feel anxious?"

I nodded.

"Oh, boy. For starters, stop taking that stuff!"

We all laughed.

Cynthia said, "Let's go over some relaxation techniques. How do you feel about yoga?"

"I love it. I hurt my shoulder a few years back and, rather than opting for surgery, I took up Bikram Yoga—you know, hot yoga—five days a week for a year. It helped me keep my physique while rehabilitating my shoulder. It made me more flexible—and limber, too."

Robert said, "That's great. I don't teach Bikram, but I've developed a system called Yogaerobics. It combines the five components of physical fitness, endurance, strength, flexibility, and balance with the five elements of cardio, breathing and meditation, yoga, upper-body workouts, and lower-body workouts. Want to try it?"

"Sign me up!" We slapped five.

Cynthia wrote it down on a sheet of paper.

"Would you like to try tai chi?" she asked.

"Yes! I've always wanted to."

Some weird feeling, deep inside me, wanted to stay at Hanley for longer than ten days.

"How about light water exercises in the pool?"

"No. I don't do light." I put up both my hands, curving my fingers to indicate quotation marks around the word *light*.

Cynthia shook her head. "We need you to unwind. How about nature walks? You can feed the turtles in the pond."

I knew it. They did feed the turtles. I couldn't help but think of Rocky Balboa's turtles—Cuff and Link—and how Rocky fed them and talked to them as if they were human beings.

I nodded, and she wrote "animal therapy" on the paper.

"You may find more joy in it than you think," she said. "These are all tools to get you better and help you chill out."

Yeah, good luck with that!

During personal time, I hung out with the guys. It felt good to pal around and connect in a less structured way. We sat on the field by the pond. As I watched a few of the guys flying kites, I briefly wondered whether Hanley was an insane asylum.

I felt more at ease than I had in the past couple days, maybe because I knew I'd be seeing Michelle, Sloan, and the rest of my family in just a few hours. As we shared crazy stories of drinking, drugging, and gambling, I felt something inside myself changing. I felt I belonged. Almost every story could make it to the movies. One of my favorite stories was about how Morty had checked into Hanley.

Morty had driven to Hanley, all by himself. He'd figured the car ride would be his last hurrah before getting clean. In the car, he took with him a suitcase of cocaine and four bottles of Jack Daniel's. He stayed up almost the whole time. He drove, cried, laughed, made ridiculous phone calls—you name it. When he finally got to Hanley, he had only about two shots of whiskey and a small bag of cocaine left. Morty walked into the detox building as high as a kite. He was paranoid, anxious, and hallucinating. He paced in the lobby for five minutes. The receptionist asked repeatedly why he was there. By the twentieth time she asked, she'd had enough.

"Sir! What can we do for you?"

Morty shot her a nasty look.

"Sir! What, may I ask, is your problem?"

Morty stopped pacing, and his face turned bright red. He walked up to her counter like a deranged maniac.

"You want to know what my problem is? Do you?" he screamed.

He put his hand into his pocket, grabbed the bag of cocaine, and slammed it down on the counter as hard as he could.

"This!" he screamed at the top of his lungs. "*This* is my goddamned problem!"

She grabbed the bag and called for medical assistance, pronto.

As soon as they began filling out his paperwork, he started to have severe cravings. He begged for that bag of cocaine. "Just a little more. Please! Just one more bump."

And soon, my entire family would be meeting this cross-dressing, flamboyantly gay alcoholic and addict.

I PACED THE HALLWAYS, waiting for my family's arrival. But while I was waiting, I realized something: *My stomach doesn't hurt.*

Usually, my stomach ached from all the pills, booze, and supplements. Those things made me constipated, bloated, and then terribly diarrheic. The gastroenterologist had thought I had irritable bowel syndrome, for which he recommended eliminating alcohol, caffeine, chocolate, and high-fiber foods. Little had he known the real amounts of *all* those things I already was consuming.

Rather than change my diet, I had added more pills: probiotics filled with digestive enzymes, essential fatty acids, and cleansing floras. If the label recommended four pills three times a day, I took ten pills five times a day, thinking that more is always better. Then I attempted to detox myself by taking lots of laxatives and vitamins, consuming lots of green drinks and fiber shakes, spending time in steam rooms, and doing hot workouts such as hot yoga. I spent hours researching combinations of cleansing supplements that I could take to make my stomach feel better while still keeping up the insane excess use of alcohol and drugs.

Now, I rubbed my concave stomach. There was no bloat. At Hanley, my body was healing quickly. I had spent all those years trying to make my excess behavior work, and the thing that would cure me was simple—total abstinence.

At 1:00 PM, my family showed up. Michelle, Sloan, Mom, and Dad all waited for me outside, next to the detox unit. When I came around the corner and we saw each other, I got choked up. I couldn't hold back the tears, even though I told myself to "man up." My joy in seeing them was mixed with my shame and guilt. That broke me. As the warm tears rolled down my face, I ran to Michelle. I put my arms around her and squeezed. She wiped the tears from my eyes while her tears flowed.

"Hi, baby," she said. "Somebody else would like to say hello to you, too."

She pointed to my mother, who was holding Sloan. I walked over to her, and Mom held Sloan out to me. Sloan was beaming with happiness.

When I took Sloan in my arms, she mumbled, "Dada," and I smiled. I held that angel from heaven and tried to at least slow my tears.

"Hi, baby. Hi, baby girl."

I squeezed her gently. I truly had not known how much being a father would change me. Now, I saw that not being around my daughter was like losing a limb, a piece of myself.

"I miss you so, so, so much. I'm so sorry."

Still holding Sloan, I looked up at my mother.

She touched the side of my face with her hand. "I'm so proud of you, Addy."

I handed Sloan back to her and turned toward my father. He wore dark Porsche sunglasses so that nobody could see his eyes, but tears were rolling down his face.

"Hey, Daddy."

"Hi, Son."

He opened his arms, and we gave each other the most sincere, loving hug we'd had in years—a hug that only a father and a son can understand. He patted my back.

I walked back to Michelle.

I opened my arms to the sky and shouted, "Welcome to rehab!"

Our laughter released the tension we'd all been holding in.

"You guys want to see my new home?"

They all nodded, and together we strolled to the men's unit.

I gave them a brief tour while they asked, "How's the food?" "How's the gym?" "Are the bathrooms clean?" "How do you feel?"

Then Michelle asked, "Have you been in the sun?"

My eyebrow rose. "Why?"

"Honey, you look really good. The color of your skin. . . . You look healthier. You're not as pale white, and your eyes seem clearer."

I thought about how I saw that same thing myself in the mirror an hour earlier. It was now confirmed. I had been that toxic, like a junkie, and other people had noticed. *What else am I not aware of?*

Just as we were about to enter the men's unit, we heard a loud bam, followed by the sound of glass shattering.

Somebody screamed, "Fuck you! To hell with this place. It doesn't make any sense. I hate all of you!"

I looked at my family and put out my hand, indicating that they should wait where they were. I ran inside the building and saw four counselors chasing somebody around the corner and down the hallway. I looked down to see a chair down on the floor and a shattered picture. Grant came around the corner.

"Hey, Grant. What the hell just happened, man?" I had an empty pit in my stomach, and my pulse had quickened.

"Matt happened. They told him he couldn't use the gym right now because of visiting day, and he blew his top. He took that chair"—he pointed at the one lying on the floor—"threw it at the picture, and stormed out."

I felt violated, by Matt, again.

"Grant, between you and me, I can't stand that kid. I hope they kick him out."

Grant made a face.

I looked down at the ground again. I was disappointed. "I was just about to take my family to see our bedroom."

"I wouldn't right now, man." Grant headed off.

I ran back outside to my family.

"I'm sorry about that. The kid who made that scene is bad news. It's just been a couple days, and I'm not a fan. Let's go find a quiet place to sit and talk."

We made our way to the nearby gazebo at a casual pace. The gazebo was located near the recreational park and the fitness trail. It reminded me of a landmark that one would see in the Deep South. We lifted Sloan's stroller up into it, and then got comfortable on the benches that lined its outer edges.

Michelle held my hand.

My mother said, "Tell us . . . what's it been like so far? What do you do here?"

"It's been a roller coaster. Yesterday, we had an amazing lecture by a man named John Dyben, the head of spiritual care. We got to the core of what spirituality is. Healthy spirituality versus unhealthy spirituality."

For thirty minutes straight, I described the lecture. The words came out effortlessly, and I felt like a spiritual teacher. I loved watching their eyes light up as I spoke.

"You really like it here, huh?" my mother asked.

"Like it? I feel like I'm in an insane asylum. I saw guys painting when I first walked in. Now, they want me to feed the turtles, fly kites, and play volleyball."

I took a deep breath.

"I plan on doing my ten days as seriously and honestly as possible and returning home good as new." I smiled.

They looked at one another cautiously.

"Look, guys. I have something to admit to you, and it's going to be hard for you all to hear."

I had built a case in my head to demonstrate not only how honest I was but also how I was poles apart from everyone else in this crazy place.

"I'm an alcoholic and an addict. But . . . I'm not like these guys. You should hear the stories. . . . You wouldn't believe it."

I told them about Seth and his heart attack, Tony's serving time, Jeremy's experience as a rock 'n' roll star, and Grant waking up in the hospital and then serving two weeks in jail for a crime he couldn't remember. "And the drugs: heroin, crack, OxyContin, crystal meth. . . . I'm getting a serious drug education in here. Trust me, I'll be home soon."

My mother and father left early so that Michelle, Sloan, and I could enjoy some time alone with one another. I ran back to the men's unit to grab a loaf of bread, and then we walked down to the pond to feed the turtles.

"It's peaceful here. I'm happy we found this place for you." Michelle ripped up little pieces of bread and threw them into the water as Sloan watched.

"I miss you and Sloan so much. I can't stop thinking or talking about you both. This morning, Jack told me I'm codependent. But I don't know how I'm supposed to do this without you here. I don't work without you."

"Adam, you need this. *We* need this." She grabbed my hand and squeezed.

"You don't work without me? You were about to leave me a week ago. You had that crazy tirade."

I looked down in utter shame. "I don't think I was really going to do that. I was just—I was so—"

"Sick!" Michelle's body looked tense. "Adam, you're sick, and you need to realize this can easily happen again if you don't continue to get help. We won't make it."

She looked at Sloan and then back at me before pulling me closer to her. "And, by the way, mister, you're no different from anybody else in here. You're in here, and they're in here. Since when did you get so judgmental?"

I broke eye contact and bit my lower lip.

"I need you to say it, Adam."

"Say what?"

"Say you're no different than they are. Say it out loud. I want to hear it."

"Are you serious?"

"Dead serious. Say it right now. 'I, Adam Jablin, am no different from anybody else in here.'"

I took a deep breath. I looked Michelle in the eye. "I, Adam Jablin, am no different from anybody else in here."

"Good boy. Here, throw this piece to those two guys over there." Michelle pointed to two adorable turtles hanging out together. One turtle was huge, and the other tiny. They each had a red streak down the shell, and the big guy had one on his head as well.

"Let's name them Spike and Taz. Spike is the big guy, and Taz is the cute, little one," Michelle said.

"Spike and Taz," I repeated.

"I want you to feed these two guys every day. It will be your daily reminder that you need to continue to get the help for our family to work. That's your job for me, okay?"

I looked at her and swallowed hard.

I nodded. "Feed Spike and Taz. Got it."

AFTER MICHELLE AND SLOAN LEFT, I went to dinner feeling depressed. Before Michelle had left, she'd made me say it aloud one more time. "I, Adam Jablin, am no different from anybody else in here."

I bumped into Jack as soon as I got to the cafeteria door. He was unhappy, too.

"Seeing them leave is a bitch, ain't it?" he asked.

I put my hand on his shoulder, and we entered the cafeteria together.

"You hear about Matt?" I asked.

"Yeah. They're keeping him here, though. The guy's nothing but trouble, if you ask me."

"I agree." I shook my head. "He's a punk."

After dinner—for me, grilled chicken, green beans, and a sweet potato—we returned to the men's unit for story time.

Frank, an older gentleman of about fifty years old, told his story. He owned a boat manufacturing company out of Key West and was worth a mint. Four years earlier, his drug use had started innocently, with Percocet to dull the intolerable pain from spinal fusion. After six more surgeries, including a discectomy and several disk replacements, he needed more medications to dull the agony. The doctors prescribed OxyContin and, eventually, Frank started using a needle to inject medications. His wife found him on his boat, overdosed and surrounded with all his drugs. She took him to Hanley. As I watched him and listened to him tell his story, I repeated to myself, *I'm no different from him*—my new mantra, although it felt fake.

High-low followed story time. As usual, Bruce went around the room.

When he got to me, I said, "My high: getting to see my family. My low . . . that scene Matt pulled. It pissed me off."

The room was united in agreement with that. I kept thinking of how much I didn't like him. But I could almost hear Michelle's voice saying, "I'm no different from anyone else in here." I stared at the ground, wrestling with that idea. I just didn't see how I was the same as him. I don't shoot heroin and throw chairs at walls.

That evening, we went to a twelve-step meeting outside the Hanley Center. I enjoyed the experience, for the most part. At the end of the meeting, everyone held hands and recited the Lord's Prayer. I wasn't crazy about holding hands with a bunch of strangers.

When they started praying, reciting, "Our Father, who art in heaven, hallowed be thy name," I freaked out. *Wait! I'm Jewish. I can't say this prayer.* But as they continued, I listened to the words. "Thy Kingdom come. Thy will be done, on Earth as it is in heaven. Give us this day our daily bread. And forgive us our trespasses, as we forgive those who trespass against us. And lead us not into temptation, but deliver us from evil. For thine is the kingdom, and the power, and the glory, forever and ever. Amen." The prayer didn't say anything about Jesus. *Maybe I can say it?*

Back in my room at Hanley, I reminisced about the day, trying to figure out how I was like these men. Their usage of hardcore street drugs made me feel healthier than them. I replayed the whole day in my head. Seeing my family and admitting to them that I was an alcoholic and an addict. The turtles. *How did I turn out this way?*

An image flashed in my mind of a confused Superman meeting his father, Jor-El, for the first time and desperately asking him, "Who am I?" I took out my pen and notepad and dug deeper into the details of my own story.

A CALL TO ACTION

- On our journey, we can sometimes be swept forward by another person's words, actions, or perspective—if we are open enough to listen. My mentor Dion does this for me every time we talk! He taught me a simple prayer. I'd like you to try it. "God, it would be nice to be closer to you." Prayer can feel like a big word and come accompanied by thoughts of whether we are doing it "right." But the wording doesn't matter as long as your heart is in it!
- The chapter ends the question, "Who am I?" Who are you? Time to start YOUR story.

CHAPTER 9

GOING DEEPER

I WOKE UP AGAIN AFTER another terrible night's sleep, shivering from the sterile, cold air. Within seconds, my thoughts were of whether Michelle and Sloan were safe in the house alone. I looked at my watch: 5:20 AM. *Damn.* Only four hours of tossing and turning. I followed the same routine as I had the previous morning. I slowly got out of bed and pinched the bridge of my nose, between my eyes. I made my way to the coffee machine in the lounge, picked up a cup, and pushed the blue BREW button. While the coffee was brewing, I flipped through the schedules and found mine. My first activity of the day would be morning meditation, followed by breakfast and wellness hour. Then, at 9:15 AM, I would go to John Dyben's office. I pumped my fist and grinned. His lecture on spiritual fitness had inspired me. Despite the sleepless night, I felt my adrenaline spike. Reading down a bit further on my schedule, another activity popped out at me: 6:00 PM psychological evaluation with

Dr. J Wirth. I thought back to the MMPI test and wondered whether "I like rainy days. A) True or B) False" and other bizarre questions actually could diagnose my personality. The rest of my schedule included group therapy, which was a step-one "powerless over alcohol" group, wellness/physical fitness, leisure education, an evening lecture, and an optional outside twelve-step meeting.

I was looking forward to the morning meditation, but I felt dead tired. I yawned for probably the twentieth time and sipped my coffee. I rubbed my crusty eyes and squinted at the two inspirational quotes I had picked—one from Michael Jordan and one from Christopher Reeve. As the morning crowd plodded in, I refilled my coffee and waited for Bruce to take a seat. Then I sat on his right so that I could share first.

We said the Serenity Prayer, and then Bruce opened up the session by reading from *Twenty-Four Hours a Day*. "And the prayer of the day reads, 'I pray that I remove all blocks that are keeping me from God. I pray that I may let God come into my life with power.'"

"Thank you, Bruce," we said in unison.

Bruce nodded at me.

"Good morning, guys. I'm Adam, and I'm an alcoholic and an addict."

"Hello, Adam," came the response in harmony.

I took a gulp of coffee.

"I picked a couple quotes I'd like to share with you before we start our day. One is, 'A hero is an ordinary individual who finds the strength to persevere and endure in spite of overwhelming obstacles.' That's from Christopher Reeve, aka Superman. The next is 'You have to expect things of yourself

before you can do them.' That's from Michael Jordan." I put my notepad to the side and looked up to signal that I was done. I sat on the edge of my chair, readjusted my back, and yawned again. I thought of the GOAT—the greatest of all time—Michael Jeffrey Jordan and that quote. If I wanted to get sober, I had to expect this rehab thing to work.

After meditation, I ate my usual breakfast of egg whites, oatmeal, and fruit, with two more cups of coffee. Then, I headed to the nurses' station to get my daily medication. I found Kat and told her, "Kat, I'm scared."

"What is it, Adam?" Her voice shook as she narrowed her eyes.

"I'm not sleeping. I haven't slept since I've been here. I don't want to get sick." I droned on and on about how getting proper rest is essential to the human body. "Studies have shown that we need seven to nine hours of sleep a night. Have you ever noticed how much a baby sleeps? Sloan sleeps twice during the day and, of course, at night, while her body grows—"

Kat grinned and rubbed my back while she led me to the medication counter. "Listen, darlin'. First off, you're not a newborn baby. Secondly, do you know how many times I've heard someone say they're not sleeping? If it gets really bad, talk to me again. You're in a new environment, surrounded by strangers. You're not in your own bed, in your own house, with your family. You're learning and growing more than you even realize. This is normal. You know what I've told thousands of patients before you?"

"What's that?"

"Nobody ever died from lack of sleep."

LATER THAT MORNING, Grant and I took another walk together. I reflected on what Kat had said about nobody dying from lack of sleep, and I resigned myself to the fact that I was just going to have to roll with it. As Grant and I talked, I felt a calm growing inside me. The sun shone on the pond, and we could see the turtles swimming beneath the surface of the water. I thought about Spike and Taz. I wondered how Michelle was managing without me. The calm feeling disappeared, and I returned to my more familiar state of anxiety, and shame.

After our walk, I showered and dressed. I could hear the ruckus coming from the hallway, and I felt as if I were at summer camp again. Hearing a bunch of guys clowning around, laughing, hollering, and telling jokes revived the little kid in me. I looked down at my schedule again: 9:15 AM John Dyben. *Yes!*

I walked from the hallway of alcoholic madness to John Dyben's office, which was two doors down from our bedroom. His small workspace felt tranquil. I think it was the aura that he emitted, like the Buddha did. Books about psychology and spirituality—the Bible, *The Tao of Pooh, Love Is Letting Go of Fear,* and *A Grief Observed*—were stacked haphazardly on the bookshelves and John's desk, mixed in with patient folders and yellow sticky notes. There were peaceful paintings on the walls—a pink and orange sunrise over the ocean and a breathtaking sunset over purple mountains in the desert. One of them made me think of my home here in Florida, and the other had me reminiscing about my college days in Arizona.

"Welcome, Adam," John said as he hugged me. He was a great hugger. He offered me a seat on a cushiony, red chair in the corner of his office. He smiled, took a deep breath, and leaned back in his own chair.

"I can see you're an open and loving guy, Adam."

I grinned and acknowledged that I am.

"Tell me a little about yourself and how you came to Hanley."

"Where to begin?" I told him about my wild, roller-coaster ride that had led to the intervention and then about the intervention itself.

"Okay, Adam." He took a deep breath and clasped his hands together. "You mentioned your family several times. You sound like a man with a lot of love to give, a lot of heart. You just lost your way, and we're going to get you back."

I couldn't contain my grin. My pulse sped up. "Sounds good to me."

"Adam, you've told me about your wife, daughter, Gaga, job, parents, exercising, pressures, and trying to please everyone. And I get it. But I want to know who *you* are. Who is Adam Jablin?"

I panicked. *Who am I?* I rolled the question around in my mind. *Who am I? Who . . . am . . . I?*

"Take a second, a deep breath, and then tell me who you are."

Who am I? Okay. Think deep here, Adam. Think deep. "I'm a lace manufacturer and fitness enthusiast."

"No. That's what you do for a living and what you enjoy. Go deeper."

Deeper?

"I'm a good, loving man who got sidetracked and wants to find his way back."

John smiled. "That's true, but go a little deeper for me."

Deeper? Whoa. Deeper. "Umm . . . all right. I'm a loving husband, father, and son. I've let the voices in my head and the pressures of life get to me, and now I need to find myself again. How's that?"

John stared into my eyes and said, "Deeper."

What? Deeper? Deeper than that? Think, Adam. Think. "I'm a . . . uh . . . an alcoholic and addict?" I hoped this was what he was looking for.

John laughed.

"Yes. Yes, you are." He chuckled. "Let me help you here. You said you love your wife, right?"

I nodded.

"She's your soul mate."

Guilt.

"You love her for sicker and for poorer, right?"

I nodded.

"You love her no matter how terrible things appear to be right now?"

"Yes."

"You'd be willing to do anything to save her life?"

I nodded vigorously.

"If she were hit by a bus and couldn't move or talk, would you still love her?"

I sat back for a second. I took a deep breath and actually visualized Michelle lying in a hospital bed, on life support, with tubes everywhere. I also saw myself right next to her, believing in her, believing she could get better, praying, and showering her with love and attention.

"John, I'd love her if she was deformed, lost her limbs, couldn't communicate, was bound to a wheelchair, bedridden, whatever. I'd love her with everything I have."

"Adam, do you know what that is? If she can't communicate with you at all, can't move, nothing, and you still love everything about her just lying there, then what is she? Think."

This was the deepest anyone had ever asked me to reflect. I rubbed my thighs with my hands and asked myself out loud, several times, "What is she?" Finally, I looked up at John. "She is a life."

His eyes opened and, like a kung fu master, he transformed from a disciplinarian into a proud teacher. "Yes! Yes, Adam. She is life, and that is the answer to the first question I asked you. Who are you? You are life. You are alive! You're God's child. You're a miracle. There is no such thing as a wrong or right life. There's just life. But a life can be healthy or unhealthy, just like our spirituality. Think about that. You're doing just fine, and you're lucky to be here, Adam. You don't ever again have to feel the way you did when you walked into the Hanley Center. You're off the hook!"

My eyes watered. I tipped my head back and closed my eyes. I didn't feel like the bad guy or the terrible father and husband. I knew I was just sick. Rehab was treating my disease, and John had made the spiritual aspect easy to understand. When John mentioned God, it didn't feel threatening, like the idea of a punishing, supernatural, white-bearded man. Quite the opposite. It felt safe.

"Adam, are you ready for your homework?"

I nodded.

"As we just said, you are life. A child of God. The only Adam Jablin on the planet. A life that deserves to be . . . observed. I want you to walk from here to the cafeteria as slowly as possible . . . slower than a crawl. You're not to speak a word. I want you to take each step with an awareness of being in your environment. At our next session, I want you to tell me everything you observed."

"Everything?"

"This is not anything that has to be perfect. Don't stress over it. Just walk, take it all in, and enjoy."

I left John's office, feeling happier and lighter. The world no longer weighed on my shoulders.

I walked slowly from John's office to the cafeteria—a distance of no more than a hundred yards. With each small step, I noticed something new. For the first time, I saw the trees—the boldness of the dark-brown bark and rich, green leaves. I noticed the beautiful marble fountains and heard the soothing sound of their flowing water. Butterflies were swarming. One was bright yellow, the other orange with a dynamic black pattern on each wing. The two of them fluttering together looked as if they were doing an exotic African dance. Another few steps, and all my senses came alive. I heard birdsong and saw a conspicuous nest. I looked up in the air and watched mourning doves flying fast on powerful wings. I closed my eyes, felt a light breeze, and heard the buzzing of crickets. All of my faculties had sharpened. I felt naturally high. My spirit revived.

A lot of guys just walked right past me, giving me privacy. Some asked me, "What's wrong?" My casual facial expression communicated, without words, that I was fine.

I learned a huge lesson from those interactions. I had become so focused on saying the right things that I had forgotten I could communicate with simple body language. I didn't need to be "perfect" or silver-tongued.

Just before I reached the cafeteria, I looked down and to my right and saw a beautiful garden of roses and other tropical delights among rugged volcanic rocks. I had passed this spot at least twenty-five times between meals, medications, lectures, and group therapy, but I had never noticed this garden. How could that be? I finally had a true understanding of the saying "Stop and smell the roses." I had ignored so much beauty in life, always going a million miles a minute and trying to get from point A to point B as fast as possible. Rehab, of all places, had slowed me down so that I could appreciate what life had to offer.

When I entered the cafeteria, I bounced from foot to foot like a fighter. I felt a warm tingling in my limbs. I went up to Jack and Tony in the lunch line and good-naturedly punched them in their arms.

Dodging the punch, Jack said, "Whoa, Muscles! What happened to you?"

"What?"

"You look . . . well . . . happy! You don't have that worried look on your face. You always look like you're in deep thought."

I'd never thought about how my facial expressions and body language revealed my emotional temperature.

"Ya get a conjugal visit from ya wife?" Tony asked, raising his eyebrows.

I chuckled. "No, nothing quite like that. I just had my first appointment with John Dyben. The guy really puts it in perspective."

In a loud voice, Tony said, "It only gets better, kid." He put both of his huge hands on my left trapezius muscle and squeezed a couple times. "It only gets better."

When Morty had joined us in line, Jack, Morty, and Tony asked me to help them make healthier food choices.

"I don't want to look like you, Adam, but I do want to feel and look better," Morty said.

I pointed at the bowl of fruit I was getting for dessert. "Try to satisfy your sweet tooth with this. If you don't like it, the chocolate cake and apple pie aren't going anywhere."

They watched me intently and listened to every word. We grabbed hamburgers, and I explained how we could make it a healthy lunch. "Here we'll put the hamburger patty inside two pieces of lettuce as our bun. Feel free to add tomato or use ketchup, although mustard would be healthier. Rather than French fries, we'll get the steamed rice and a side of vegetables."

They heckled me a bit, especially about the French fries, but they listened.

We walked over to the drinks area.

"Try this." I pointed at the Crystal Light. "It has zero calories and tastes refreshing. Trust me. Eliminating sugary sodas saves hundreds of calories and makes a world of difference."

We placed four healthy plates on a table and sat down. Everybody around us noticed and, one by one, the questions came in:

"Do you think you can teach *me* to eat right?"

"Can you help me lose my gut?"

"How do I put on more muscle?"

"Can you show me how to get a bigger chest?"

To each question, I answered yes. I loved that they all were coming to me for help and wanted my advice. I felt like a leader. But a leader of sickos.

"YOU SOUND SO DIFFERENT, and it's only been a few days." Michelle sounded surprised.

"I'm learning who I am all over again. . . . And get this: A lot of the guys want my help to get in shape and eat right."

"Shocker."

"What do you mean?"

"Everybody loves you. That the guys are asking you for help doesn't surprise me one bit. I'm surprised at how much it surprises you."

Her kind words meant a lot, but in my head I heard another voice say, *She doesn't know you. Nobody knows the real you. You're a fake, a phony. You could have been someone special, but you're not. And now, you're in rehab, putting your family through hell. You're just another businessman who doesn't like his job and works for his father. Another fitness junkie who does absolutely nothing useful with his body. You're nothing special, Adam. You're a bum!*

This getting sober thing was very up and down.

IN GROUP THERAPY—the step-one "powerless over alcohol" group, I looked around the room and read some of the posters on the walls. HOW DO WE REMEMBER THE

PAIN? WE GO TO MEETINGS. *That makes it sound like going to twelve-step meetings will remind me of how bad my substance-abuse problem is.* WE ARE NOT HUMAN BEINGS HAVING A SPIRITUAL EXPERIENCE. WE ARE SPIRITUAL BEINGS HAVING A HUMAN EXPERIENCE. *I like that one!* The sunlight shone in through the windows, and the warmth, in contrast to Hanley's usual arctic chill, was welcome.

"Today's group topic is our inner child," Brent said. He looked down and read, "The inner child dwells at the core of our being. With great enthusiasm, it constantly explores the world. It knows feeling: When angry, it screams; when hurt, it cries; when happy, it smiles. As time goes by, the child runs into adult demands. The voices of grown-ups begin to drown out the inner voices of feelings and instincts. With time, these qualities are forced into hiding."

He stopped reading, looked at us, and spoke softly. "Guys, we'll look at this closely throughout your time here."

Brent slowly and deliberately leaned back in his chair and made eye contact with each of us. "Today, gentlemen, I want to go around the circle and have each of us talk about our childhood. Tell me what you liked and didn't like, your beliefs and your behaviors, some specific events and how they felt. Remember, guys, no fixing one another and no interrupting. This exercise is deep and personal. Let's all just listen and learn."

Jeremy had served as the scapegoat of his family. He had broken all the rules and grown into a defiant, hostile kid. He had channeled the pain of being the problem child into his lyrics and music.

Tony was the chief enabler of his family. His father had been a made guy—a fully initiated member—in the mafia and had taught those values to his only son. Tony had grown into his role in both his own family and the mafia family. He had felt obligated to protect his mother and sister and take responsibility when his father was gone for days at a time. He picked up the cash from the bank. He bought the groceries. He acted as the man of the family while he was still a kid. He hid his vulnerability by acting the part of a self-righteous know-it-all: telling his mother what she should cook for dinner and his sister when to be home. Tony experienced hurt, anger, and low self-esteem.

When it was Matt's turn, I lowered my head and pressed my lips together the moment he opened his mouth. He shared his difficult childhood in an abusive, chemically dependent home. He had grown up as a lost child—shy, quiet, withdrawn, and alone. He shared horrific details of his life—how his father would get angry and break things—Matt's body parts, lamps, chairs, TVs, whatever he got his hands on.

"I'm sorry about yesterday." Matt bowed his head and rubbed the back of his neck. He was sweating visibly. "My dad breaks stuff. . . I break stuff. But I'm working on it."

I listened actively and experienced Matt's emotions as if they were my own.

As each guy—even Matt—shared about his childhood, I achieved a better understanding of him as a spiritual being and, in the process, learned about myself. I became conscious of my insecurities and strengths and more accepting of their personality quirks and my own. As each guy shared an intimate account of his childhood, I felt the heightened emotions pulling us closer together, bonding us.

LATER, I HEADED TO THE psychology wing to meet with Dr. J Wirth about my test results. When I entered the wing where his office was, I noticed a bright flower garden at the left of the entrance. I stopped, scratched my cheek, and narrowed my eyes. I didn't remember having seen the garden at my first appointment with him. I thought of Ferris Bueller's famous quote: "Life moves pretty fast. If you don't stop and look around once in a while, you could miss it."

Dr. J's office door was open, and he waved me in. "Adam, how are you?"

"Good, Doc. Umm . . . hmm . . . I'm doing good."

I plopped down in the yellow recliner for his patients.

"You sure?"

"Yeah. Just anxious about what that crazy test told you."

"Why don't you first tell me a little about yourself and how you ended up here at Hanley?"

"I'm pretty wound up all day every day. I have a lot of responsibilities, and I can't stop worrying about everybody. I'm always trying to be perfect. Perfect husband. Perfect father. Perfect body. Perfect businessman and son. You name it, and I want to be my very best at it. As a consequence, every little thing affects me. I feel like I'm constantly stressed out and being judged. I overwork or do favors or run around, all trying to make everybody happy." I shook my head in disgust. "And *I'm* the one in here. Why don't they ever try as hard as I do? If they all cared as much as I do, things would be

different. I run around trying to keep everything peaceful, and I'm in here while they're still out there."

"You sound angry."

"I'm not angry. I'm disappointed." I scowled.

"I don't think we need to even go over your test score, because you just told me exactly what it said. I give you a lot of credit for your honesty. You're going to make it if you keep that up."

"Really? Thanks, but I'm curious what the test said."

"I'll read you it briefly." He looked down and began reading from the paper on his desk. "The MMPI-2 validity scales indicate that this individual answered in a frank manner as well as displayed a healthy balance between self-praise and self-criticism. The clinical scales indicate that individuals such as these may tend to present themselves as being in psychological turmoil and discomfort. They may be tense, anxious, and agitated and may have difficulty with concentration. These individuals usually report feelings of sadness and being unhappy, and they are generally pessimistic about the future. They tend to be introspective and have high standards of performance for themselves and others and usually feel guilty when not living up to these standards. The Addiction Acknowledgement Scale was extremely elevated, showing that the patient admits to having a substance abuse condition at this time." He looked up from the paper.

I scratched my head. "So, what do you think?"

"You need to calm down, stop worrying about everybody else, and focus on yourself. You have an exaggerated sense of responsibility."

"It's *all* my responsibility! I love my wife and daughter. I want to give them everything they want. I need to keep the extended family together and help run the family business. I have my parents, sister, brother-in-law, sister-in-law, grandfather, my in-laws. . . . Can you help me manage it all without drinking?"

Dr. J sighed and leaned closer to me. "You can't give everybody what they want. That's impossible. You can't be everything to everyone. You're not Superman."

I raised an eyebrow and slid back in my chair. "Have you been speaking to my family, Doc?"

"No. Why?" He gave me a blank stare.

"What made you say I'm not Superman?"

"It's just what I thought of, what came to mind. . . . Adam, you're trying to be Superman. Why?" He squinted at me.

"I have this . . . thing . . . with Superman."

"Well, you're not him, buddy!" Dr. J laughed as he put the test scores away in my file.

THAT EVENING, I THOUGHT LONG and hard about Dr. J's words—"an exaggerated sense of responsibility." That made sense. I tried so hard to please others, at my own expense, and my reward was drinking followed by pharmaceuticals. I thought back to "going deeper" with John Dyben. I thought about my slow walk to the cafeteria, how all my senses had felt alive, like superpowers. I couldn't explain it, but something inside me was shifting. I no longer felt like a prisoner.

A CALL TO ACTION

- In Chapter 9, I freaked out because I hadn't been sleeping and was scared to get sick. Kat set me straight, "Nobody ever died from lack of sleep." We all have excuses of why we are not accomplishing our dreams and visions, like not enough sleep. Arnold Schwarzenegger said, "Just, sleep faster."
- So, how much are we all not accomplishing each day because of a fear? Take a look!
- John Dyben, who is still one of my closest mentors and best friends to this day introduced me to the long, slow walks to wake up the basic five senses! I use this exercise with my clients to this day. I want you to start incorporating this walk into your daily life the next few days. Record what you experiences; How was the weather? What did you hear? What did you see?

CHAPTER 10

SEEING GOD

ANOTHER NIGHT, another awful night's sleep. Despite a week of averaging only four hours rest each night, I felt better than I had in years.

I carried out my morning ritual: made coffee, grabbed my daily schedule, and slowly walked to my favorite bench by the pond. But this time, as I had been doing for the past few mornings, I moved through it all slowly, remembering to "stop and smell the roses." In rehab, I had learned so much about the disease of alcoholism and addiction, healthy spirituality, my story, my inner child, my exaggerated sense of responsibility and, of course, the importance of calming down.

I'd been at Hanley a week, and only three days remained before my ten-day evaluation. To my surprise, I realized that part of me wanted to stay at Hanley the full twenty-eight days. I liked the guys and all that I'd been learning. But a strong voice in my head still wanted out. It wanted to point out how different—how much better—I was from the other

patients. I reviewed my options—stay or go. I sighed and bit the inside of my cheek.

Three things on my schedule held my attention. First, I had another one-on-one appointment with Brent. Second, at 1:00 PM, I would meet with Father Ron at his office in the chapel and meditation center. According to the stories I'd heard from the guys, the man could walk on water. Third, at 2:20 PM, I had wellness and exercise. *Yes!* I rubbed my hands together and felt my heartbeat increase. The previous night, when I had gotten my meds at the nursing station, I finally had been given the green light to exercise as intensely as I desired.

During morning meditation, I sat back with my eyes closed, sipped coffee, breathed deeply, and digested the readings. I listened to the words and tried to process the meanings behind them.

When it was my turn, I read from the *Tao Te Ching*. "Better stop short than fill to the brim," I said, raising my eyebrows.

Most of the guys chuckled.

I continued. "Oversharpen the blade, and the edge will soon blunt. Amass a store of gold and jade, and no one will be able to protect it. Claim wealth and titles, and disaster will follow. Retire when the work is done." I looked at my new friends. "This is the way to heaven."

At breakfast, seven guys tried the egg whites, and three others experimented with oatmeal instead of their usual artery-clogging breakfasts. I gave a wink, nod, or pat on the back to each new buddy who was trying the fit menu. When a couple of the counselors walked by our table, they gasped at all the wholesome food. I smiled proudly. When John Dyben

walked by, he handed me one of his business cards. On the back, in his handwriting, were the words "God, teach me to love the truth." He patted my shoulder and walked away without saying a word.

WHILE GRANT AND I WERE stretching before our morning walk, Jeremy ran over to us. It was the first time I'd seen him in sneakers. He'd been wearing beaten-up, dirty Adidas flip-flops ever since I'd met him. He blinked several times and leaned toward me. "You guys mind if I join you?"

"The more the better," I said. Grant nodded his agreement.

We walked at a fast pace while sharing crazy war stories and our thoughts on whether we could make it through the rest of our lives sober. If you saw the three of us outside Hanley's walls, you would never expect us—the thin, shaggy rock star, the preppy, Southern English teacher, and the buff, metrosexual businessman—to speak to one another . . . but in Hanley we were family.

After an hour, drenched in sweat, I explained to Jeremy and Grant that we needed simple sugars because we had just burned up a lot of electrolytes and glycogen and needed to replace it in our bodies. "This is why athletes use products like Gatorade."

"Whoa, Adam! You're really smart with this stuff. How come you're not a personal trainer?" Jeremy asked.

"You'll hear when I tell my story."

"Okay, looking forward to it." Jeremy raised his hands in the air to stretch. He took off his Rolling Stones concert T-shirt, revealing even more tattoos on his chest and back, and tied it around his long hair like a bandana. "Ahh, this feels so good. I may even try to quit smoking while I'm here. And remember, Adam, you said you'll help me put some meat on these bones."

"Yes, sir. We'll hit the gym." With a smile on my face and my chest thrust out, I made a fist and pumped it. I was loosening up. I was making friends. I was becoming real. The old Adam Jablin was returning. *I, Adam Jablin, am no better than anybody in here.* I thought of Michelle. I missed her more than ever.

I WAITED OUTSIDE Brent's office for ten minutes.

I can't believe this guy. If he were in my business, he'd be suspended or even fired. Never keep them waiting, Adam. Always be on time. I could hear my grandfather and father in my head, and I grew frustrated.

I paced back and forth with my arms crossed.

Brent casually walked toward me to unlock the door.

"Hey there, Adam. How long have you been waiting?" he teased loudly. I thought I saw a smirk on his face.

"I'm always five minutes early. Maybe ten, fifteen minutes." I narrowed my eyes and tapped my foot.

"Hmm. You sound angry."

"I'm upset and annoyed, not angry."

"Uh-huh. I see." Brent rolled his eyes and opened the door to his office. "Well, you look and sound angry now. You're also a good communicator, good with your choice of words. We'll take a look at that."

We walked into his office. I took a seat and looked out the window. My nostrils flared as my face turned red and

I cracked my knuckles. *You want to push my buttons? Keep it up. I'll show you angry.*

Brent unbuttoned his sleeves and rolled them up. "Adam, do me a favor. Close your eyes and take a deep breath."

I did.

"I know you're upset and annoyed with me for being late. I apologize. Do you accept my apology?"

I hesitated and then cleared my throat. "Yes."

"Okay. Open your eyes. You all right?"

"I'm good." *Just don't ever be late for me again.*

"Good. So you're almost finished with your ten-day evaluation. What do you think of Hanley?"

I pulled back slightly while staring at nothing for a moment, "Well . . . it's an experience."

"A lot of the other men have taken a strong liking to you. I hear you're a leader."

I glanced around uneasily. "I wouldn't say that."

"Why not? You should be proud."

I shook my head and rubbed my beard. "I just want to get better for my family. I don't want to be a leader."

"Why not both?"

I sat there thinking quietly about Brent's remarks.

He looked at me steadily as I fidgeted in my seat, trying to get comfortable.

"Thank you. I appreciate the compliment. I do want to be a leader. It's just that I don't think I'm going to be here much longer. A leader stays with his men. I—I just want to get healthy and back home."

"So do they, Adam. So do they."

He scooted closer to me and leaned in. "Think about what you just said—'to get healthy and back home.' It will parallel perfectly with the homework assignment I'm about to give you. I want you to write two letters to your daughter, but twenty years from now. In one letter, I want you to write to her from twenty years of sobriety. I want you to write down memories, fun times, how you and Michelle have watched her grow and accomplish wonderful things. What it has been like to be a father to this beautiful girl."

Brent paused, and his voice went lower. "Now, in the second letter, I want you to write from the viewpoint of remaining a victim to the disease—twenty years of drinking and drugging. I want you to tell her the memories of her seeing you drunk or high repeatedly. Tell her what it did to you and Michelle. Explain to her the decision you made to reject the help that was offered to you. I want this assignment completed before your ten-day evaluation is finished. I may ask you to read it at group."

I rubbed my jawline and contemplated the amount of emotional pain that would be involved in writing that letter. I left Brent's office feeling as if he had punched me in the stomach. A letter to Sloan after twenty years of drinking and drugging? *Ouch.*

AS I WALKED INTO the chapel and meditation center, I heard soothing music played in the background. The light-blue and white walls provided a bright environment. Through the skylight, a sunbeam shone directly onto a Recovery Bible sitting on a wooden bookstand. The floor was made of beautiful, light-colored cedar. The room smelled of roses and vibrated with peace. It could seat thirty people comfortably. Behind the bookstand was a small entrance hall that led to Father Ron's office. I stood outside and looked at my watch: 12:55 PM. *Never keep them waiting, Adam.*

I read the name on the door: (MSGR) RONALD BESHARA, STL, JCL. Underneath, his title was given: VP, MISSION & SPIRITUAL CARE.

The door opened, and an elderly female patient walked out.

Father Ron, with his New York accent, said, "Come in, Adam."

When I walked in, I saw that Father Ron was tall and had brown eyes and light-brown hair. Although probably in his sixties, he looked in his late forties. I chalked it up to good, healthy living. He rose from his chair and walked around his desk to greet me.

"Wow, look at those muscles!" He embraced me warmly and then felt my left arm.

"You work out a lot, son. That is fantastic. It will help you in your recovery."

He had sealed the deal. I loved him.

I looked around his office, at the posters of dolphins and butterflies. Father Ron explained that he loved dolphins, because they're spiritual animals that represent harmony and balance. The butterflies represent growth, because of their sensational metamorphosis from caterpillar to cocoon to growing wings to finally gaining the strength and courage to break free and fly away.

"Take a seat, Adam, please."

I chose one of the two chairs in front of his desk.

Rather than going back behind his desk, he sat down next to me and studied me for a few moments, seemingly deep in thought.

Finally, he said, "Do you have a close relationship with a higher power, whom I refer to as God?'"

"Father, I've been searching. I was Bar Mitzvahed. I've studied Kabbalah, the Tao, Buddhism, Jesus's teachings, parts of the Koran, all types of new age literature. . . . I want to be close to God. I'm just not sure how."

He scrunched his eyebrows and squinted. "Tell me more."

"Well, growing up, religion was confusing. There's just no way around it—Santa Claus and a Christmas tree are cooler than a menorah and a dreidel."

Father Ron belly laughed.

"My whole life, I've read spiritual books, and . . ."

I stalled, licked my lips, and swallowed hard.

"I don't speak of this often, but my great-grandfather, Harry Jablin—my Poppa Poppa—was a spiritual and holy man. He was given the honor of lighting the eternal flame at Yad Vashem in Jerusalem. And then there's my favorite story, about my great-grandfather and the pope."

"The pope?" Father Ron's eyes sparkled.

"Yes!" I clapped my hands. "My Poppa Poppa was given a gift of honor. Archeologist friends of his discovered parts of the original Wailing Wall in Jerusalem during a dig. For his good works with Israel, the Masons, and the Jewish community, he was bestowed one of the five sacred stones found. The pope knew of the excursion and asked to bless one of the stones. My great-grandfather offered his stone and flew to the Vatican City in Rome. He was escorted to Pope John

XXIII, and the two men got along like old, dear friends. The pope, at the papal blessings, blessed the stone in front of millions of people gathered outside his balcony in St. Peter's Square. He asked Poppa Poppa if he'd like to join him. 'But I'm not of your faith,' Poppa Poppa said. "The pope said simply, 'I don't know anyone who couldn't use the blessings from two old men.' My great-grandfather followed the pope onto the balcony and gave a blessing in Hebrew as the pope blessed the giant audience. There is a documentary on Pope John XXIII that captures the whole encounter."

"That's incredible!" Father Ron pressed his hand against his heart.

"Thank you." I sighed with satisfaction.

"You mentioned books you've read."

"I own a small library of them. You see, I always wanted a strong connection to God, but no one religion or one way made any sense to me."

"I understand." Father Ron tilted his head. "Do you pray?"

"No. Well . . . I did pray in Sunday school—Hebrew school—but the prayers were in Hebrew, so I didn't really understand them. Also, all the prayers were about only Israel, which is smaller than the state of New Jersey, where I grew up, so it confused me." I showed my palms and shrugged.

Father Ron laughed. He crossed his legs, slowly leaned toward me, and gently touched my arm.

"Adam, do you see that mark I left on your arm just now?" he asked.

I stared at my arm, looking for a physical mark.

"No, Father, I don't."

"Please, look again. Look deeper." There's that word again—*deeper. Deeper, Adam, deeper.* I stared at my arm, still seeing absolutely nothing.

"Sorry. I see nothing. Maybe because I'm Jewish?"

Father Ron laughed and then, in an almost bubbly voice, said, "Adam, wait right there."

He slowly got up, grabbed a handheld, portable UV-detection black light and turned off the lights in his office. The room got very dark. Then he turned on the UV light and aimed it at my arm.

I looked down and saw his fingerprints glowing on my skin.

He sat down next to me. "I left my fingerprints . . . and, even though you could not see them, it didn't mean they were not there."

I felt Father Ron connecting the dots, as if I knew what he would say next, but I still deeply desired to hear it.

"It's the same way with God. You can't see *Him,* but He is there, son. You have to. Are you ready?"

I didn't blink. My jaw unlocked, and I felt as if I had entered another dimension.

"*Trust.* You have to trust that He is always with you, around you, inside of you . . . and in everything this universe offers. Just like when the lights go back on, you have to trust my fingerprints are still there."

He was describing a source, an energy with an intelligence that knew exactly who I was. I felt it. My body and mind stayed within the room with Father Ron, while my spirit opened its arms and finally welcomed in the light. Just because I couldn't physically see it, did not mean a Power was not there.

Father Ron turned the lights back on.

"Let us begin with prayer. First off, God knows you, Adam. You may speak to your Higher Power any way you'd like. Just be yourself. Be authentic. Talking to God is considered prayer. It is communicating with your newfound friend. So, let us use what you are comfortable with—fitness. I bet you eat a healthy diet. Three square meals a day?"

"More like five or six."

"Perfect."

He stood up and picked up a sheet of paper and a pen.

"Now, we are going to get you spiritually fit. I want you to have three "meals" a day of prayer to make your connection to your Higher Power big and strong like your muscles. The soul needs nourishment just like the body. In the morning, I would like you to say a prayer of greeting and praise—a thank-you to God for life, a new day, your loved ones, and all of creation. Also, I would like you to give an offering. Offer yourself—your talents—to God for the good of others."

Father Ron paused and inhaled deeply.

"Add to this morning prayer some words of remembrance for the needs of your loved ones. At the end, please feel free to improvise a bit. You can even end with the Serenity Prayer."

"I can do that, Father!"

"Meal number two: This you will do in the afternoons. I want you to practice looking for God where He reveals Himself. One place is nature. Appreciate God by observing His creations and thanking Him for them."

He clasped his hands under his chin as if in prayer.

"Also, look for God in words: scripture, the Big Book of *Alcoholics Anonymous*, poetry, music, and inspirational quotes. In this afternoon prayer, I want you to look for people being kind to one another. Watch how people feel, react, and play when they are nice to one another. See God's work in the act of kindness."

I felt lightheaded. I locked my hands together tightly.

"Adam, your third and final meal for your newfound muscles is in the evening before you go to bed. First, I would like you to thank God for the gifts of today. I want you to find three reasons to be grateful. Second, ask for His forgiveness. Ask that others forgive you for stupid things you said or did, but also forgive others who harmed you. Pause and reflect on this act, as forgiveness is sacred. Lastly, ask for blessings upon your loved ones and yourself. If you like, you may end with the Lord's Prayer or something from the Torah."

I felt goose bumps on my arms and the little hairs on the back of my neck standing up. The room brightened, the air settled, and I felt an electric jolt shoot through my body.

"Are you getting to know your brothers here, Adam?"

Brothers? I did not see them exactly that way, but I knew that something inside me was changing. I nodded.

"Good. I also see a wedding band on your finger." He pointed at my left hand.

"Yes, sir. Wait till you meet Michelle. And we have a six-month-old daughter, Sloan—an angel."

"Adam, you are blessed. I feel you opening up. Your homework assignment, Adam, is to reread Genesis, chapter 1. I want you to write down what God is telling us about

nature, Himself, and us. Secondly, I would like you to read Matthew 22:34 through 40. Please find three lessons in the two commandments in that passage. Your next homework assignment is to add your name to the list for my Cenacle Retreat tomorrow night. Last, find a way to practice giving to your brothers and being of service to them. Can you handle all of that on top of your three square meals a day of prayer?"

That same feeling from my intervention had possessed me. I felt weightless and boundless. Time had frozen. I leaned in toward Father Ron. "Yes! I can!"

Father Ron jotted down some notes and handed me the paper, on which he had written everything we had discussed. "Good. I knew you could. You have been chosen. You are having a spiritual awakening. Try to enjoy the ride."

A CALL TO ACTION

- In Chapter 10 John Dyben handed me his business card with a handwritten note, "God teach me to love the truth." What are you afraid of being honest about right now? Do you want to get a new job? Are you not happy in your relationship? Are you sick and tired of being sick and tired? Say this simple prayer... "God, teach me to love the truth."
- The UV light moment with Father Ron changed my entire life. Those glowing fingerprints opened me to a Higher Reality. I've learned to trust in God and the spirit world. I would like you start your Prayer-Diet. 3 square meals—morning, noon, and night... just as Father Ron prescribed for me!

CHAPTER 11

MOMENT OF CLARITY

THE TURTLES SCURRIED UP to the surface, fighting for grub, as I ripped off another piece of bread and threw it into the water. Spike and Taz scrabbled on the outskirts, trying to get into the crowd. I chucked another small piece of bread as a decoy, farther away from my new pals, and the birds that had been hovering pounced on it. Then I rocketed two balls of bread right in between Spike and Taz, and they got them! Mission accomplished. I felt connected to Michelle.

It was time for my first "meal" of the day. I looked over the sheet of paper that described my prayer ritual and thought back to my session with Father Ron. ("I would like you to say a prayer of greeting and praise—a thank-you to God for life, a new day, your loved ones, and all of creation. Also, I would like you to give an offering. Offer yourself—your talents—to God for the good of others.") I closed my eyes and said, out loud, "Yo, God. It's me again. Good morning. Umm . . . thank you for another day alive. Thank you for Michelle, Sloan, and my family. Thank you for all of creation. I offer myself to you today by helping the guys more with their diet and exercise. That will be my service."

Also, Father Ron had asked me to "Add to this morning prayer some words of remembrance for the needs of your loved ones. At the end, please feel free to improvise a bit. You can even end with the Serenity Prayer." I thought of Gaga and all the good times we'd had together. Gaga had had the deepest belly laugh, the greatest laugh in the world. Once she'd started, she hadn't been able to stop. She would laugh so hard that she wouldn't be able to catch her breath. You'd hear this wonderful roar, and then it would get deadly quiet as she turned red in the face and tried to catch her breath before letting out another huge belly laugh. I missed her terribly. But I had to learn to accept the things I couldn't change. She was gone, and she wasn't coming back.

As I stared out at the pond, I thought about last night's outside activity—the Cenacle. It had been held at a monastery, but many religions of the world were represented. About fifty people had shown up. A big, white candle had stood tall in the middle of the room. Chairs had been placed in a circle around it. The new age music that had been playing took me to a relaxed state in the beginning, as Father Ron opened the Cenacle with a meditation and prayer. One by one, we went around the room introducing ourselves and describing how we felt at that precise moment. I enjoyed the experience, because I didn't have to label myself an alcoholic and addict. I said simply, "Hi. I'm Adam, and I feel happy to be here."

Father Ron brought up a topic—gratitude. First, he asked us to define it.

One woman raised her hand and said, "Gratitude is a feeling of appreciation."

Father Ron asked us, as a group, to "go deeper." As various ideas, definitions, and feelings of gratitude—including "Gratitude is smelling a newborn baby's head," "Gratitude is an action word, not just a feeling," and "I've never seen a grateful alcoholic drink again"—were given by people from various races, genders, and religions, I felt more and more connected to the concept. The hour flew by. At the end, we said a prayer, and whether someone went home, back to jail, back to a halfway house, or back to rehab afterward didn't matter. We all felt better!

I planted my feet on the grass and shook my hips and butt on the bench, trying to get more comfortable. I closed my eyes and felt the breeze on my face. I heard the Hanley campus start to wake up as I contemplated leaving rehab in less than twenty-four hours. How was I supposed go home? Everything I had been taught at Hanley resonated with me. I tilted my head from side to side and ran my left hand through my hair as I muttered to myself, "Can I live sober?" Tonight, I would have to tell my story to the guys, and before that I had to finish writing my two letters to Sloan. I hunched over and sighed. It was too much for me to process, so I headed to the gym.

On my way to the gym, for the first time ever before a workout, I said a prayer. "Thank you, Creator, for giving me the strength and discipline to work out. Please keep me healthy and sober." I thought of those handicapped or those who didn't have the freedom to exercise, and I said a prayer for them, too. I liked the idea of talking to God. "Yo, also please take care of Michelle and Sloan for me. Amen." I winked at the sky and hit my upper chest with the side of my fist.

I strutted into the gym with my chin high, shoulders back, and chest thrust out. My muscles, joints, tendons, and ligaments all felt rejuvenated. Although I still wasn't sleeping much, I felt bigger, taller, and stronger. The lack of gym equipment had forced me to come up with unique, new exercises, like Arnold Schwarzenegger had done back in the seventies.

Some of the guys walked into the gym and asked whether they could join me.

"Absolutely!"

My morning prayer of service had rekindled my desire to share my knowledge with the guys. I set up eight stations, starting with the physioball for balancing on while doing crunches. The second station was kettlebell goblet squats. The third was lat pulldowns. The fourth was overhead dumbbell presses. Fifth was bent-over rows. Sixth was to run over to the chest press machine, do a set and then drop down to the floor to do a set of pushups. Seventh was supersets of thirty seconds of standing dumbbell tricep kickbacks and thirty seconds of dumbbell bicep curls. The eighth and final station was standing calf raises. We would all rotate from one station to the next after one minute, with forty-five seconds of rest between stations. My role was the coach, or trainer. First, I demonstrated each exercise slowly, showing the guys what to focus on and what muscles it would develop. I went over proper form, breathing patterns (negative breathe in, positive breathe out), and simple tricks, such as doing squats by

breaking first at the hips rather than at the knees, squeezing and contracting the weights rather than just lifting them, and tucking the elbows to get better arm contractions.

"Guys, in order to feel the back muscles contract, think of your hands as hooks and let the lats do the work of pulling down the weights."

I got behind the bench and spotted Grant.

He pushed up the weight, his arms wobbled sporadically, and his face turned red. After doing ten sloppy reps of dumbbell bench press, he said, "Adam, I feel all over the place. When you do it, you're in total control. Your focus is so intense. It's like nobody else is even here. It's just you and the weights in your hand."

I patted him on the back. "Buddy, it took me years of hard work and discipline to train the mind-body connection. Things take time."

On my way back to the men's unit, I had an epiphany: I could use the same mind-set and determination to learn the prayer-God connection. Just as I had faith that bench pressing would build my chest, I could believe that saying prayers would build my spirituality. As in bodybuilding, spirituality building would take time and concentrated effort. Rome wasn't built in a day.

"REBT. THAT'S TODAY'S TOPIC: an introduction to Rational Emotive Behavior Therapy," Ed said.

Ed was one of the counselors on the men's unit. He was about five feet seven inches tall, and he had short, dark-brown hair with a few grays sprinkled in. Ed was also a major yoga junkie, and it showed in his long, strong, lean body. He wore a white button-down shirt, red tie, and khaki pants. He also was an alcoholic.

"REBT was developed by a man named Albert Ellis. One of the key elements of this view is . . ."—he surveyed the room—"how the events in our lives truly affect us by how we *perceive* them. Alcoholism is a disease of *perception.* This will determine our resulting feelings and behaviors. REBT tells us that it's important to understand the difference between distorted, or unhealthy, feelings and undistorted, or healthy, feelings."

I was taking notes diligently, worried that the explanation was a bit over my head but determined to hang on.

"Some examples of distorted feelings are anxiety, depression, rage, and shame."

That got my attention.

"Some troublesome behaviors resulting from unhealthy feelings are drinking and drugging, aggressive language or physical violence, avoidance, sleeping too much or too little, eating too much or too little, low self-esteem, and strained relationships."

Now I was getting it! *Don't forget overexercising and doing a million favors, Ed.*

"Let me give you some examples of healthy feelings: love, remorse, sadness, anger, grief, and hope." Ed cracked his knuckles loudly. "Now, let's begin your REBT. I want you to write down, on four lines, the letters A, B, C, and D. After A, write down the words "External event." After B, write down "Resulting self-talk." After C, write down "Resulting mood." And after D, write down "Behavior." Now take a few

moments to fill out these four lines to describe something that normally would occur in your life."

I wrote the following:

A. External event: Michelle is upset with me.

B. Resulting self-talk: What can I do to fix it?

C. Resulting Mood: Anxiety.

D. Behavior: Drink or work out.

I studied what I had written down. I couldn't believe it. I could see a pattern in how I reacted in not just my marriage but all situations.

Ed continued his lecture. "Now, the next step in REBT is to challenge the distorted belief or thought. Ask yourself if there is any evidence behind the resulting self-talk. Think of several interpretations of the external event. What else could be happening? Stick to the facts. Avoid speculation. Let me list some of the most common negative self-talk and beliefs: I must be liked by everyone,"—*Yup, definitely me*—"I must be perfect."—*Me again*—"I must have everything go my way."—*Me*—"If I worry about things, they'll get better."—*Also me*—"I can rescue others from their situations."—*Is Ed reading my life story?*

I sat in awe. How do these rehab people know me so well? How do they know what's inside me?

Ed clapped his hands and then rubbed them together. "All right, let's take a look at what's doing this. There are three main culprits in the negative belief system. One is the should–must–ought culprit. This turns desires into demands, or creates unbreakable laws. Culprit number two is awfulization: turning hassles into horrors, disappointments into disasters, and difficulties into impossibilities. Third is self-devaluation: I'm worthless, this is what I deserve, and this is how it will always be."

I frantically wrote everything down.

Ed put his hands in his pants pockets and cleared his throat. "Guys, I'm here to tell you that this is all based on fear. It's all based on our *perceptions*. If we can change the questions we ask ourselves in these moments, our lives will turn out very differently. Questions like 'Could this be worse?' 'What good things may come from this?' 'Why is this awful?' or, even better, 'Can I give my worries over to my Higher Power?'"

Ed clapped his hands together and exhaled loudly. "Okay, guys, that's it for Rational Emotive Behavior Therapy. It's time for lunch."

I found Grant already eating at one of the tables in the cafeteria. I grabbed an apple and sat next to him, my brow furrowed.

He took a bite of his chicken and looked up at me. With his mouth full of food and chomping away like a pig, he mumbled, "What's up, pal?"

"Grant, I don't know about this ten-day evaluation thing. I feel like I have so much more to learn here. Something is changing in me. I'm afraid to leave."

He took a quick drink and washed down his food. "Did you speak to your counselor and your wife about this?"

"Well, not at great length. Last time I saw Brent, he asked me to write two letters to my daughter, both twenty years from now—one letter after twenty years of sobriety, the other after twenty years of drinking and drugging—and to tell my story. He just said he wanted them done before my tenth day. As for Michelle, I'm afraid to bring it up. It's not right leaving her alone with the baby, but I think I need to stay. But that would mean another nineteen or twenty days. I'd really be letting her down. I'd be letting everyone down."

Grant took another huge bite of chicken and studied me for a few seconds. Chomp, chomp, chomp. "Well, you may be surprised" Chomp, chomp, chomp. "She asked you to come here, right?"

"Yes. But twenty-eight days?" My voice choked up. "That's not fair to her. It's just not!" I put down my apple, unable to eat.

"That's between you and your wife, Adam. But you seem to be feeling better, and you're helping us." He gestured to our buddies, who also were eating lunch. "You're helping us with fitness and nutrition. It'd be nice if you stayed." Chomp, chomp, chomp. But the tape in my mind started to play again: *Twenty-eight days. That's a long time. I don't need that. I'm different. I want to go home.*

When I trudged to the 1:30 PM counselors' meeting on safety, I still was wrestling with the voices in my head. *It's time to go home. You're really not that bad, Adam.* A few more slow, painful steps. *Stay. Stay for Sloan. Stay for Michelle. Stay for Gaga. Stay for you!*

The counselors' meeting was short and sweet. We reviewed where to go in case of an emergency or a hurricane, where the fire alarms were located, and where to go if there were a fire. Then came the moment we'd been waiting for—the crowning of a new peer leader. It was a changing of the guard and an honor for the next man chosen. Bruce was holding a piece of paper that the counselors had handed him before the meeting, and on it was the name of the new peer leader.

Bruce looked down at the piece of paper. "Gentlemen, the new peer leader is . . . drum roll, please . . . Jack!" We all stood up and cheered, hooting and hollering, "Jack! Jack! Jack!" I thought Jack was the perfect choice. He was able to speak with everyone, and I could see his recovery getting stronger. "It's now time for the peer-leader-exchange ceremony!"

Bruce took the necklace and loudly, as if he were a dramatic actor on stage, recited, "Roscoe is the carved tooth of a walrus brought to Hanley Center by an ancient mariner named Goo Goo Achoo. Roscoe symbolizes leadership, commitment, and respect for self, community, and the twelve-step recovery. In order to keep it, you must give it away. I take the spirit of Roscoe and pass it on!"

Jack took the necklace and put it around his own neck. He looked down at the paper and recited, "I accept, and I, too, shall pass on the spirit of Roscoe!"

We all hollered in celebration.

After the meeting, I went back to my room. I sat on my bed, cracked my knuckles, and flipped through my notepad until I found the page where I had written my story. I closed my eyes and took a long, calming breath. It was almost time for me to share.

A CALL TO ACTION

- Wayne Dyer had a famous quote, "Change your thoughts—Change your life." This is a major theme of what this chapter is about. Are there troubled areas in your life that you look at from a different point of view?
- In the beginning of Chapter 11, I said my morning prayer of service and decided to help my brothers in rehab exercise and eat healthier. What can you do as an act of service today?

CHAPTER 12

MY STORY

I WAS THE FIRST ONE TO arrive in the men's unit lounge. I looked around. It was set up for story time, with the couches and sofas facing a large, brown leather chair in the center of the room. The late-afternoon sun was shining into the room.

Tony's deep voice blasted over the intercom, "Adam's story in five minutes. I repeat, Adam's story in five."

I felt warmer than usual and wondered whether the warm was from nerves. I had butterflies in my stomach. I took a seat in the center chair and then bounced my right knee while I went over my notes.

The guys shuffled into the lounge. Grant, Jack, Jeremy, Tony, and Morty sat closer to me, and the newer guys sat farther away.

Brent came in and performed a quick head count. He smiled at me and said, "Gentlemen, our story today is Adam's. Let's give him our attention and support."

They applauded, and then the room grew silent.

"Hi, guys. I'm Adam, and I'm an alcoholic, addicted, codependent musclehead."

All the guys shouted back, "Hi, Adam!"

I laid my notes to the side. Suddenly, something strange happened. Everything became clear and bright, bringing about a subtle clarity of mind. I felt extremely focused or, as athletes say, "in the zone." I felt both slightly chilled and lighter in my body. I easily found my words.

"My full name is Adam Moshe Jablin. I was born on May 19, 1976, at North Shore Hospital in Manhasset, Long Island. I lived in Queens, New York, for two years and then moved to Tenafly, New Jersey."

I closed my eyes briefly as I reminisced.

"Tenafly, New Jersey, in the late '70s and '80s was an amazing place to be a kid. The town felt like one big happy family. Have you guys ever seen the movie *Big*, starring Tom Hanks?"

I slowly looked around the circle and made eye contact with each guys. They all nodded. I remembered thoughts and feelings from those times, and I placed my hand on my chest and took a deep breath.

"Well, it was just like that. I still consider my old friends from there like family."

Scenes from my childhood played in my head. I could see all the old faces, Stillman Elementary School, the house I grew up in at 24 Malcolm Court. My old phone number even randomly popped into my head: (201) 569-8740. All of this happened while I remained connected to the guys in the lounge. It was as if I were simultaneous in two different dimensions.

I cocked my head to the side and lowered my voice. "Wow, it's been years since I took the time to think about those days. But growing up, there was one thing always on my mind—my weight. I remember shopping for school clothes with my mother . . . and while all the other children could shop in the entire store, there was a special rack for kids like me, called the husky section. That's where *we* shopped. I don't remember the first time I heard that I was pudgy, chubby, or fat, but hearing it over and over again killed me. I hated it."

I clenched my fist tightly, and veins rose to the surface up and down my forearms.

"It left a dent, a deep scar. The teasing squashed my self-esteem. If someone brought it up, I would try to laugh along, but I'd be crying on the inside. I felt humiliated and insecure. But being the fat kid taught me something wonderful, too. Since I felt I wouldn't ever be noticed for anything but my appearance, I created an extroverted and funny personality and became the class clown.

"Having this insecurity made me idolize muscular physiques. I knew how I wanted to look. My whole world changed one night when my parents took my sister and me on a trip to Washington, DC. I must have been around six or seven. It was way past my bedtime, and my dad and I were hanging out on the hotel couch. 'Son, you want to watch *Rocky* with me?' I looked at the clock and back at my dad. 'Yes! Of course! . . . Dad, who's Rocky?' It was *Rocky III*, the one with Mr. T and Clubber Lang. I was mesmerized by Sylvester Stallone. That's what I wanted to look like!"

As I spoke, I started to think to myself, *What the hell does this have to do with alcohol and drugs, Adam?* I looked across the lounge and read one of the posters on the far wall. *To thy own self be true.* A sense of peace took over, and I half shrugged and grinned.

"I remember going down to our basement and pretending to be Rocky Balboa. I'd play-fight for hours and make up training routines. My dad got a kick out of it, and so he bought me a play weight set. We kept it right next to *his* barbells. I wanted to be like my hero—Rocky Balboa. I shadowboxed and used my toy weights, hoping the very next day I'd wake up and look like an Adonis and not El Chubbo. It was my great obsession."

Getting this all off my chest felt so good. I was unburdening myself of so many years of pain that I'd held deep inside. These strange alcoholics and addicts were learning more about me than most of my friends already knew.

"When I was ten years old, my grandfather sold his company, and my father opened a new one in sunny Boca Raton, Florida. I hated the move and the town!" I clenched my jaw. "I missed my friends, my home, my bedroom. Plus, South Florida was a place where I could be at the beach or the pool every day with my shirt off and the fat hanging out. Around that same time, I also started to go to an overnight summer camp in Maine. These two events, together, were huge in my life. My two new homes meant meeting a lot of new people. My wanting friends and wanting to belong were put on maximum intensity, as was my insecurity about my weight."

I sighed deeply.

"Going to summer camp turned out to be one of the best experiences of my life." I clasped my hands together, and then rubbed my thighs. "It was the ultimate freedom. I made lifelong friends. Something about Hanley and our group's camaraderie has reminded me a lot about those days, which is a great compliment. At camp, I learned how to work out, swim laps, exercise, and transform my body. Camp was also where I had my first kiss, first beer, and my first joint. A bit of everything, like here in rehab."

That got a few laughs.

I explained my middle school years: puberty and other changes. Alcohol was there, but it didn't yet play a major role. We were young kids.

"In those three short years, I went from being the heaviest kid in the class to the best-built kid. No longer did kids tease, 'How many Oreos you eat last night?' Now, they asked, 'How much can you bench press?'

"When I turned fifteen, my father was offered a lot of money to sell his company. While contemplating the decision, my mother and father asked me if I would go into the family business. I said yes. That decision was a burden I never understood. I was always taught that the family business came first, that when you take care of the family business it takes care of you. I never thought, *What do I want to be when I grow up?* I knew my direction, my destination, from a very early age. It was a promise I'd made to my parents."

I felt good in my body. My posture grew erect as I gazed out the window and continued to tell my story.

"As I grew up, the gym became my home, my sanctuary, my church, my place of worship. I worked out for every reason imaginable: to deal with anger, frustrations, and pain or to just feel good and compete with myself. I obsessed over bodybuilding and making my physique perfect. Everything else became secondary. I read every muscle magazine I could get my hands on. I educated myself about proper nutrition and studied Arnold Schwarzenegger's *Encyclopedia of Bodybuilding*.

"Every day I went into battle with myself to get bigger, stronger, and more defined. At sixteen, I entered my first bodybuilding competition. What an experience! I was posing up in front of three hundred people, in a little bikini. That helped with my confidence." I winked.

The guys laughed.

"For that show, I learned what real, old-school dieting was: lowering my carbohydrate intake, not eating past 8:00 PM, tracking my calories and macronutrients, supplementing and measuring every single thing I ate. It taught me another level of dedication and discipline. It showed me what I could achieve if I put my mind to it.

"Something else happened in high school. I fell in love with alcohol and partying. It felt normal. We were having a blast. But to me, it was more than a way to get loose. It fixed something inside me that was broken. When drinking, I stopped worrying about my body, my family, the business. I felt like a leader, and my personality got even happier and more confident. Unconsciously, I dedicated my life to finding that fix. I was the first one of my friends with a fake ID. It said I was from Iowa, and it slightly resembled me, but it worked. Most weekends, we'd buy a bunch of beer and hang out at somebody's house or the beach. I loved booze and having fun so much that I chose Arizona State University—ASU—for college, because it was the number one party school in the country."

I explained how ASU offered amazing weather, gorgeous women and, of course, alcohol and drugs. I pledged a fraternity and went to parties and lots of bars and clubs. "I dibbled and dabbled with this and that, but nothing was like alcohol for me. I loved to drink, man. If I ever took a narcotic or hallucinogen, it was really just so I could drink more. You see, building my body was great, but it never cured my underlying insecurities. But the alcohol relaxed me. It turned me into Mr. Cool. I wasn't constantly worried about how I looked, what I was saying, or how I said it. Alcohol was the best confidence builder I knew. A couple cocktails, and, yo! The man was here! I could schmooze with the best of them. I could talk to anyone any time. You want to meet the hottest girl in the room, no problem. You want to skip the line to get into the club, I'm your man. I combined that fake confidence with my outgoing personality and my muscles, and I turned into Ferris Bueller. Everyone loved me, and I loved everyone. What could ever be wrong with alcohol? It was my best friend!"

I shook my head as I saw myself more and more clearly.

"College did put my drinking into perspective, though. I was pulled over and arrested for driving under the influence. It was awful.

"I remember getting pulled over and knowing that I'd soon be in handcuffs. Thank God, my dad helped me with an attorney. I had to do something like ten hours of community service, a two-day course on alcohol and its effects, and twenty-four hours in jail.

"Jail? The worst. They never shut the lights off, and there were no clocks, so you never knew what time it was. It gave me a good scare . . . for maybe a month. Soon, it became a distant memory . . . and I kept on drinking. I drank every night. I'd usually start right after my daily workout."

My voice cracked as I sank deeper into the chair. "I slowly became dependent on alcohol to feel comfortable. I lived up to my word, though. After college, I went straight to work in the family business."

I paused and stared down at my hands.

"It was nothing like I expected. I thought the plan was to train me as the salesman for the company . . . to use my personality and people skills as a strength to get more business, like my grandfather had. But those days were in the past. They'd died with his generation—death of a salesman, so to speak. The world had changed, and my father's business had become more of a pure production facility. My charisma wasn't needed or useful. I worked inside the office and manufacturing plant. I mastered production charts, yarn inventories, costings, designs, and machinery. I was always running on idle. If our customers called I'd be busy, but if the phones were quiet I was bored out of my mind. I felt trapped like a rat in a cage. But I believed I'd been given the opportunity of a lifetime, and I'd given my word. . . ."

I thought about the last nine years I'd spent working for my father. *Why am I so unhappy?*

"But hey, what can you do? I made a commitment to my family, and I stuck by it. After a few tough years, I started to make decent money at a young age. My boozing increased, too. It was work hard, play hard. I'd go to work with the nastiest hangovers, after drinking all night, but I made it to work. I thought that meant that I didn't have a problem. But it was tough. My head would pound, and my stomach would be terribly sick."

I told them about Michelle.

"The one thing that always got between us was my drinking and carrying on. She always questioned whether I'd been drinking, and I'd lie to her face while reeking of alcohol. This happened over and over again. One fight we had early on in our relationship, she told me she wouldn't be with an alcoholic. I remember staggering back and covering my mouth in shock. 'What? An alcoholic?' I was so offended. How dare she! How could I be an alcoholic? So, with my razor-sharp mind, I decided pills would be my relief. That way, Michelle couldn't smell the alcohol on my breath."

I took the guys in the circle from my thrill of getting married, through the grueling IVF process of Michelle getting pregnant, and finally to Gaga dying in my arms.

"And then, it all stopped working for me—the bottle and the pharmacy. No matter how much I took, I couldn't shut my mind off. I couldn't relax. I was miserable. My mind kept telling me I'm a loser, that I could have done something great with my life. What's the point to it all? I stopped caring. I lost any and all moderation."

I dropped my chin to my chest and pulled my arms inward.

"I wanted to stop drinking and taking pills—so many times—but I had no willpower. The worst part is my body craved it. I needed it."

I slowly shook my head and wiped my lips with my left hand.

"Guys, six months ago, on December 9, 2005, my little angel, Sloan, was born."

I told them how it killed me that Gaga didn't get to meet Sloan and that the responsibilities of being a father were tougher and more exhausting than I'd ever imagined. Finally, I described the last fight Michelle and I'd had two weeks earlier and my behavior during that week, right up to the intervention.

"And that, gentlemen, is how I got to Hanley."

Everybody stood up and cheered. One by one, each new friend came up to me to give me great big hug and thank me. Each one told me how he was the skinny kid or the heavy kid, about high school years, or about moving from state to state.

"Adam, wow—your story. I had no idea."

"Bro, I had a DUI in college, too."

"Adam, you made me think about my first fake ID. It was gold."

"Muscles, I felt the same exact way."

Smiling, I hugged each guy. I felt a tingling and lightness throughout my body. Then it hit me. *I belong here.*

LATER THAT EVENING, during personal time, I went for a walk around the Hanley campus. Patients and staff alike were outside, enjoying the cooler evening weather. I strolled down the fitness trail, past the recreation park. A bunch of my newfound friends were playing on the sand volleyball court, and a group of women were shooting basketball. Some older men were fishing by the pond, and there was a baby boomers' meeting (ages 46–64) on the park bench by the shuffleboard courts. *Everything seems so peaceful. Am I getting accustomed to the rehab way of life?*

I reflected on my story: childhood in New Jersey, summer camp in Maine, adolescence in Florida, college in Arizona, drinking, drugging. As I made my way back to the men's unit, I noticed that an intensive, co-ed, outpatient session was taking place in the gazebo. I heard about that group. The participants were men and women who'd graduated from the inpatient rehab program to living back at home, in the outside world. They seemed so happy, so comfortable in their own skins. I licked my lips and swallowed hard. *I don't know if I have all the tools to make it out there yet. How am I going to do this?* The angel on one shoulder was telling me to stay, while the little devil on the other shoulder was saying, "Go home already. You're different from the others." I was tearing myself in two.

A CALL TO ACTION

- I finally told my story in Chapter 12 and realized I was just like my brothers in rehab. I was no better, no different. My ups and downs, my successes and failures, my joys and fears—I was a garden variety alcoholic and addict.
- Finish writing your story!
- Have you ever felt torn in two making a major decision that was hard, but you knew would benefit you? What did you do?

CHAPTER 13

MY SURRENDER

"WHY A THREE-FOURTHS medallion?" I asked as I watched the guys slowly line up and take seats for Bruce's departing medallion ceremony.

Ben cleared his throat. "The reason the medallion is only three-fourths is for it to be a constant reminder that we're not complete, we're not whole. If you make it to your one-year anniversary, Hanley gives you the last fourth of the medallion."

"Pretty cool. Do they give them out for ten-day evaluations?"

Ben smirked. "No, they do *not* give them out for ten-day evaluations." He shook his head and sighed. "We'll pass a little wooden block with Bruce's medallion inside it. When it's your turn, knock twice on the wooden block. Bring up some good memories, wish Bruce well, knock twice on it again, and pass it on."

Knock, knock. Jack passed the wooden block and medallion to me.

I looked at Bruce and thought of the past week. "Bruce," I said in a low voice as if I were chanting at a Bruce Springsteen concert. "Ever since I came here, you've been there for me. My very first day down here in the men's unit, you asked me to participate in high-low. I liked you from the beginning. I really want you make it out there. I don't want you to ever pick up a drug or drink again. You have so much going for you. Take care of yourself, pal."

I knocked twice and passed the medallion on.

Bruce hit his chest once and pointed at me. "Adam, stay here. Stay!"

I felt as if I was about to go crazy. *Stay or go?*

Later that evening, Bruce and Jeremy jammed on the guitar while Tony played the harmonica. The acoustics invigorated the room. We all shared funny stories of the craziest things we had done while drunk or high. There was so much laughter. I couldn't believe that I was having a good time.

BEFORE BED, I SAT AT my desk and worked on my second letter—the drunk–druggie one—to Sloan. I glanced at what I'd written before, and it felt fake. I crumpled it up and threw it on the floor. I didn't know what to do. I glanced over at the sheet of paper from Father Ron, and it hit me—pray.

"Yo, God. Me again. How are you up there? I'm sure you're good. I mean, of course you're good. You're God! Look, this letter to Sloan—It doesn't feel honest. I keep writing it as if I know she'll excuse the twenty years of my being a bad father, drinking and using drugs. Please help me."

Like a vacuum, I sucked in a deep breath of air so the oxygen went directly into my stomach. I closed my throat and held my breath, pushing out my belly. I looked at the photo of Sloan and felt every bit of love I had inside me. Then I pushed all the air out, with force, and put pen to paper. My hand felt as if it were being guided, and I knew that I was connected to a Higher Power.

Dear Sloan,

I don't know how to begin this letter. All my apologies over the years only make this letter pathetic. Another weak try to reach you. Another awful method to try and explain my drinking. My drugging. My selfishness.

I'm so sorry I've done this to you. Your mother had me go to rehab in July 2006—seven months after you were born! I still have all her letters, e-mails, and gifts. At that time, she was behind me, loving and supportive. I was taught all about the disease of alcoholism and addiction and the steps of recovery. But I felt different than everybody else who was in rehab. I felt better than them. I felt like I could control it. That my "disease" was somehow just a lack of willpower on my part. I was in major denial.

Then I relapsed. You were so little. Things spun out of control. The drinking, the pills, and the denial got worse and worse. Your mother and I split up. My fault. She got custody of you, of course. I wasn't able to be the father I always wanted to be. The guilt ate me up, so I covered it with more alcohol, drugs, and selfishness.

Sloan, I know this letter won't do much. But I'm so sorry. Sorry for all the destruction. All the tears. All the mess-ups.

The violin recitals I didn't make. The dance shows I didn't attend. The graduations. Not being able to be trusted to drive you to school or pick you up. The times my mind was so twisted that I forgot special days or embarrassed you in front of your friends.

I want to make things right. I'm checking myself back into rehab at the Hanley Center. It's twenty years too late, but maybe this time I'll learn? Maybe I can finally admit to myself that I'm truly sick! I pray that I'm in your life when I get out and we can have a nice, quiet dinner. I hope so. Until then, baby girl, I'll leave you with this—Be better than your old man.

I love you with all my heart,
Daddy

Tears ran down my face. I felt as if somebody had beaten my chest with a sledgehammer. *I can't lose them!* I rested my head on the desk and begged for mercy. *Please, God. Please! Don't let this happen. Please. Please. I'll do anything you want.* I wiped away my tears, shut off the desk lamp, and collapsed into bed.

I tossed and turned. Tortured by the mental strain, I didn't sleep a wink. *How am I supposed to leave? I don't think I can stay sober outside yet. I'm learning so much in here.* My body stiffened. I squeezed my pillow and scrunched it into a ball. *What will Michelle think of me? What will my whole family think of me? I told them ten days.*

I shivered. My mind split in two again.

I need to stay.

How can you leave your family for a full twenty-eight days? Loser.

But . . . I believe everything they're teaching me. I believe I'm an alcoholic and addict.

You're not like these guys, Adam! They take the hard stuff. You're different. You're better than them.

I don't think that's true anymore. I like these guys. I think this is real.

C'mon! You don't need twenty-eight days. Hey, what will everyone at work think?

I don't care. I'm not ready to leave. I can't lose Michelle and Sloan.

The two of me fought twelve hard rounds. Upper cuts, hooks, jabs, body punches, hard lefts, straight rights, and combinations. It was nonstop action, a barn burner. Adam versus his disease. I couldn't turn it off. The imaginary bell rang again. Another round? The tightness in my chest became unbearable. My heart was racing. Cold sweat poured off my body as I trembled. I hyperventilated. I couldn't take it anymore.

Annoyed by my ruckus, Grant rolled over in his bed. "Adam! Please go to the nurse's station already. You've been up all night!"

I looked down at my watch. It was 4:00 AM. I got up and left the room.

Outside, I felt the warm summer air. The stars were still out. When I looked up at the sky, I immediately felt dizzy and faint. I was losing control. My hands went numb. *What's happening to me?* Somehow, I managed to make it to the detox unit. I threw open the door to the nurses' station and stumbled through.

"Help! Please!"

Two nurses ran to me and then escorted me to a chair.

Kat sprinted to me. "Adam, what is it? Talk to me!" She sounded frantic.

"I—I can't breathe. I—I'm freaking out. Help. Please."

Kat shouted to the other nurses. "Get me a paper bag over here."

I looked at her as if she were crazy. *A paper bag? A paper bag ain't gonna cut it. I need something strong to calm me down: a Valium, Xanax, Ativan, or Vistaril.* I was insulted.

"Adam, what happened? Speak slowly. Try to calm down. Take deep breaths."

It was difficult for me to get air. The room was spinning.

"Kat, I'm going crazy. I can't sleep. I feel like there are two of me. I—I—I think I may have to stay here for the full twenty-eight days."

Saying it out loud threw me into deeper panic. My lungs started to close, and I felt a tight squeezing on my heart. I bent over in pain, closed my eyes, and squeezed my hands tightly.

Kat handed me the paper bag. Out of the corner of one eye, I saw that she had a fat grin on her face.

"Breathe into the bag, darlin'. Take long, deep breaths. In . . . out . . . in . . . out."

I listened and followed her instructions. After six repetitions, I grabbed her hand.

"This is serious, Kat. I need a drug, a pill. Something to calm me down. Please?"

Kat just sat there and slowly shook her head.

"No, Adam. No more pills for you. No more alcohol. This is it. This is your moment. This is your surrender."

I lowered my head, closed my eyes, and collapsed back in the chair.

"Kat, I admitted I'm an alcoholic and an addict the first day I got here. This is way more serious. I think I'm having a heart attack." I raised the paper bag back to my mouth and continued taking deep breaths.

"You're not having a heart attack. You may have *admitted* that you're an alcoholic and an addict, but now you're *accepting* that you are. And that's a *huge* difference. So what if you have to stay here twenty-eight days. Is that so bad?"

"What will my wife think? What will she do without me? What about my parents? They'll feel like failures. I can't do this to them. I just can't. I love them too much."

"And they love you, too. Don't you think they knew that you staying here was a big possibility? Did they mention it to you in your intervention?"

I thought hard about that. I nodded.

"Adam, call your wife this morning. Tell her how you feel. I think you may be surprised."

"HONEY?"

"How did you know it's me?" I asked.

"Who else would it be at 5:30 in the morning?"

"I have to talk to you. It's pretty serious. Are you sitting down?"

I heard the phone receiver rattle in her hand. "Oh, my God. What is it? Are you okay?"

"Are you sitting down?" I was terrified of the shock I was about to give her.

"I'm *lying* down. I'm in bed. It's 5:30. You woke me up. I think you woke the baby up. What is it, Adam? Are you hurt? Are you all right?"

"No, baby, I'm not all right. I'm sick. You were right. I'm an alcoholic and an addict. I couldn't sleep all night. I'm so afraid to tell you this. I think I have to stay here the full twenty-eight days."

Silence.

More silence.

"Are you still there?"

I heard laughter, hysterical laughter.

"Adam, I was never going to come pick you up today."

I stared at the pasty-white wall. Time stopped. *She was never going to pick me up*?

"Don't you see? It's *you!* It's you! It's always you. Adam can't do this. And Adam won't do that. And Adam needs to work out. And Adam needs to drink. And Adam needs to go to the office. And Adam can't do twenty-eight days. Adam, Adam, Adam, Adam!"

Oh, my God, It's me! I'm the problem. At that moment, I saw clearly two versions of myself. I had a choice. One Adam Jablin got defensive and angry, and screamed back at Michelle, "You think it's me? No, it's you!" That Adam pointed a finger at her and the rest of the world. He demanded to be picked up or he'd take a taxi home. He was right, and they were wrong. He thought he was better than everyone else. But now I knew better, especially after having written to Sloan from the perspective of twenty years of drinking and drugging. I knew where that road would lead me.

Then there was the other, enlightened Adam Jablin, the one who stopped fighting and just listened. He was sober,

humble, willing, and open-minded. I didn't know exactly where that road would lead, but it would be a lot better than the one the other Adam wanted to go down.

Michelle's soft, low voice came out of the telephone. "I'm proud of you, Adam. You're a real man. You're confronting your demons. I always knew it was twenty-eight days, baby. Always."

Relief set in. My chest loosened up, and I could breathe more easily. I sighed.

"Are you kidding me? What about the whole ten-day evaluation thing?"

"That was just to get you there. We all knew you, and we knew the idea of twenty-eight days would scare you. Michael told us to do whatever it took to get you there." Michelle giggled.

I thought of what Tony had said on my first night at the Hanley Center: "Ten? Ya kidding? Nobody comes in for ten!" and then "We'll share stories. I'll make sure I tell ya mine on ya day eleven. We'll go fishing or something."

I was so grateful to Michelle. "Honey, I love you so much. Thank you for saving my life."

THE REST OF THAT DAY FLEW BY. It was an easy, fun day at Hanley. Even on no sleep, it felt like spiritual camp to me. I experienced so much joy telling all the guys that I'd be staying for the full twenty-eight days. The day consisted of interesting lectures, enjoyable group sessions, delicious, healthy meals, sunbathing, and a meaningful evening lecture.

At 9:00 PM, I called Michelle to say good-night and send her my love. Afterward, I decided not to join the guys horsing around but rather to lie in my bed and think about the previous twenty-four hours. *Wow. What a ride.* I stared at the ceiling. My eyelids slowly got heavy. My body went numb. I passed out cold and got my first good night's sleep in years.

A CALL TO ACTION

- In Chapter 13 we went over the two letters I had to write to my daughter twenty years in the future. One clean and sober, the other active alcoholism and addiction. Please write two letters to a loved one or yourself twenty years in the future on something you would like to change!

CHAPTER 14

HAPPINESS VS. PEACE

I TAPPED MY FINGERS anxiously as Brent read my two letters to Sloan. Finally, he looked up and grinned. "Adam, I'm impressed. Your openness and honesty say a lot about you."

I exhaled with relief. I looked into Brent's eyes.

"I thought long and hard about it, Brent. If I were writing a letter to Sloan twenty years from now, after all the drinking, drugging, and pain I caused her, it wouldn't be a long, sympathetic letter trying to make excuses for my behavior. I would have begged for forgiveness millions of times while she was growing up. At twenty years old, she wouldn't trust me. The only way she would even think of speaking to me again is if I went for help."

"You're probably right."

He looked back down at the letter, "And you're 110 percent right in thinking your marriage would have ended in divorce. If Michelle had the strength to perform an intervention already, she'll have the courage to protect her daughter from her alcoholic, addict father."

That stung.

"Adam, I'm proud of you for your decision to stay. Acceptance is a huge part of recovery. You're really doing the work."

"Work? This didn't feel like work. Sitting in an office looking up lace patterns—that's work. Running around to accommodate others—that's work. This is more like I'm getting to know myself all over again. Like a retreat, kind of fun in a sick way."

Brent rubbed his stomach. "Now, we just have to get you to be more honest about that anger you're carrying around inside your belly." He leaned back. The fine wool of his three-piece suit shimmered in the sunlight.

"I'm not angry!" I cracked my knuckles.

Brent's shifted his body weight, leaning back in his chair. "No, Bruce Banner. You're not angry. We wouldn't like you if you were angry. What is this emotion right here, right now?"

My muscles tensed, and my veins strained against my skin. I cracked my neck from side to side. Watching him sitting there in his satin shirt, double-Windsor, vintage tie, and Italian dress shoes, hearing him tell me about my feelings, I felt as if I were a child and he were the principal of my school.

"I'm annoyed you keep telling me I'm angry. You want to see angry, Brent? Just keep pushing my buttons by telling me I'm angry. This is ridiculous. You want me to be angry about you being late, angry that my parents asked me to take over the family business at fifteen years old, angry at

the kids from twenty-five years ago for calling me 'fatso'. That's silly! I'm disappointed that you're constantly late, and thank God you're not out there in the business world with that lackadaisical mentality or you'd be filing Chapter 11. Life isn't always fair, but you do what you have to. Like my dad says, 'Cowboy up!'"

Brent just sat there for about a minute.

Then he lifted one eyebrow and cocked his head. "Adam, you put the world on your shoulders. You don't give yourself permission to feel anything, and it comes out sideways, like it did just now. Wouldn't you like a drink right now? To calm those nerves?"

I panted. I was still short of breath. I spread my fingers and shook my hands as I tried to calm down. *A drink or a pill* would *be nice. Is this a test?*

"Just stay open to this process. We have some time now. Just stay honest. Can you do that?"

I pressed my lips together and softly nodded.

"Adam, I don't think you're lying to me. I just don't think you know what anger is. I think you've been taught that it's a bad emotion to feel. Just stick with me."

"Okay."

Brent pulled out a sheet of paper and handed it to me. "I'd like you to sign up for the family program next weekend, starting a week from Friday. I think it will be a great help to your recovery."

I looked at the top of the page: GUIDELINES OF FAMILY PROGRAM PARTICIPATION. PATIENT: ADAM J."

"Your counselor has referred you to this program, and we, the family program staff, welcome your participation."

I continued reading:

- Orientation is Friday at 8:00 AM in the cafeteria. Please be on time.
- All Family Program participants, including you, dine together for all meals during the Program. This is an important part of the group experience.
- You are expected to attend each session of the program, all three days.
- We want you to be comfortable and appropriately attired. Please adhere to your unit's dress code.
- The Family Program concludes at 3:00 PM on Sunday. Please let your visitors know that you will be unavailable until then. You will be able to receive visitors between 3:00 PM and 5:00 PM.
- Thank you. We appreciate your cooperation.

I pointed at the mention of visiting hours. "Brent, if this is going to interfere with my time with Michelle and Sloan, I'd rather not."

"Adam, you and your wife are completely codependent. You both need the family program. I have good news for you, though. With your new life in recovery, you and Michelle can have more time together over the next few weeks to get reacquainted. If possible, I'd like her to come this Saturday and register for the following weekend's family program so you both can attend it . . . if she'd like to. You'd have an hour or two of visitation, and she could stay until 6:00 PM on the Sunday of the program. How does that sound?"

"Great!"

"I thought you'd like that. The family program is set up like this. Three men from the men's unit and three women from the women's unit are paired with outside family participants. Addiction is a family disease, it doesn't just affect you, the addict. It affects the family members and the family system itself. Most of the time, the families who sign up are relatives of your fellow patients. You guys will all learn quite a bit from one another. It's an amazing journey. There will be a lot of sharing. You'll tell your group what the disease is like and its effects. In return, you'll hear how alcoholism and addiction are devastating to them. Together, you'll gain knowledge about the family disease, family systems and roles, recovery skills, relapse education, and more.

"If Michelle signs up, she'll be here on the following Friday, Saturday, and Sunday. You can see her every day. Afterward, Adam, you'll be on your final days here in Hanley. I'll speak to you and Michelle together a couple times, about your new life.

Thrilled, I clapped my hands loudly. "Thank you, Brent."

Brent had gone from foe to friend in minutes.

"Don't thank me, Adam. You're doing all the work." He paused. "You understand that?"

"I guess." I shrugged. *This still doesn't feel like work.*

"No, don't guess. Know! *You* are doing all the work."

On the way to lunch, I thought about my anger. I felt uncomfortable in my own skin. *If I ever get truly irate while clean and sober, what will that look like? How will that feel?*

A scene from the original Superman movie popped in my head. After having saved millions of lives from a vicious missile attack, Superman finds Lois Lane dead in her car.

She has suffocated from an avalanche caused by one of the missiles in Lex Luthor's evil plot to take over the world. Superman lifts the buried car out of the dirt and rubble and pulls Lois's body into his arms. As he kisses her lifeless lips, he lays her body gently on the ground. He whispers, "No, no, no, no, no, no, no . . ." while feverishly shaking his head, his face bright red. Heartbroken that he couldn't save her, so full of pain and anguish, he lets out a furious scream and launches himself into Earth's atmosphere. That look on his face, that despair . . . *I never want to feel that way.* Anger comes from pain, and it scared me.

At lunch, I met three new, interesting guys who had just completed detox. Ethan, a fifty-year-old heroin addict from Washington, D.C., had made a fortune helping design some fuel system for airplanes. He spoke some genius engineering language that I couldn't comprehend. He looked terrible—gaunt with white skin. He was sweating and shivering despite wearing two sweatshirts, a jacket, and a pair of jeans. It was summer in South Florida.

Dwayne, a top stuntman in show business, was my age, thirty. He had a beautiful wife and one child. Five years earlier, he'd injured his back doing an acrobatic motorcycle stunt called the Leap of Faith. Dwayne had stood on the seat of the motorcycle and leaped high into the air, intending to land back on the tank of the motorcycle. He had missed—and instead landed in the hospital for six months. His downward spin had started with the morphine he was given in the hospital, followed by a prescription for OxyContin. During his recovery from the accident, Dwayne's life had changed forever. He had

become addicted to opiates and put them before anything else in his life, even his wife, child, and career.

Nolan—a salesman and co-owner of a private airline company—was forty-eight years old and handsome. At first impression, Nolan had everything going for him; in reality, he had a crack addiction that was so bad he'd sold all his assets and drained his bank account of nine million dollars.

After I'd eaten a lunch of grilled swordfish, steamed spinach, and a fruit platter, Ben, the director of the men's unit, called me into his office.

"Adam, I need a minute of your time."

"Sure. What's up?"

He took a deep breath. "Before I ask, please know that you don't have to say yes. I have a favor to ask of you. We feel you've grown here and are strong enough for the task." He folded his arms across his chest.

I cleared my throat. "Task?"

"Yes. This week you would typically be moved into a two-bedroom. But we're currently running short on beds. Would you mind staying in the swamp, the four-bedroom, for a few days with Ethan, Nolan, and Dwayne? If not, one of them will have to stay up in detox."

That's all he had to say. *Nobody* should have to stay in detox.

"Sure, Ben. Not a problem. Where are Jack and Grant going?"

"Jack is moving in with Morty, and Grant is moving in with Tony."

Lucky bastards.

I scratched my chin. "Where are you putting Seth, if he ever wakes up?"

"I'm not at liberty to say. Why don't you ask Seth yourself?"

That threw me off guard.

"Thanks a million, Adam. You're helping everyone out on this." Ben extended his right arm for a fist bump.

We fist bumped.

"When the time's right, just make sure you give me a good roommate."

I went to my room. Seth was out of bed and packing his stuff.

"Yo, welcome to sunlight! What room are you assigned to?"

His face turned bright red. "Room? I'm leaving. My parents think I have a more serious problem. They're putting me in a long-term treatment facility somewhere in Minnesota. Can you believe that crap?"

He sighed as he chucked crumpled clothes into his duffle bag as if he were skimming rocks across a lake.

"This *is* your fourth rehab stint this year, and it doesn't seem like you care. You never even get out of bed. The move could be good for you."

"You think I have a problem, too?" He shook his head.

My mouth fell open. It hit me. *This is what the disease can do to someone. It can make them so blind they have absolutely no clue they're sick.*

I spoke in a soft, comforting voice. "Yes, Seth. I do think you have a problem. I just accepted that *I* have a problem. You're nineteen, and you've already had a heart attack. Do

you think that's normal? Look, man, you can hate me all you want, but if you were my kid, I'd do whatever it takes to save your life."

I patted his arm and then left the room. That was the last time I ever saw Seth. Years later, I learned that he died from alcoholism and addiction.

On the way to my second appointment with John Dyben, I made a great effort to walk a little slower and "smell the roses." The fragrance from the flowers. The flight of the birds overhead. The gentle ocean breeze. This one simple exercise taught me that I had always hurried. The situation never mattered. I wanted to get everything done fast. Even my drinking! I slammed back Patron Silver tequila. I guzzled cocktails so that the fourth one was in me when the first one hit my bloodstream. My life philosophy was to get from point A to point B as quickly as possible. I want it now. More now. More now. More now. More now.

I sat back, casually, in the comfortable, red recliner in John's office. I told him about the previous morning's massive panic attack.

"Sounds more like a spiritual awakening to me, Adam." His eyes softened, and he put his hand on his heart. "A true surrender of your ego." He seemed to contemplate something for a moment, and then he asked, "What are your hobbies?"

Hobbies? Hmm. I quietly reflected on the question. I still wanted John to think I was Superman, but I didn't want to lie. I didn't want to make grandiose claims like "I help out with the Peace Corps," or "I mountain climb, ride horses, and skydive."

I was honest. "Bodybuilding and drinking."

He grinned. “Ha! I love your honesty, Adam. Well, exercise is mostly a good thing.” He shrugged. “I could use some more of that.” He pointed at his little belly. “What else do you enjoy?”

“I don’t know. I think that’s it. I love watching movies.”

“We can count that. No other hobbies, though? Maybe music? You play an instrument?”

“No. I always wanted to but just never had the time.”

He leaned toward me and rubbed his hands together.

“Being sober, you’ll have more time on your hands. I want to explore who you are and what you like. Let’s start with this simple exercise. I’m going to give you two choices.” He fiddled in his chair and leaned toward me. “Just go with me on this.”

He stuck out both of his arms, both hands in fists.

“In this hand, you have peace, and in the other, you have happiness. Which one do you want? Don’t say both, because that’s not an option.”

“I’ll take happiness.”

He smiled as he lowered his arms.

“Okay. Why happiness?”

“I have so much to be grateful for, but I’m not happy. I have close relationships, a beautiful home, job, cars, security, and . . . I’m just not happy.”

He closed his eyes and took a deep breath. Then he opened his eyes again.

“I hear you. I hear you, Adam. I think you want peace, and let me explain why. Many things can and will make you happy. But sooner or later that happiness fades. Remember when you got your new car?”

I thought of how pumped I'd been in my new, black Hummer H2.

"You loved that car. All you wanted to do was drive or sit in that car. The car made you so happy. But, after some time, that brand-new car became just your car. You started losing the pleasure in driving it. It didn't give you that same satisfaction anymore. Before you knew it, it became just another thing you have to take care of. It constantly needed gas. It needed to be cleaned. But, in the beginning, all of that was a pleasure. You see, a new car made you happy but only for a little while. All material things will make you happy for a while. You know what else can make you happy? Getting married. Having a new baby. But, soon, the same things can happen with them. The happiness starts to dim. They become just another part of your life, another responsibility for you to take care of."

He has a point. All things seem to lose their magic eventually.

"You know what else can make you happy, Adam? A drink. You have a few drinks and feel, 'Ahh, instant gratification!'"

He clapped his hands and again stuck them out to indicate the two choices. "In this other hand here is peace. Adam, I believe it's peace you're looking for. When you're a man who lives in peace, you can take the good and the bad and it won't change you or make you react. If something amazing happens in your life, you're appreciative, joyful, yet steady. You don't need a drink to celebrate. If a tragedy happens to you, you're able to deal. You can have faith, see it through, and handle it without a drink or drug."

I leaned in closer. John's delivery had hypnotized me. I felt that same buzz I had felt during our first meeting.

He stopped for a minute to let me absorb the wisdom he'd imparted.

I forgot everything else going on in the world. I was in the now.

"Have you ever heard of the painting of peace?" John asked.

I shook my head.

"A few years back, they held a competition for a piece of artwork that would best symbolize the feeling and definition of peace. Countless works were submitted—everything from statues of animals to interpretations of heaven. It came down to two paintings. The first was of a gorgeous lake—water like glass except for the slightest ripple. You could feel the water just by looking at it. Behind the lake were two mountains. You could see the rising sun just over the horizon. The sky was magnificent, with shades of blues, purples, and pinks. A couple birds were flying in the distance. One look at this painting, and the first word anyone would say is peace. It symbolized tranquility to a T."

John's voice easily put me into a meditative state.

"The second painting was quite the opposite. It depicted a darker pond with rough waters. The sky was full of every weather system known to man: a tiny bit of sunshine, clouds, deep, dark thunderclouds with lightning bolts, a hurricane, a tornado causing a torrential downpour."

I furrowed my brow as I tried to understand how that painting was peaceful.

"On one side of the painting stood a large tree, tortured by the massive effects of the weather."

John's voice grew louder. "The commotion and destruction of branches and leaves was scary. All the way in the top, left-hand corner was a nest. In it, a mother bird protected her little baby bird from the horrendous weather outside and kept him safe. Adam, that's the painting they chose."

In my mind, I compared the two paintings: the beautiful, serene lake that reminded me of my childhood days at summer camp and a vicious lake where a mother bird was protecting its little one from the craziness all around their nest. I rubbed my chin.

John saw my confusion.

"You see, Adam, they picked that one for its symbolism of how life really operates. Life is full of every situation imaginable. We've all experienced those moments by the peaceful lake, but they're only moments. Life is much, much more. The baby feels safe with its mother. No matter what weather comes, Mama Bird will protect her baby. Through all the lightning, hurricanes, and tornados, she'll watch over her baby. The symbolism of every weather system known to man crashing down and a mother looking after her child moved the judges, because it was real life. No matter what happens in your life, if something is important to you, you protect it with all your heart. Nothing can knock you off. Wouldn't you do the same for Sloan and Michelle?"

"Of course."

"And, God is there for you, Adam. You're His baby. Peace is what you want. Peace isn't the opposite of war. Peace is connection to your Source and knowing everything will be okay."

I felt lighter and slightly euphoric. I thought about the two paintings. If this God, this Higher Power, is the mother bird, then I'm always safe. Once again, John had gotten my adrenaline pumping, and I'd entered another dimension.

He stood up, walked over to me, and placed his hand on my shoulder. "This, my friend, is what you want. You want to feel connected to your Higher Power. You want to know everything's going to be all right."

I could hear Bob Marley in my head singing, "Everyting's gonna be all right, yeah! Everyting's gonna be all right!"

"You want to feel protected, Adam. You want to feel peace."

When I left John's office, there was a bounce in my step. I needed to share this knowledge. It wasn't fair that people needed to have this disease or hit bottom to learn these invaluable lessons. *They should be teaching this to every child in the world. Everyone should know this stuff.* I didn't know one person who wouldn't benefit from a little rehab. Not one.

A CALL TO ACTION

- In Chapter 14 John Dyben taught me the true difference between happiness and peace. Please think of three things that made you happy this year! Has it faded already? Does it still truly make you happy? Be honest!
- Now, write about what peace of mind would look like in your life. How would you respond to daily events? What does your behavior look like? How would the tone in your voice sound? Visualize having this peace not just in the good times, but also in the storms of life!

CHAPTER 15

THE PRODIGAL SON

"YOUR PROGRAM? What's that?" Michelle asked.

"Sorry. I've been learning this new terminology every day—my new second language, of recovery. They drill it into our heads. My program is how I work the twelve steps of recovery—how I'll use the steps as a new way of living to stay sober."

I filled her in on every detail of my session with John Dyben. In a loud voice, I babbled about the painting of peace, God, and walking slowly. When I had finished rambling, there was a long pause on the other end of the phone line.

"Honey? You there?"

I heard her breathing heavily and sniffling.

"You all right?"

She spoke softly through sobs. "No. No. I'm *not* all right." She sighed. "I hear you doing the work, and I'm proud of you. But . . . you have no idea how hard this is on me—alone here in the house. Sometimes I don't feel safe. I'm raising our baby all by myself. I'm not sleeping. When friends call, I don't want to pick up the phone. It's hard to lie all the time. I'm constantly worried about you. I panic, thinking, 'What if this whole thing doesn't take?' Your family is upset with me over you being in treatment and not at work. I don't believe they think you're really sick. They think *I* did this to their poor son. I feel so lonely, so scared."

Now I could see the family disease clearly. It was affecting everyone.

I hit the wall with my fist. My eyes watered. I felt low. Ashamed. Guilty. One minute I was proclaiming the will of God. The next minute I was a scumbag alcoholic and addict.

I cleared my throat and then said, "Do you want me to come home?"

"No!" she yelled. "I want you to listen to me. Just listen. Can't you do that?"

"Okay, I'm sorry."

She inhaled deeply. "I'm not asking you to apologize." She let out another long sigh.

I could feel her frustration, but she continued.

"I'm asking you to understand. This isn't easy. I know it's difficult for you in there, but it's just as hard for me out here."

I closed my eyes and shook my head. *I can't fix this. I can't put on a red cape and save the day.* I couldn't say the right words to calm the situation and make it go away. I had to allow myself to feel it, and that hurt.

Meanwhile, I could hear my disease talking to me. *How do* we *deal with this now, buddy? You can't drink. Oh, and no*

more pills. You gonna talk to God again? Ha! Is He even real? Is the Great Almighty even listening to you? Some shmuck in rehab instead of, let's say, starving kids in Africa?

I shook it off.

"Michelle, I'm so sorry I've done this to you and our family. I'll get better. I promise."

I hung up the phone and then pinched the bridge of my nose and closed my eyes. When I opened my eyes again, I looked around the tiny, pale phone room. *What do I do now?*

I had to work a new muscle—I had to talk to another alcoholic or addict about my feelings. The old me would have kept the pain inside, beat myself up, and maybe gone to work out. Now, I needed a friend who understood how I think.

In the hallway, I found Grant and Jeremy horsing around on the computer. "Guys, you mind if I talk to you real fast?"

"What's up?" Jeremy asked.

"I just got off the phone with Michelle, and it's starting to get to her."

"What is?" Grant asked.

"This. Rehab. My being away for so long. Raising our baby on her own. Lying to our friends about where I am."

I rubbed my hands over my face. "I hate this disease!"

Grant walked over to me and put his hand on my shoulder. "You're not alone in this, man. We all hate this disease. It'd be nicer having this talk over a cold one."

I thought about having a drink.

"Your wife still has to go on with life out there in the real world. It's like *we* all hit the pause button, but she doesn't get to do that. It's good she shared her pain with you. That'll give you the motivation to stay on track so you never have to do this again."

I thanked the guys and then made my way to the cafeteria to grab a coffee. It had been years since I'd leaned on friends for support, years since I'd trusted people. I couldn't believe it, but I felt better. Sharing did cut the pain in half.

THAT NIGHT, I FELL ASLEEP easily and slept peacefully. Sharing my worries had relaxed me. I was recovering.

BUT THE NEXT MORNING, I woke up, from a dead sleep, to screaming and a loud bang. I jerked my head up off the pillow. I heard more shouting and commotion in the hallway. I jumped out of bed and ran to my door, where I saw Jack, in his light-blue Life Is Good sleepwear, pacing back and forth in the hallway and Morty, in one of his many Hawaiian shirts—this one with hot pink hibiscus—sitting on the floor. The fluorescent lights blinded me for a few seconds.

"Guys, what's going on?" I rubbed my eyes, trying to wake up.

Jack's face was bright red. "I'll tell you what's going on, Adam!"

He pounded his fists against his thighs. "Matt's been smoking crack in here! Morty saw him last night in his room."

Morty looked up at me. "Matt begged me not report him. He threatened to kill me. But I couldn't not say anything. I told Matt, 'Either you confess or I turn you in.' Matt flipped out, and I called Father Ron."

Confused, I walked over to Morty. "When?"

"Last night. He didn't realize he'd left his blinds open. It looked suspicious to me, so I walked closer to the window, and there he was, lighting up a pipe."

I scratched the two-day stubble on my cheek. "How did he get crack into rehab?"

Jack shook his head. "Seth. That idiot! The other day, when he packed his stuff, he asked Matt to help him take his bags to his car. Inside his car, he had some leftover crack rocks, a stem, and a pipe."

"How do you know that?" I felt like a cop gathering evidence.

Jack looked down the hallway, checking for counselors. "Jeremy saw it. He didn't know what to do, either. When Morty told Jeremy what had happened, he shared what he saw."

"So, what was the yelling and that loud bang just now?"

"The loud bang was Matt hitting our window from the outside. The yelling was Matt threatening—again—to kill Morty."

I turned toward Morty, who was still sitting on the floor.

"You all right, pal?" I reached out my right hand. When he grabbed my hand, I slowly pulled his overweight body onto his feet.

"I'm okay." He moaned loudly. "Help me lose this spare tire?"

I chuckled.

AT BREAKFAST, THE GOSSIP about Matt circulated fast. I felt bad that my new roommates were coming into such drama when they were just starting to get clean. To make them feel more comfortable, I asked them to join us in our morning walk. Ethan felt too weak from detoxing, but Nolan and Dwayne joined Grant, Jeremy, and me. After twenty minutes, everyone else had slowed down, so Grant and I were able to have a private conversation.

"Can you believe Matt smoked crack here in rehab?" Grant asked, slightly out of breath.

I raised my eyebrows and swallowed hard. "He's been nothing but trouble. Sometimes I can tolerate him, but this is it for me. I hope they kick him out of here."

Grant gasped for air. "But where would he go?"

I picked up speed. "None of my business. Look, I live forty-five minutes from here, and nobody's smoking crack in my house. I'd feel a lot safer sleeping there. I doubt I'm the only one thinking this way. They should get rid of him. They need to do something."

"I don't know, Adam. I'd feel bad kicking somebody out and then finding out they died a week later."

I stopped dead in my tracks. With that one simple statement, Grant had opened my eyes to the truth of addiction. I thought about the evening prayer that Father Ron had taught me and how he'd said I could say the Lord's Prayer at the end of it. *And forgive us our trespasses, as we forgive those who trespass against us.* Each evening, I asked forgiveness for the stupid things I'd said and done, but then I had to forgive other people in order for God to "work." It was a paradox, I tell you! I felt torn. A part of me wanted to destroy Matt for the greater good. *This spirituality thing isn't easy.*

I decided to seek out Father Ron.

KNOCK, KNOCK, KNOCK.

"Who is it?" Father Ron asked.

"It's Adam, Father. You have a few minutes?"

"Absolutely. Come on in."

I opened the door, and Father Ron greeted me with a hug. "Are you feeding yourself those prayers like you would those muscles?"

I stood tall and proud. "Yes, and I'm actually enjoying it."

"Have you done your homework?"

I nodded.

"Would you like to go over it now?"

"Well . . . I'm here for a different reason. I—"

"I know why you are here, son. But first, what were the three lessons in the two commandments from Matthew 22:34 through 40?"

I closed my eyes and tried to recall my homework. "One is to love God with all of your heart."

He pulled out his Recovery Bible and flipped to the page containing the assigned bible verses.

"Adam, before we read this together, I want you to remember that Jesus was a rabbi. So, just because our faiths differ on what He truly symbolizes doesn't mean that He didn't say it. Are you uncomfortable with any of this?"

"No, not at all. . . . I've always been fascinated with religion, spirituality, and the holy books. I told you that. I got a kick out of doing the assignment."

"Good." He handed me the book. "Please read it for me." He pointed out where to start in the book of Matthew.

"Hearing that Jesus had silenced the Sadducees, the Pharisees got together. One of them, an expert in the law, tested him with this question: 'Teacher, which is the greatest commandment in the Law?'

"Jesus replied: 'Love the Lord your God with all your heart and with all your soul and with all your mind.' This is the first and greatest commandment."

I looked up at Father Ron, and he winked at me.

I continued reading, "And the second is like it: 'Love your neighbor as yourself.' All the Law and the Prophets hang on these two commandments.'"

I glanced up from the book.

"What is the third lesson from the commandment?" Father Ron asked

"That all the laws and prophets hang on those two commandments?"

"No. I want you to think. Go deeper."

Oh, great. Here we go again. Deeper? I stared at the two commandments, and a flash went off inside my head. *"Love your neighbor as yourself . . . as yourself. . . . Love yourself!*

"The third lesson is to love yourself?"

"Bingo! You got it. To love yourself. That is something we need you to work on. To keep the focus on you and not . . ."—he paused and grinned in an all-knowing way, like the Mona Lisa—"others. Keep your attention on yourself, and concentrate on your own lessons instead of somebody else's. Now, I am ready to talk to you about Matt."

It was like visiting a great, powerful, all-knowing oracle who could read my mind.

I thought about the commandment "Love your neighbor as yourself." *Would I want to get kicked out of rehab for making a mistake?*

I shared my thoughts with Father Ron. "This spiritual way of living, it's not easy. I know I should forgive Matt. I know *I* wouldn't want to be kicked out of here, so I shouldn't want him to get kicked out. But, Father . . . the guy just rubs me the wrong way. And, if he'd touched a hair on Morty's head, I think I would have gone after him."

He lowered his head and studied me. "Adam, do you know the parable of the prodigal son?"

I shook my head.

"In the Gospel of Luke, Jesus tells the story of a man who has two sons. The younger son demands his share of the inheritance while his father is still alive, and he goes off to a distant country where he spends his riches on riotous living. Say, he squanders his money on alcohol and drugs. As of result of his recklessness, he eventually has to work as a swineherd. There, at his bottom, he comes to his senses and makes up his mind to return home and throw himself on his father's mercy. When he returns home, his father greets him with open arms and hardly gives him a chance to express his repentance. He is thrilled to have his son back home. The father even kills a fatted calf to celebrate his son's return. We can say he serves filet mignon. The older, good son becomes jealous at the favored treatment of his faithless, foolish brother. He is furious at the lack of reward for his own faithfulness during all those years. But the father responds, 'Son, thou art ever with me, and all that I have is thine. It was meet that we should make merry, and be glad: for this thy brother was dead, and is alive again; and was lost, and is found.'"

I nodded. "'I once was lost, but now I'm found.' Sure, I've heard that."

I was reminded of how much I enjoyed the conversations I had with the Hanley staff, especially Father Ron and John Dyben. I wanted what they had—real faith and definite purpose. I felt fortunate to be in the company of such holy, divine men. They urged me to think on a more profound level. I finally was seeing how religious people were right.

Father Ron continued his explanation of the parable. "Adam, there are many lessons in the story of the prodigal son, the lost son, but the one I want to focus on is forgiveness. I teach that the father in the parable is God and that all you have to do is go to Him and seek His forgiveness. Not only does He forgive, but He celebrates. You see, He never condemned you, and He wants you home with him. *You* were the one who left *His* side. He did not kick you out."

I sighed deeply. And then it hit me: *Matt is the prodigal son*. I stared at the floor. Father Ron could see the recognition in my face.

"Would you like to say a prayer for Matt with me, Adam?"

I nodded meekly.

Father Ron reached for my hands and led me in prayer.

One second, I'd wanted to knock Matt out. The next second, I'm praying for him. Is this my new life?

WHILE I WAS ON THE WAY to my next group therapy session, I heard an announcement over the loudspeaker: "Emergency men's unit meeting in five minutes. No group today. Everybody, including counselors, please meet in the men's unit in five."

It didn't take a genius to figure out what the emergency meeting was about. I felt more centered after having met with Father Ron. I no longer wanted Matt to be kicked out of Hanley, but I still didn't trust him.

As everyone filed into the lounge and grabbed seats, Ben walked to the center of the room. He angled himself so that he could see down a hallway out of everyone's view and, when all the counselors and patients were settled in, he signaled someone to come in. Whispers filled the room. Ben lowered his head and pressed his lips together tightly. Finally Matt walked into the room.

Ben said loudly, "Gentlemen, may I have your attention? We have a situation. Before we start the meeting, Matt would like to say a few words."

Matt's face turned pale. He swayed slowly back and forth. After a moment, he cleared his throat and then began.

"A couple of days ago, when Seth left, he asked me if I'd help him take his bags out to his car. He had some leftover crack and a pipe stashed away there. We both got high. He gave me the pipe and the crack he had left. For most of the day yesterday, I was high. Last night, I decided to finish what was left, and Morty caught me. I flipped out and threatened him."

Matt raised his head and found Morty in the room. "I'm really sorry, Morty. I didn't mean it. I'm an idiot. I never would have laid a finger on you. . . . I'm sorry, all of you."

Matt turned, walked back into the hallway he'd come from, and shut the door.

Ben started the meeting. "Gentlemen, this is a serious problem. My first question to you all is, 'Do you still feel safe here?'"

We went around the room, each patient answering that question.

Taylor said, "I feel safe. I know this isn't anybody's fault, but what if that wasn't crack? What if that was a case of beer? What if he'd invited me to join him? Would I still be sober? I don't know."

I thought about that long and hard. *Would I be sober now if it were my favorite tequila? Yes.* I felt confident and sure of that. This was a breakthrough. I wanted to be sober.

By the time we finished going around the room, everyone had reported still feeling safe.

Ben asked, "Would anybody like to vote Matt out of Hanley? We can't have him jeopardizing your sobriety. Anyone who'd like Matt to be removed, please raise your hand."

My heart felt full. I formed a steeple with my hands and pressed them to my lips. An hour earlier, I'd have voted him off. But since then, I'd spoken with Father Ron. Something strange was happening inside me. I was seeing and participating in my life in a whole new way. I was changing.

"It's settled, then. Matt stays. Let's close out the meeting with the Serenity Prayer."

We all stood up and held hands.

"God, grant me the serenity. . . ."

THAT AFTERNOON, WE WENT on a field trip to Rapids Water Park. It had thirty-five waterslides, a big wave pool, and raft rides. There we were, a group of grown alcoholic and addicted men playing together in a children's water park. We fooled around with the kids, competing on the six-lane rapid racer slides and shooting squirt guns. Many adolescents recognized Jeremy from Stalker and swarmed around him, asking him a million questions. It was cool to watch. As he rode down the waterslides and played in the wave pools, he preached to the minors not to smoke, drink, and take drugs. The irony made me laugh.

Dwayne showed off his crazy stuntman moves on the high dives and in the FlowRider simulated wave system that went forty miles per hour. He looked like an action hero, flipping, turning, and contorting his body in crazy positions. I felt as if we were at Disney, watching the spectacular extreme stunt show.

I laughed so much. I rode down waterslides. I told jokes. I bounced around on the rafts. I relaxed on the park's lazy river. I played pool basketball. And I did it all without alcohol or drugs. I couldn't believe how much fun, relaxation, and excitement we had. Over the years, drinking and pleasure had had such a direct relationship in my life that I'd completely forgotten how to have fun without alcohol. I was finding my smile again.

A CALL TO ACTION

- Forgiveness! This is a huge topic. I had to forgive Matt in this last chapter and realize that him getting kicked out of treatment would be awful for his chance at recovery. Jesus's main teachings were based on forgiveness. Forgiveness is not reconciliation. Forgiveness IS allowing yourself out of a prison in your own mind. Whom do you have a deep resentment toward that if you were able to forgive, you'd be free? Why don't you just let that go?
- When was the last time you experienced pure joy, like I did that day in treatment at the waterslide park? Have you found your smile?

CHAPTER 16

BOUNDARIES

WE GOT BACK FROM the water park thirty minutes before dinner.

Ben found me in the hallway. "Adam, you mind coming to my office for a second?"

I nodded and followed him down the hallway. When we got to his office, I saw that all of the men's unit counselors were there.

"Whoa—"

"Please close the door behind you."

I panicked. "Is it Michelle? Sloan? Are they okay?" I felt a chill run through my body.

Brent said, "Everything's fine, Adam. Nobody's hurt. We have a couple things to speak to you about. Just chill."

He leaned back in his chair, with an easygoing grin.

I sighed, raised my hands, and placed them on top of my head.

"Let's start with the easy topic," Ben said. "Soon, we crown a new peer leader, and we unanimously voted for you."

John Dyben chimed in, saying, "What would you say you bring to the table as peer leader?" He winked at me.

I was taken aback, and I took a second to answer him. I felt uncomfortable speaking positively about myself. I'd become accustomed to pointing out what I needed to work on, what I could improve about myself.

"Well, all the guys seem to respect me. And I haven't missed one lecture, group, meditation, or high-low."

"What else?" Brent was drumming his fingers against his leg.

I closed my eyes, scratched my beard, and thought about my leadership assets.

I opened my eyes and said, "I've taken the dedication and discipline I learned in bodybuilding and applied it to my sobriety. A lot of the men come to me for nutrition and fitness tips, and I love showing them the ropes and seeing them get stronger and healthier."

"Anything else?" Brent asked.

"I guess I lead by example. And I've become a good friend."

"Good answer, Adam. We agree," John said.

"There's a 'but' here, Adam." Brent locked eyes with me, and I knew I wouldn't like what he was about to say. "Yes, you're a great leader but, having said that, you're still practicing some of your old habits. People pleasing. You think you need to be there for everyone—your Superman complex. Our job is to get you better so you can deal with life outside of rehab. There's no doubt you're the most enthusiastic and motivated patient we've ever had. But you need to learn boundaries.

This exercise is not just for you at Hanley but also for your recovery outside these walls."

I stepped back and crossed my arms, unwittingly showing how defensive I was. "What exercise?"

Brent enjoyed seeing me get angry. My emotions were coming to the surface. I couldn't pretend anymore. . .

"The world isn't always going to hand you the best conditions for your sobriety. You'll be challenged day in, day out. As your counselor, I've decided to room you with Matt."

Pause.

Long pause.

Very long pause.

"What?" My hands trembled. "You roomed everybody together in order to get them stronger for the outside. This isn't right."

I looked at Ben. "What about that deal we made? I stay in the swamp to help out Hanley, you give me a good roommate like Grant. Come on, guys! Christ! Two nights ago, Matt smoked crack in that room." I wanted to hit something.

Brent said, "Ben told me about the deal he made with you, but I'm your counselor. This isn't debatable. I need you to learn boundaries. I want you to learn the truth about yourself. Your stay here is almost complete."

John Dyben put his hand on my shoulder. "I agree with his decision, Superman. It's the best thing for you."

Hearing it from John made it seem more like a spiritual exercise than corporal punishment.

"Fuck. He'll hound me, constantly ask me about workouts and dieting. He's dirty. He'll get on my nerves about everything." I ground my teeth. "This sucks."

"That's why I believe it'll be a great tool for you." Brent was looking directly into my eyes. "Boundaries. We don't need to teach you how to get along with people out there. You have wonderful charisma and a pleasant personality. We need to teach you how to keep your energy for yourself—not let it spill out all over those people, places, and things that add stress to your life—how to stay within yourself, protect yourself, protect your sobriety. Inside, that's where your power is. You're always giving it away."

I understood his point. I couldn't save the world, and when I tried I failed—and I got thirsty. If I didn't learn this lesson, I'd end up trying to gain relief from alcohol, drugs, work, supplements, exercise, eating, you name it, and back in rehab. They call that cross-addiction—the substitution of one mood-altering drug or behavior for another. Their decision made sense, but I needed time to process it.

"When do I move?"

Brent's eyes glanced around the room, looking at each of the staff members and then at me. "Soon," he said, smirking. "You in?"

The room went silent.

I closed my eyes and swallowed hard. *God, help me.* "I'm in."

A FEW DAYS LATER, after morning meditation, I packed my bags. It was finally time for me to leave the swamp, the four-bedroom. *But to move in with Matt?* I rolled my eyes. *Here we go.* My new living quarters were fifty feet down the hallway. Each step felt like an eternity. *What am I going to find in Matt's room?* I envisioned his unmade bed smothered by dirty clothes, the floor covered with filth—crack stems, dirty needles, and rotting food with fruit flies buzzing over it—and shaving cream and toothpaste all over the bathroom walls. I cringed.

I knocked twice. No answer. I slowly opened the door and peeked inside. My mouth fell open. The room was spotless. Matt had left a note on the unmade cot that would be mine. The note said simply, "Welcome." I grinned and unpacked.

AFTER BREAKFAST, I RAN INTO Matt outside the men's unit. I asked him for a quick chat.

"Mind if I smoke?" he asked.

I shook my head.

He took out a yellow pack of Camel nonfilters, sparked his lighter, and lit one. He inhaled and then exhaled a giant cloud of smoke.

"I asked to room with you, Adam. I don't get this spiritual mumbo jumbo. I'd do anything for some more crack or a stiff drink. How do you do it? How do you just believe in all this recovery nonsense?"

How am I doing this? It was difficult to put into words. "At first, I just didn't want to lose my wife and daughter. And then . . . umm . . ."

My hands had grown sweaty. *How does one describe coming to believe, acquiring faith, almost overnight?*

But I tried. "Look, start by doing what I'm doing. Follow my lead. Wake up early, go to morning meditation. Continue making your bed and keeping the room clean. Go to every group. Share honestly with your counselor. Participate. Just be willing, man. Try."

THAT AFTERNOON, Matt showed me several notebooks he'd filled with poems and stories about his life using drugs. He taught me what a speedball is.

"You see, first I'd shoot up the heroin and get real mellow, almost nod off. Then I'd take a hit off the crack pipe."

He lifted his hands up and pretended to light white rocks in a pipe and draw from it.

"It raced up my heart. I'd feel my heart pounding through my chest while I was high as a kite and comfortably numb."

He pounded on his heart with his fist. "Boom! Boom! Sweat covered my body instantly. The chemicals left a sweet taste in my mouth. I loved it."

Matt's dark, twisted drug world scared the hell out of me.

AFTER MY TALK with Matt, we went to another experiential therapy session. This time, it was karaoke. The last time I'd done karaoke was at Maloney's bar, on campus at Arizona State University. I must have been twenty-one and on my fifth or sixth Long Island Iced Tea.

The music from the karaoke machine blared through the men's unit.

"You know you make me wanna—"

"Shout!" the gang yelled.

"Kick my shoes off and—"

"Shout!"

"Throw my hands up and—"

"Shout!"

"Take my pants off and—"

"Shout!"

"Come on now!"

I dropped to my knees as if I were performing on stage.

We felt like kids again . . . or like we were at a bar. I jumped on the couch, microphone in hand. The Isley Brothers backed me up as I sang my heart out.

"Hey-hey-hey-hey!"

The guys answered, "Hey-hey-hey-hey!"

"Come on and *shout* now!" I belted the words with my eyes closed.

"Shout!"

We all jumped up and down, wildly screaming, "Jump up and shout now! Jump up and shout now!"

What's happening to me? I feel safe here. Like Morgan Freeman's character in The Shawshank Redemption, Red, says, "These walls are funny. First you hate 'em, then you get used to 'em. Enough time passes, you get so you depend on 'em." I felt dependent on the structure of Hanley to keep me sober. I had a daily schedule. I went to spiritual classes. I painted. I played at the water park. I was chaperoned to outside Alcoholics Anonymous meetings. Now, I sang karaoke. I was institutionalized just like Red had been.

THE REST OF THAT DAY consisted of what had become my usual routine: Big Book study, step-three group, one-on-one counseling, and wellness time.

On my way to dinner, I saw Tony fishing. I jogged over, grabbed a fishing rod, and joined him.

"Hey, kid. How ya doin'?"

"I'm doing okay. How about you?" I pulled my rod back over my right shoulder and threw out the line.

"I was just reflecting on my life." He cast his own line into the pond. "I did a lot of bad stuff, kid. Ya name it, I did it. I started at five years old, as a pigeon."

"What's a pigeon?"

"A messenger. They used kids back then to deliver notes, envelopes, ya name it. No cellphones in the sixties."

He told me about how he'd moved up through the ranks. "When you had respect in your neighborhood, everything worked for you. And if you were a made guy like my old man . . . everything was given to you."

While Tony told me about his life in the mafia, serving time in prison, and later joining the Hell's Angels, something occurred to me: Tony would do anything for love, for a feeling of family. If he loved you, he'd take a bullet for you—literally.

He choked up every time he mentioned his son, Junior. Like Tony before him, Junior had wanted to emulate his father. But times were different. There were a lot of drugs. Junior grew up on the streets and fell in love with heroin. They found him in his car, dead from an overdose. He'd been in there for three days. Tony found out when he was behind bars, and he blamed himself. Tears filled Tony's eyes as he told me about it.

"If I'd been there to raise him, it all would have been different. That's why I couldn't go back to the family. And believe it or not, they understood. I did my time, but I needed out. It wasn't like the movies. They just cared about my well-being."

We sat there, staring at the pond.

After about ten minutes, I broke the silence. "So, what's your drug of choice?"

"Gambling. I'm in here for gambling. I've tried lots of drugs, but nothing can replace the excitement of a large bet. The rush I get from the action just can't be described. A big win at the tables or a huge return from a parlay at the sports books. . . . Boom! I chase it, I get desperate, and then I get helpless. I can't stay away from the action. It got real bad." He jerked his fishing pole.

"How bad?"

I tugged on my line, hoping to make the bait seem attractive to fish.

He lifted up his shirt and revealed a huge scar, from his upper belly across his chest and up into his armpit. "Three heart attacks. That's how bad. I'm gonna die, kid, if I keep this up. That's why I've been in here so long. I feel safe here. I don't trust myself out there, and I'm not ready to die."

As Tony reeled in his line, I noticed that he wasn't wearing his fancy Rolex. Today he was wearing a simple Timex that carried the Caesars Palace logo.

"What's with the new watch?"

He fiddled with his lure. "Tonight they take me outside for a Gamblers Anonymous meeting. Every time I go, I wear this watch. This is the most expensive watch I own. It cost me 1.5 million dollars. I gave Caesars my cash; they gave me a suite, champagne, and this beautiful watch. It's my personal souvenir to remind me of how bad I get. It and the scar."

He bobbed his fishing rod up and down. "Say, you want to come with me tonight? I always go alone, but I sure would love the company."

"Sure!" *Where else will I get to experience a Gamblers Anonymous meeting with a former gangster?*

THE ROOM WAS COMPACT AND DIM. There was a small podium with a GA banner and about seventy old, wooden folding chairs. And the room was full. I enjoyed hearing Tony and the others share their stories. I realized how strong the high from winning is. On the wall opposite me was a giant banner listing the twelve steps of Gamblers Anonymous, which were almost identical to those of Alcoholics Anonymous, with just the slightest differences in wording. Step 1: Admitted we were powerless over *gambling*—that our lives had become unmanageable. Next to the banner was a bulletin board that displayed meeting times for a list of various twelve-step programs, including Sexaholics Anonymous (SA), Cocaine Anonymous (CA), Overeaters Anonymous (OA), Narcotics Anonymous (NA), Co-Dependents Anonymous (coda), Heroin Anonymous (HA), and Al-Anon/Alateen, a group for friends and families of alcoholics. The list went on. It occurred to me that anybody in the world can use the basic approach of a twelve-step program to achieve freedom from addiction and greater connection to a higher power. I'd discovered a new world.

I HAD HIT MY REHAB STRIDE. Having gotten in the sober zone, I bounced around the Hanley Center campus. Brent said I was starting to feel a "pink cloud." Pink cloud is a recovery term that means high on life. I was in the flow, and I felt amazing—until I had an awful nightmare about drinking.

> The sun is setting. I'm coming home from work—wasted. I have a large red, plastic cup between my legs, filled with warm tequila and chopped limes. I pull into the driveway,

> feeling nervous, and I take a swig. It goes down smooth. I rub my five o'clock shadow and try to straighten my rumpled clothes. Even in my dream state, I know that Michelle will be upset with me for being intoxicated. I rest my head on the steering wheel and try to think. I can't go inside like this. I take another big gulp and shake my head to deal with the stiff drink. I decide not to go inside, not yet. I put my Hummer into reverse and pull out of the driveway without checking my rearview mirror. After a second or two, I hear an incredibly loud bang. I try to stop the Hummer, but my reflexes are impaired. My foot slips off the brake, and I hear a loud thump-thump. I finally hit the brake again and look at my rearview mirror. I see a bicycle—a toddler's bicycle. I jump out of my Hummer. A little boy is lying on the ground. Dead. What just happened? What did I do? I'm terrified. Do I call 911? Do I drive away? Did I just think that cowardly idea? Oh, my God! What have I done? The world caves in on me. I can't breathe.... I can't breathe....

I startled awake, gasping for air and soaked in sweat. I tried to swallow, but my throat was choked dry. Quivering, I sucked in air. The dream felt real. *Is this nightmare a sign?* My senses started to readjust to reality, and I heard Matt snoring. The room was nearly pitch-black. I squeezed my eyes tight and rubbed the bridge of my nose. I shuffled to the bathroom and took a hot shower. I tried to wash off the nightmare of having relapsed, but the sensation stayed with me. The guilt and remorse felt real.

I got dressed and headed to the coffee machine in the lounge. I sipped my coffee as I rubbed Roscoe, the walrus-tooth necklace—the symbol of the peer leader. The previous night, we had had another peer-leader-exchange ceremony. Jack had yelled to the group of men, "I take the spirit of Roscoe and pass it on!" I had received the necklace and placed it around my neck. I had put my fists on my hips and stood tall like Superman. "Thank you! I, too, shall pass on the spirit of Roscoe!" The other men had cheered.

Now, I just wanted my sober friends—the same way I'd craved a margarita—to kill the fear. *I'll do anything for this feeling to go away.* I closed my eyes and took slow, easy breaths. A gust of cold air whooshed over my face.

"Hi, Gaga," I whispered.

I felt as close to her as if she were standing next to me, holding my hand. I tipped my head back and said the Serenity Prayer. *I may be going crazy within these rehab walls, but I'm safe.*

A CALL TO ACTION

- "The world isn't always going to hand you the best conditions for your sobriety. You'll be challenged day in, day out. As your counselor, I've decided to room you with Matt."
  Can you imagine how I felt?! But, the counselors were right. Life will NOT just deliver you the best conditions. People, places, and things will confuse you. Are you strong enough to stick to your goals even when times get tough? Are you able to look loved ones in the eyes and say, "I love you. I respect you. But, I don't need your approval."
- I love that in this chapter Matt asks me how one acquires faith. By following a set of spiritual principles and actions laid out before us. Maybe by the Church, or Synagogue, or Mosque, etc. You can work and practice your way to faith, just like working out a muscle. Do one thing today that will strengthen your faith.

CHAPTER 17

A LOTSAHOLIC

EARLY ON FRIDAY MORNING almost a week later, family members and we patients who would be participating in the family program met for orientation in the cafeteria, where an area had been blocked off as a classroom. Grant's parents, Taylor's parents, and Morty's partner, Gary, were in my group. There were also family members from the women's unit, baby boomers unit, and senior unit.

I sat with my legs crossed and bounced my knee. I took a few quick breaths as I looked around the room. Each participant introduced himself or herself and gave a reason for signing up for the family program. We patients maintained our traditional form of introduction.

"My name is Adam, and I'm an alcoholic and addict."

"Hello, Adam," about forty people responded.

Winona, the head counselor of the family program, stood up and walked to the blackboard at the front of the classroom area. "First and foremost, alcoholism and addiction is a disease. It's primary (meaning that it's an illness in and of itself), chronic (an illness that can't be cured), progressive (an illness that will worsen over time), and fatal (an illness that damages internal organs—the heart, liver, and brain—and leads to premature death). Those are the four qualifications that make up a disease and why one can use insurance to pay for treatment of substance abuse. This isn't a bad habit or lack of willpower."

Winona was a heavyset woman with striking, silver hair, smooth, youthful skin, and a sweet smile that put the focus on her charm. She turned away from us and used a large, red marker to write on the blackboard. As she wrote, she said, "When a loved one, spouse, child, or parent suffers from alcoholism or addiction, the whole family suffers. That's why we call it 'the family disease.'"

When she turned around to face us again, she pointed to the words FAMILY DISEASE, which she had written in large letters.

We went around the circle, and each individual shared an example of his or her personal relationship with the disease.

Gary shared about all the empty liquor bottles he'd found and all the secrets he'd kept to protect Morty from their friends and family knowing how bad his disease was. "Even now, I feel like I'm breaking his trust by sharing that."

We nodded in empathy.

Grant's parents shared about losing their other son, Robert, to this awful disease two years earlier.

"Our home felt so empty, and we were lost," Melody said, her eye makeup running down her cheeks.

Her husband, Allen, put his arm around her.

"Robert's death weighed on Grant terribly. The boys were very close," he said as he stared vacantly.

The room went deadly silent except for the sound of their crying. I felt a deep sadness, and I was sure the others did, too. It killed me to watch them weep.

Eventually, the mood in the room lifted. Within just a few intense hours, the family members gained an understanding of the real torture of alcoholism and addiction—how our minds and bodies are different from those of normal people, how the first drink or drug is a choice but the addiction that follows is not. They gained more compassion for us. At the same time, we patients grew more appreciative of our loved ones and realized the destruction we had caused.

"My goal through this process is to teach you to detach with love," Winona said.

We participants looked at her like deer in headlights.

"To love *more* by caring *less,* to allow your loved ones to feel *consequences* and to become *independent!*" Winona made a fist to emphasize her point.

I swallowed hard and repeated under my breath, "Love more by caring less." That sounded like quite the conundrum.

WE ALL ATE LUNCH TOGETHER and, of course, when people saw my plate—grilled chicken, steamed spinach, fresh berries, and a side salad—I got a round of questions about my eating habits.

"I wouldn't have thought someone like you, so healthy . . . so . . . you know"—Grant's mother made a muscle—"could be in a place like this."

"Oh, trust me. He's one of us. Maybe even worse!" Jeremy gave her a big grin.

She raised her eyebrows and giggled. "How can he be worse?"

I leaned into Jeremy. "Yeah . . . how can I be worse?"

Jeremy patted me on the back. "Adam here is a . . . lotsaholic!"

Everyone at our table chuckled.

"And what exactly is a lotsaholic?" Grant's father asked.

"Whatever my friend Muscles does, he does *a lot*—the craziest extremes. You name it—alcohol, drugs, exercise, his family's business, being on time, eating healthy, worrying about his wife . . . no, *talking* about his wife and daughter."

He made a duckbill mouth with his hand, opening it and closing it quickly as if it were a talking puppet. "Michelle, Sloan, Michelle, Sloan, Michelle, Sloan. God! He doesn't shut up about them."

Everyone roared.

"Ask him if he's missed one activity here. No, even better than that, ask him if he's been five minutes early to every appointment."

All of them looked at me, and I closed my eyes and nodded.

"It's amazing! He's a freak. A sweet, muscular, neurotic, obsessive, extreme freak. I've never met another cat like him. Whatever he does, he does it *a lot.* A lotsaholic."

I thought about a few of the events of my life. No matter the situation, I wanted to have more, be first, or be better. I was competitive, anxious, and abnormally sensitive. I remembered the epiphany I'd had on my third day at Hanley: *I'm*

an alcoholic, addicted, codependent musclehead. No matter what I do, I go to extremes. I'm a lotsaholic.

We finished lunch and headed back to the portion of the cafeteria that had been set up as the classroom. The afternoon sun was shining through the room as we took our seats.

"Hello, my brothers and sisters."

Father Ron, in his usual clerical garb, entered the room abruptly, like Kramer in the television sitcom *Seinfeld*. He handed out copies of a document about integrating spirituality into a family's recovery. He looked around the room and made direct eye contact with each of us, ensuring that we were paying attention.

"Spirituality is the art of revealing and experiencing a life of consciousness and a consciousness of life—an appreciation for and a gratitude of life. It is waking up to the mystery of life within and being fully alive. Spirituality is a way of living. We can be asleep or awake, a survivor or a celebrator. Our spirituality reveals the quality of our relationships, our conversations, and our daily lives."

He gave an amazing presentation—more like a performance. His presence brought a special energy to the room. I felt as if I had left my body. I drew a deep breath and looked around the room. Everyone was engaged, listening, and healing.

Father Ron paced back and forth at the front of the room. "The twelve-steps program treats the whole person—spiritual, emotional, and physical. My specialty is the spiritual realm. A recovery program based on spirituality focuses on our awareness, on changing, and on practice. It includes our relationship with self, with others, and with God."

He paused and then continued in a softer voice. "Many people are afraid of the word God. Please do not be. We are not a cult here. Spirituality is not a religion but rather a way of life. It is not acquired, you see, but discovered and nurtured, since we are born with it."

I couldn't hear these lessons enough. My past attempts of studying and seeking in the Bible, the Torah, Kabballah, and Buddhism flashed through my mind. I'd searched, but it had been impossible for me to find the truth when I was drunk. I'd truly believed that one day it all would just click into place in a white-light moment. I hadn't realized that I would have to change to understand spirituality. *What a breakthrough I'm having!* I watched the faces of the family members in the room light up, like mine had been doing during my time at Hanley. Father Ron had broken down their walls and taught them to believe. *I want to do that!*

Father Ron pointed to the back of his handout. "On the back of the handout, I provide you with a brief guide to Twelve Stepping through Life."

We followed his lead and flipped over our handouts. He read the twelve steps aloud:

1. We admit we are powerless over alcohol, drugs, people, places, and things and that our lives are unmanageable. This is honesty.
2. We believe God can restore us to sanity. This is hope.
3. We turn our will and lives over to God. This is awareness and faith.
4. We take a moral self-inventory. This is courage.

5. We admit to God, ourselves, and another human being our wrongs. This is integrity.
6. We become entirely ready to have God remove these character defects. This is willingness.
7. We humbly ask God to remove our shortcomings. This is humility.
8. We make a list of those persons we have harmed and become willing to make amends to them. This is transformation and discipline.
9. We make direct amends to those people. This is forgiveness.
10. We continue to take personal inventory and admit our wrongs. This is acceptance.
11. We pray and meditate to improve our contact with God and carry out his will. This is awareness.
12. Having had a spiritual awakening, we share this message and live these principles. This is service.

He put down the piece of paper and, with his hands steepled together, paced slowly in front of us. "This is my abbreviated version. To all family members, these are the same exact twelve steps you can use in your own recovery."

Father Ron looked around the room and smiled genuinely. "Please remember that life is a precious gift. God bless you all, and be well."

Everybody stood up and applauded as if we were at a rock concert and wanted an encore. Father Ron waved and walked slowly out the door. We all seemed to feel a surge of energy.

After a few intense group sessions followed by dinner, day one of the family program was in the books. At the beginning of the day, it had felt as if we were on different sides—family vs. patient. Now, we were playing for the same team.

AFTER DINNER, I PLAYED volleyball with the guys in the men's unit. We clowned around as if we were in third-grade gym class. And then, it happened—a miracle. In the last point of the game, a fresh, alive Ethan spiked the ball inbounds to win the game. He pranced around the sand court, celebrating and getting high fives. I watched him come back to life from a horrendous detox. Afterward, as a unit, we broke the rules and jumped into the pool. As acting peer leader, I would bear the brunt of any penalty or scolding. I didn't care. We were bonding, forming friendships and trust. We were becoming a true we.

THE NEXT MORNING, my family program group met for breakfast. We were more comfortable with one another than we had been the previous day. Grant's mother gave me a nice, warm hug. Gary, Morty's partner, had his arm around Jeremy as they walked into the cafeteria to grab a coffee. I answered all of the others' questions about the egg whites, avacado, and oatmeal I was eating.

"My doctor keeps telling me I need to eat more like you, because of my heart and cholesterol." Taylor's father was shoving a chocolate muffin into his mouth and washing it down with some ice-cold whole milk. "I already suffered a heart attack and had a stent put in. How do you do it, Adam?"

I responded gently, saying, "Years of practice. It's just habit now. Eating healthy makes me feel good. Try to listen to your doctor. You'll feel a world of difference."

We all suffer our own addictions. Don't we? A doctor tells this man that he needs to cut back on junk food for the good of his heart, but he can't stop. *Maybe he could use a little time in here with us.*

WINONA WALKED AROUND the classroom portion of the cafeteria and passed out copies of a handout. "This morning we'll be learning the family systems. Let's take a look at an open family system."

She wrote on the blackboard: OPEN FAMILY SYSTEM.

"In an open family system, the rules and consequences are consistent, reasonable, and clearly stated. There is a minimal amount needed to provide structure and ensure safety. The family is flexible, and the rules and consequences are based on choices.

"Now, let's take a quick look at a closed family system. You'll notice just the opposite."

She wrote on the blackboard: CLOSED FAMILY SYSTEM.

"In a closed family system, the rules are inconsistent—too lax or too harsh—and very confusing. There is absent or excessive effort used to maintain them. The family is rigid, and the rules and consequences are based on control."

We participants were taking notes intensely.

Winona summarized, "In an open family system, the children learn they have choices and they develop problem-solving skills. The child is taught to talk, to trust, and to feel. On the other hand, children in a closed family system learn they have no choices."

My stomach turned. I couldn't stop thinking of the day I'd been asked to go into the family business. *How could I have known at such an early age what I wanted to do? How could I have chosen?* That thought stung.

Winona continued, "These children feel inadequate and insecure and ill prepared to meet life on life's terms. They also feel helpless and confused. They're taught not to talk, not to trust, and not to feel."

And that real men don't cry—to cowboy up. Memories bubbled up to the surface. Looking at them through this lens scared me. I thought of an ice-cold Coors Light. I suddenly had a flash, in my mind, of drinking sweet, prickly pear margaritas all day at the luxurious Phoenician resort in Scottsdale, Arizona. The movie in my mind could have been produced by the Tyler Durden character from the movie *Fight Club*. This phenomenon is called *euphoric recall*. It's a way that my disease reminds me of only the good times that I had when I was drinking. In reality, those days were dead, behind me, and I had to *feel* this—all of it.

LATER THAT AFTERNOON, during a short break between sessions of the family program, Michelle and I met with Brent.

"Adam is lucky to be married to you. You're supportive and understanding, definitely not the norm. Has Adam spoken with you about his treatment here at Hanley?"

Michelle raised her eyebrows. "Well . . . he told me about his new roommate and that he's peer leader now."

"Well, for your information, on a deeper level, we're having him work on boundaries and getting in touch with his anger."

I felt like a child. *Don't they see me sitting here right in front of them?*

"That's great. I'm happy about him working on his anger."

"*You* think I'm angry, too?" I felt tricked. I bit my lower lip and slowly shook my head.

"Honey, you lose your cool with me over nothing. When I ask you to please put your shoes away and not leave them by the bed, you freak out. Is putting your shoes away or cleaning up after yourself a little more such a big deal?"

I shook my head. "No." I looked at the floor.

"Michelle, this is excellent. You're going to help me in this project. I've been trying to make him angry for three weeks now. I've purposefully been late to many of our appointments, just to get a rise out of him. I could see lack of punctuality gets under his skin."

My eyes popped out of my head.

"On purpose?" I asked. *Is this a game show? Are there cameras on me?*

Michelle slapped her leg and smiled. She clearly was amused. "I'm late all the time," she admitted, still smiling.

"I can say clinically, Adam truly doesn't know he's angry. He has a million different words for it—upset, disappointed, discouraged. I could go on. Somewhere down the road, he learned that being angry is a bad thing, that anger is a bad emotion to feel."

"Brent, you'd have me get angry over every little thing in my life. Do you know how depressing that sounds?"

Brent lowered the brim of his glasses and made direct eye contact with me before answering. "Adam, do you know what depression is? Anger not dealt with and held inside. If you want relief from your life, from your emotions, you have to *feel anger.* After anger, we can get to blame, doubt, frustration, hopefulness, and maybe even happiness. But, first you have to *feel,* Adam. You're human, right?"

I crossed my arms over my chest and looked out the window.

Michelle grabbed my hand and squeezed it. "Honey, you have every right to be angry. Gaga passed away in your arms. The family business and its drama. You have a massive amount of responsibilities, and you feel like you have to get it all perfect. . . . There's a lot to be angry about."

"You know your husband well," Brent smirked. "As I work with you and Adam during the rest of his stay here, we can work out the kinks in your relationship and your lives. Miracles can start now."

Michelle and I squeezed each other's hands, and I let out a long, low sigh.

After the counseling session, Michelle and I walked down to the pond to feed Spike and Taz. We saw some of the guys playing volleyball, and they hollered at us to join in.

Michelle yelled back, "We're all good, boys! Need some time with my man."

At sunset, the colorful sky seemed to glow. We ripped off little pieces of bread and threw them into the water.

"It was intense, huh?" I asked.

"It's impressive. We sent you to the right place. Brent really knows you." Michelle chuckled under her breath while she continued to rip off bread to throw to the turtles. "I can't believe he knew to get to your appointments late to get a rise out of you."

"Yeah. I guess . . . I'm angry."

For a few minutes, we both looked out at the pond, in silence.

"Your being away, here in rehab, it's hard on me, but I see the way you look and sound, and I know we did the right thing asking you to come here."

I nodded. I gave Michelle another piece of bread and then threw the rest of mine to the turtles. I looked down at the ground and kicked a rock. "I've been thinking about Gaga a lot . . . and . . . sometimes . . . I think I hear her."

"What does she say?"

"She tells me to stay here, or I hear her singing to me. Crazy, I know."

Michelle smiled.

Again, there was silence. We weren't totally comfortable being together. In a way, we were strangers. This was a new beginning to our marriage.

Michelle threw a chunk of bread to Spike.

"Speaking of anger . . . I think your parents are mad at me that you're in here. I don't think they realize how sick you are."

I understood. On paper, I did all the right things. And I turned Michelle into the bad guy in every situation. If she got mad at my drinking, exercising, you name it, I made her look like an angry, controlling wife—a woman who didn't know how to loosen up and have fun. Now, my parent's son, Mr. Make-Everyone-Happy, was in rehab. I could see how that would be hard for my parents to accept. Blaming Michelle would be easier for them.

"Don't worry. I'll talk to them when the time is right. It must be hard to digest that your son's an alcoholic and addict. Just wait till I tell them I'm a lotsaholic!"

We laughed and then hugged.

THE FINAL MORNING of that weekend's family program was devoted to a discussion of codependency, enabling, communication, and relapse.

Winona wrote on the blackboard: CODEPENDENCY.

"Codependency is a popular psychological concept loosely defined as someone who exhibits too much, and often inappropriate, caring for people who depend on him or her. It's another type of addiction. Relationship addiction. A good example is that while your loved one is addicted to a substance you're addicted to them. You can become overprotective and not allow the alcoholic or addict to learn from their mistakes. You enable them. You try to control them. These codependent relationships are filled with shame and guilt, and they lack intimacy. Then we have the distrust, the perfectionism, depression, frustration, and emotional pain."

As the lecture progressed, Winona taught us how to detach with love. She pointed to a handout.

"When I feel responsible *for* others, I try to fix, rescue, protect, and control them. I don't listen. I feel tired, anxious, fearful, and liable. I'm concerned with answers, with circumstances being right. I manipulate feelings, people, and outcomes. I expect others to live up to *my* expectations. When I feel responsible *for* others, I'm caretaking. Can I see a show of hands? How many of you feel this way?"

All the family members raised their hands.

The funny thing was that I, too, felt that way.

"We want to detach with love," Winona said. "When I feel responsible *to* others, I'm sensitive. I show empathy. I encourage, share, confront, level, and listen. I feel relaxation, freedom, awareness, high self-worth. I can feel my feelings. I can express them and eventually let go and trust. I expect others to be responsible for themselves and their actions. When I feel responsible *to* others, I'm practicing self-care."

I want that!

Winona wrote on the blackboard: ENABLING.

"Enabling is doing for others what they need to do for themselves. It's reacting to a person in such a way as to shield them from experiencing the full impact of the consequences of their behavior. Enabling behavior differs from helping in that it permits or allows the person to be irresponsible."

We went around the room, each of the family members sharing stories of enabling their loved ones while my peers and I felt guilty.

Some of my confused anger finally had made it to the surface. I raised my hand, and Winona called on me.

"I'm the same as the family members on this one! I'm an enabler. I shield all my loved ones and make them feel like life is perfect and good. I'm the protector. I'm the caretaker. I take on more responsibilities than I can handle. I do more and more and more, and then I want to get out of myself with a drink, drug, workout, you name it—"

Jeremy said, "You see, everyone. You see what I'm talking about? He's a lotsaholic."

We all went into hysterics.

WHEN THE MORNING of lectures, videos, and powerful sharing was finished, my family program group ate lunch together.

As Charlotte was finishing organizing the food in the buffet line, she asked me, "What's wrong, dear? You're usually bouncing off the walls."

"Too much family therapy. My head is spinning."

"Aww! That's how it goes around here, dear." She placed a cup of plain brown rice on my tray. "When do you leave?"

"Next week." I opened my eyes wide. "I can't believe I'm saying this, but it went fast."

"That's because you're doing what you're supposed to. Just to cheer you up, I'm going to serve you an extra piece of the grilled mahi mahi and some strawberries."

Charlotte winked as if she were giving me a piece of homemade apple pie.

"Thank you, ma'am."

WE RETURNED TO THE final afternoon of the family program to find COMMUNICATION written on the blackboard and two sheets of paper waiting on every seat. The first handout listed the dirty dozen of communication:

1. Criticizing
2. Name-calling
3. Diagnosing

4. Praising manipulatively
5. Ordering
6. Threatening
7. Moralizing
8. Excessive inappropriate questioning
9. Advising
10. Diverting
11. Logical argument
12. Reassuring

As we went down the list, defining and giving examples of each, I heard the small voice in my head: *I can't believe they don't teach this stuff in first grade. Imagine if everyone could learn how to communicate with one another.*

After going through what *not* to do, we focused on the second part of communication: listening. Winona read aloud an anonymous letter that summed it up:

> When I ask you to listen to me and you start giving me advice, you're not doing what I asked. When I ask you to listen to me and you tell me why I shouldn't feel that way, you're trampling on my feelings. When I ask you to listen to me and you feel you have to do something to solve my problem, you're failing me, strange as that may seem. Listen! All I ask is that you listen, not talk or do. Advice is cheap, and I can do that for myself. I'm not helpless. Maybe discouraged and faltering, but not helpless. When you do something for me that I can and need to do for myself, you contribute to my fear

> and weakness. But when you accept, as a simple fact, that I feel what I feel—no matter how irrational—I quit trying to convince you. I can get about the business of understanding what's behind this irrational feeling. And when that's clear, the answers are obvious and I don't need advice. Irrational feelings make sense when we understand what's behind them.
>
> Prayer works, sometimes, for some people, because God is mute. He doesn't give advice or try to fix things. God just listens and lets you work it out yourself.
>
> So, please listen to what I say. If you want to talk, wait a minute for your turn, and then I'll listen to you.

That letter hit me like Bruce Willis realizing he was dead in the movie *The Sixth Sense. It all makes sense! I'm a poor listener!* Sometimes, people just want somebody to listen rather than fixing things for them. *This is another skill set I have to work on.*

Winona wrote on the blackboard: RELAPSE PREVENTION.

I found that session informative, too. The formal definition that Winona read out loud was "Relapse is a process that occurs within a person; it manifests itself in a progressive pattern of behavior or characteristics that allow the symptoms of the disease to become reactivated in a person who previously has arrested those symptoms."

The bottom line is that relapse is what happens when you stop doing what you're supposed to and you instead drink and drug again. End of story. The word *relapse* scared the hell out of me. Winona explained the various patterns of denial and what to watch out for: exhaustion, dishonesty, impatience, argumentativeness, depression, frustration, self-pity, cockiness, and complacency, just to name a few. Then we discussed our triggers—what could make us dishonest about our feelings and make us want to drink or use drugs again.

At the end of this three-day marathon, we held a goodbye, or medallion, ceremony in honor of completing the family program. My brain felt fried from all the emotional and psychological information that had been crammed into it in such a short period of time. I had what felt like a recovery hangover. But that hangover was from getting too much of a *good* thing. I missed my normal rehab schedule, though, and was glad to jump back into it that evening. I missed group. I missed story time. I missed working out with the guys.

THAT NIGHT, I RECEIVED a special treat. It was as if the Big Man upstairs knew exactly what I needed. The Hanley staff took us out for a twelve-step recovery meeting, but this was no regular meeting. It was an all-men's meeting filled with the biggest, baddest, toughest guys I'd ever seen. These guys looked as if they'd served hard time. Their 26-inch arms bore old, faded tattoos of green eagles and American flags that looked as if they'd been inked by a buddy. Most of them were wearing sunglasses even though it was night. They called themselves the "old timers." They ranged in age from late forties to early eighties. These guys were bad dudes, and I loved meeting them.

The format of the meeting was topic discussion. In other words, somebody brought up a topic and then we all discussed it. The old timers wanted one of us "young rehab pups" to choose the topic. All of my friends seemed scared to raise their hands. They were frozen stiff.

I raised my hand.

An enormous man whose nametag said HANK pointed at me. Hank was about six feet six inches tall and about two hundred ninety pounds. He'd obviously seen the gym before and, based on his arm decorations, he'd served our country, too.

"I think I have a topic."

In a deep, raspy voice, Hank said, "What's the topic?"

"Triggers. What makes us want to drink."

The room grew silent. A few of the old timers ground their teeth.

Uh-oh. Have I awoken the living dead? What the hell did I say wrong? I'd never felt so many people so furious with me at one time. I wondered whether a war was about to begin.

Hank shook his head and motioned with his hands for the other old timers to calm down.

"Go on, son. Continue. What do you mean 'trigger'?"

I bit my lower lip. "Well, let's say my wife and I have an argument. She's stubborn and won't listen to reason or, at least, to my side of the story. I become nervous, agitated. I want to drink. Wouldn't that be considered a trigger?"

My eyes scanned the room of snarling dogs.

Hank raised his hands slowly. All eyes were on him. His face reddened. "Okay, gentlemen, today's group topic is triggers. Raise your hand, and today's share leader—that's me—will call on you. Please don't talk too long. Keep it to three minutes. After that, nobody's listening."

The old timers chuckled like evil pirates ("Arr. Arr. Arr.")

"We want to give everyone time to talk. I'll start."

Hank shrugged and then stretched his neck so that his right ear touched the boulder that was his right shoulder. His neck cracked as loudly as a firecracker.

"Young man, you guys come in here from a treatment center and push all this Freudian, psychological, rehab mumbo jumbo on us. Your wife is not a *trigger.* There's no such thing as triggers! When I grew up, Trigger was a horse."

My hands grew clammy. Though afraid, I felt comforted that, having been raised by my father, the cowboy, I knew that Trigger was Roy Rogers's famous horse.

"That's all bullshit, and you can tell your teachers and doctors I said so. You can't cope with stress, young man. You're an alcoholic, so you thought of a drink. That's it! That's what alcoholics do: They think of alcohol. Plain and simple. There are no triggers. I have twenty-four years of sobriety under my belt, and I've dealt with a hell of a lot harder life than you can imagine."

He glared at me. I saw a vein in his forehead pulsing. "My triggers will outdo yours anytime. You have to deal with life on life's terms, and if you can't do that, you have to deal with life on God's terms. Do the steps."

When Hank leveled with me, my fear of the situation vanished. I felt my ego melting away and my headache from the family program subsiding. He was right. It wasn't complicated. *When I can't cope, I turn to alcohol, pills, and workouts rather than dealing with my problems. How many others like me are out there?* They can't cope, so they turn to work, eating, bulimia, gambling, shopping, and so on. *I need to learn a way to cope.* What Hank said is what I needed to hear. It's not that I didn't love the education I'd received from the family program. I did. But this was real. Truth. The basics.

Soon, the old timers were arguing among themselves about whether rehab and treatment centers were good or bad for society. Their argument didn't faze me, though. I was continuing to connect the dots.

I, Adam Jablin, am an alcoholic and addict. Extreme. A lotsaholic. I don't cope well with stress. I need to learn to listen better. I need to continue working on my relationship with God—a Higher Power. I need friendships. I need a support system. I need to feel my emotions. I need to be honest. I need to be leveled with every now and again. I need a new perspective. I need to acknowledge what's truly important to me—my sobriety. I need to work the twelve steps of recovery!

At the end of the meeting, every single one of those old timers walked up to me and gave me a gigantic, bone-shattering hug.

"Listen, kid, you got balls."

"Nobody else in your whole group said a word. You took your lesson like a man."

"Keep coming back."

It felt like my inauguration into the gang. I received many pats on the back, and each of the old timers had some private words for me. Their messages were the same: "You can do this. We believe in you. Keep coming back."

When we returned to Hanley, I went to the men's unit lounge and looked at the bulletin board. Tony's goodbye ceremony was scheduled for the next evening. Jack's goodbye ceremony would be in two days, at 8:00 PM The following day, also at 8:00 PM, would be Morty's turn. The guys were leaving, one by one. A deep sorrow filled my heart. The end was near.

A CALL TO ACTION

- A Lotsaholic! Addicted to MORE. Going to EXTREMES. Are there areas in your life where you have created the disease of more? This could be watching Netflix. Gossiping. Exercising. Shopping. More—Now—More—Now! For now, I just want you to examine your life. Where are things a bit too radical or immoderate?
- Simple question here…and be honest. WHAT ARE YOU ANGRY ABOUT? Journal it!

CHAPTER 18

MY MASK

THE NEXT MORNING, now that the family program had ended, I could no longer avoid the mess in my room. Crumpled, dirty underwear, socks, T-shirts, and shorts covered Matt's side of the room, including his desk, the floor, and his bed. He smelled ripe, too. He was like the *Odd Couple's* Oscar Madison on crystal meth. During my time in the family program, Matt never had woken up for morning meditation, attended group, or participated in treatment. He had closed the blinds, blocking out the sunlight. He barely had left our room. I think he saw me as a big brother who had abandoned him. He had rebelled by not caring and so descended into a black hole. It took all of my energy not to scream, pull his lazy ass up and out of his disgusting bed and throw him in the shower.

I read a handout about boundaries, which Brent had given me in our most recent counseling session.

> The boundary lines that we draw around ourselves delineate a safe area within which our recovery can flourish. We set limits on what we do and say, how we spend our time and money, and whom we choose to be our friends. I will move toward recovery today by setting limits.

Setting limits. That was it. I needed to do something, and fast. But first, I had to go to group therapy with John Dyben.

"Today, we'll work on our masks." John handed each of us a worksheet. The title at the top of the page was MY MASK. The middle of the page had been left blank, and on the bottom inch of the page contained the heading DESCRIPTIVE WORDS followed by four blank, horizontal lines. I flipped the paper over and found two additional sections. The top section, labeled BENEFITS OF WEARING THIS MASK, had blank lines numbered one through six. The bottom section, labeled, THE PRICE I PAY FOR THIS MASK, with another set of six numbered blank lines.

John took a deep breath as he paced the room. "Guys, let me tell you about one of my masks. Before I came to work at Hanley, I served as head of a drug abuse foundation. I made great money, and my job title wielded great power. Every decision had to go through me. As a control freak, I felt like a big shot. I bought a BMW and fancy suits to help me with my mask. My mask looked like Mr. Know-it-all, Mr. Confident, Mr. Connected-to-God. I had to show the world that I could handle everything. A huge staff reported to me, and that

made me feel even more powerful. On the surface, things looked great for old Johnny boy here. Any time anyone asked me how I was doing"—John glanced at me—"I'd shout back, 'Great! Never better! How are you?'"

John's style of teaching reminded me of the maverick English teacher John Keating who Robin Williams had played in *Dead Poets Society*. ("Carpe Diem! . . . Seize the day, boys. Make your lives extraordinary.")

John stared at the floor for a moment. When he began speaking again, his voice had softened. "But I was miserable. I hated my job. I hated acting like I had all the answers. I started smoking. I went up to a pack and a half a day. My apartment turned into a mess. I gained weight. My values changed from the way my father and mother raised me. I lost myself. I was sick. I wore this mask until it almost killed me. Not from drugs and alcohol. From stress."

John and I locked eyes.

John said, "I wore that mask for eight years. Today, I would like you to draw the mask you've been wearing out there." He pointed out the window, at the real world outside the Hanley Center's walls. "You have thirty minutes. Start now."

I realized that John had hidden that part of his life from me, saving it for this precise moment, perhaps for this very exercise. I thought about my mask. I picked up my pencil and drew my face, envisioning all the lies and bullshit I told everyone else and, more importantly, myself. My hands grew sweaty. I bit my lip as I concentrated.

My Mask:

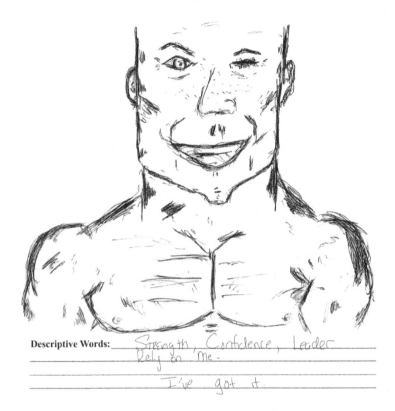

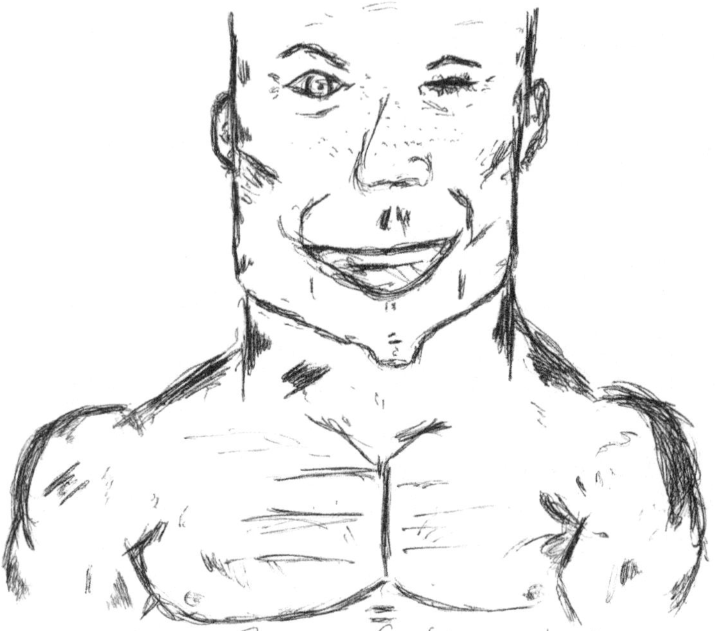

Descriptive Words: Strength, Confidence, Leader
Rely on me -
I've got it.

I drew my left eye winking, because I often wink. It's part of how I exude confidence and "No sweat. Leave it to me." I drew a confident smirk. I drew my upper chest, trapezius, and deltoid muscles. I knew that my mask included more than just my face. My mask was my whole body. Under the heading DESCRIPTIVE WORDS, I wrote the following:

Strength, Confidence, Leader.
Rely on me.
I've got it.

I acknowledged how I continually fabricated an image of how happy I was, how I loved what I did for a living, and how I felt like the luckiest guy in the world. It was all deception—a mask.

I flipped over the piece of paper and filled in the six items under the heading BELIEFS OF WEARING THIS MASK:

1. Strength
2. Dependability
3. Leader
4. Success
5. Respect
6. Honor

I took a hard look at the bottom section of the page, with its heading THE PRICE I PAY FOR THIS MASK. I jotted down my feelings:

1. Isolation
2. Confusion
3. Fear
4. Loneliness
5. Anger
6. Sadness
7. Lack of intimacy

I realized I didn't let anybody get to know the real me. They met Superman. They met Mr. Life-of-the-Party. They met Mr. Happy-Go-Lucky. They met Adam-the-Body. They never ever met me.

Twenty-five minutes in, John walked around the room and observed everybody's work. When he got to me, he stood over my desk and picked up my worksheet. He looked it over, reading the front and the back.

Curious about his thoughts, I looked up at him and raised my eyebrows.

"Stand up, Adam."

John gave me a big bear hug. "It's a pleasure to know you, brother! You're truly on your way. You're healing."

I knew how special that moment was to both of us.

John said, "Guys, take a good look at your masks. Here's the interesting part of this exercise. Your masks are *exactly* what the real you looks like. When you're true to yourself, you *will* look just the way you do with that mask, but you'll be at peace. You'll know a confidence beyond your wildest dreams."

I stared at my drawing and smiled.

I felt calm, relaxed, poised, and ready to take action about living with crazy, bipolar Matt. I went to Brent's office and knocked on the door.

"Come in," he called out.

I opened the door. "You have a minute?"

"Sure. Have a seat."

I walked over to the patient's chair in his office, sat, and then stared out the big window, bouncing my knee.

"What's on your mind?" he asked.

I took a deep breath. "It's living with Matt. It isn't working."

"What exactly isn't working?"

I took a moment to think carefully about my words. "Look, Matt isn't making any effort. I know he's bipolar, and maybe he's having an episode, but . . ."

I felt hot. My face reddened. My forehead grew sweaty. *I feel . . . angry? Finally!* For my entire time in treatment, Brent had been trying to artificially produce this emotion. I wanted to defend myself, justify my argument, and win. And that made me angry.

"But what, Adam?"

But I think you should take care of this wacko yourselves. You're the goddamned doctors. Why don't you worry about me a little bit? I'm your patient, too. What kind of facility are you running here? I thought all that, but I didn't say it.

Instead, I cleared my throat and then threw my hands up in surrender. "I've tried to help him. I've tried. But you can't help somebody who doesn't want the help. I have an old friend in Phoenix who worked with Mike Tyson in his training camps. For the fight he lost against Lennox Lewis, Tyson paid millions for the best trainers, coaches, and nutritionists in the business. He wanted the best. You know what my friend told me? Tyson didn't want to do the work that time around. And he got destroyed, knocked out in the eighth round. You can be surrounded with the best of the best, but if you don't want to do the work it's all flushed down the toilet."

I bit my lip. "I'm surrounded by the same help as Matt, but he's not accepting it and I am. I have just a few days left here, and I'd like to live with Grant. I feel—"

"Enough said. Your new roommate is Grant. Starting tonight."

"Umm . . . you don't want to hear why?"

"No. You just came into my office, calmly, and said what you felt was best for your recovery. No people pleasing. You set a healthy boundary. You protected yourself. Of course, you can room with Grant. I planned to room you guys together for your final days, anyway. I never reassigned anyone to his room when Tony left."

I bounced out of my chair, put on an Italian New York accent, cocked my head, and shouted, "Get ova' heah!"

Brent stood, and I opened my arms for a hug.

We hugged.

"You're doing so well, Adam. You should be proud of yourself."

"I'm getting there."

That was our last one-on-one counseling session.

A CALL TO ACTION

- What MASK do share with the world? Do you have different masks for different people? Please draw YOUR mask.
- Describe your mask.
- List 6 Beliefs of Wearing This Mask.
- Then, The Price You Pay For Wearing This Mask.

CHAPTER 19

DISEASE OF PERCEPTION

THE VOLLEYBALL HIT the water hard and splashed out of the pool.

I pointed at the spot where the ball had made contact and, laughing, yelled, "That was in!"

Grant splashed me and then pointed at Ethan. "What? It hit off his hand."

He splashed Ethan, who splashed him back.

"In!" Ethan and I yelled together.

"Out!" Grant and his teammates shouted back.

The ball rolled toward the new kid, who was sitting on a lounge chair, and startled him. Shaking, probably from nerves, he leaned over slowly to get the ball and push it to me. His ribs looked as if they were popping out, his arms were like twigs, and his face was covered with a bushy beard. I empathized with his nervousness—identical to mine twenty-seven days earlier.

"You all right?" I asked him.

"Dizzy." He rocked in place, sweating.

I grabbed the volleyball and threw it to the guys who were still clowning around in the pool. "What's your name?"

He swallowed hard and then answered in a weak voice, "Josh."

His Adam's apple stuck out of his neck like a golf ball in straw. I could see every muscle twitching from the detox that his poor body was going through. I jumped out of the pool.

"What's your drug of choice?"

His mouth fell open. He looked at me as if I were speaking a different language.

"That's how we talk here, get to know one another. What are you here for? Mine is alcohol, pills, opiates, barbiturates, uppers, downers, exercise, supplements, basically anything that can make you feel good."

"Alcohol and heroin." His chin dropped to his chest.

"Look, man, I know how you're feeling. I've been there. I mean, exactly there"—I pointed at him—"in that same chair, detoxing and freaking out the same way, just a few weeks ago. Please trust me, and join us in the pool. Try to loosen up and have some fun with us." I slapped his shoulder. "It'll take your mind off the detox. I wish I had. . . . I was a complete mess."

Josh trudged into the pool, and I followed. Ethan, Dwayne, and Nolan were still wrestling about the previous point. Grant jumped on Ethan's back and dunked him. I thought back to twenty-seven days earlier, when Morty and the gang had

been play-fighting about the score, just like the guys were doing now. I remembered the one sentence that had settled the score and had made me feel different from everybody else.

I shouted, "Hey, boys, who gives a damn? There's no score in alcoholic, cracked-out volleyball!"

After the game, I walked back to the men's unit with Josh and talked to him about my stay at Hanley. I showed him around campus and took him to lunch. So much had changed. Not only had my physical body healed, but my insides felt calm. Cheerful. Hopeful. I grinned from ear to ear.

After lunch, I met with the entire group of men's unit counselors. It was my good-bye and passing of the torch. The Hanley Center had become my home. Now, with the end of my stay near, I was abnormally relaxed. I leaned back and stretched out my arms wide.

"So, guys, who's the next peer leader?"

Brent's body posture perked up, and he tilted his head to the side. He loosened his GQ-worthy tie. "Adam, before we get to that, we have a matter of business to discuss with you."

I looked around the room and each counselor wore an expression of concern.

"Oh, my God! What is it? Did I do something wrong?"

"Is it true that while serving as active peer leader you broke our rules and led the guys in jumping into the pool after volleyball?"

My shoulders hunched forward and my chest caved in. "Um. Yeah."

John Dyben said, "And is it true you did this knowing it was a violation?"

God teach me to love the truth.

"Yes. Yes, I did. Well . . . we did. I thought it would be good for us as a team—to bond as sober brothers."

They all applauded, hooted, and hollered.

Brent put his hand on my shoulder. "You're ready, Adam. You learned the most important rule."

"What's that?"

"It's a *we.* It's always a we. We need each other to stay sober. We can't do this thing alone. Ask any leader in the world, and they'll tell you that. You've been one hell of a peer leader, Adam."

Brent gave me a big hug.

The counselors' reaction had given me a huge burst of confidence, which made me feel more ready for the outside world.

"So, who's the next peer leader?"

Brent handed me a piece of paper.

I opened it and then read out loud, "Grant."

I scratched my temple. "Um, Grant was here when I got here. Isn't he leaving here the same time as me?"

"He told us he thought he needed a couple extra weeks. You should talk to him about it."

I grew gravely concerned, and headed to my room.

"Yo! You in here, buddy?"

Grant came out of the bathroom, still damp from a shower.

"Hey, my man. What's up?" He twisted a Q-tip in his ear and pulled it out.

"Not much. Everything all right with you?"

"Great. Why?"

"The counselors told me you signed up for a couple more weeks."

"Why'd they tell you?" He looked worried.

I pulled out the piece of paper with his name on it and tugged on the peer leader necklace that I wore around my neck.

"No kidding?" He quieted down. "I'm the new peer leader? That's awesome."

"Yeah, very cool. But why are you staying? Talk to me."

I sat on my bed.

Grant said, "Listen, I know I have an allergy to alcohol, but when I drink, I break out in handcuffs."

I laughed. "That's a good one."

"It's true, man. I can't wake up in a hospital again, handcuffed to the bed. I somehow hurt people when I'm drunk or high. I need to make sure I get this thing right before I leave here."

I thought about hearing Grant's story four weeks earlier. It was still hard for me to believe everything he'd gone through. Unlike me, who faced going home to resume my life, he faced a major court battle later in the year. I realized, once again, how serious and destructive this disease is.

On my way back to the lounge, Brent found me.

"Adam, what do you have scheduled right now?"

I stuck my hand into my pocket and pulled out my schedule to check.

"First-step group."

"Perfect. You've done that plenty. Come to my office for a sec."

We trotted down the hallway, making small talk along the way. When Brent opened his office door, I saw that John Dyben was waiting for us.

John was leaned against Brent's desk, holding a piece of paper. He said, "Hey, Adam, how are you?"

"Good. What's up?"

"We want to promote you. Fourth-step work."

Brent said, "Adam, we have you in touch with your anger, finally."

We all chuckled at that, and then Brent continued his explanation.

"Adam, the fourth step is to make a searching and fearless moral inventory of ourselves. We want you to begin to write accounts of all your anger, resentments, dishonesty, fears, shame, guilt, sexual conduct, and harms to yourself and others."

John pointed at the piece of paper he was holding. "This worksheet is an outline of how to do the inventory properly. We want to uncover your character defects. They're what your mask has been hiding."

I scratched my temple and bit my lip. *A fearless moral inventory of myself? Resentments? Dishonesty? Fears? That sounds more like an immoral inventory.*

John put his hand on my shoulder. "Adam, this will be a good exercise for you to do before you go home. This will help change your perception. By setting these resentments down on paper, you'll see how *you* have contributed to every event in your life—good and bad. You'll learn you're not a victim of other people or circumstances. Alcoholism is a disease of perception. Change your perception; change your life."

I walked down to the pond, carrying my journal—a black-and-white composition book—and some bread for the turtles. I looked at the inventory worksheet and bit the cap

off my pen. I followed the instructions, drawing two vertical lines to make three columns.

I labeled the first column PEOPLE & INSTITUTIONS—all in caps. Underneath and in parentheses, I wrote, "I'm resentful/fearful at."

I labeled the second column WHAT HAPPENED/CAUSE—all in caps. Underneath and in parentheses, I wrote, "Why I'm upset."

I labeled the third column AFFECTS MY—all in caps. Underneath and in parentheses, I wrote, "My relationships, self-esteem, security, sex-life."

I had to take stock of the damaged goods and get rid of them, just like I did all the time in the family business.

I closed my eyes and bowed my head. *God, Gaga, and spirit, please give me the strength to be fearless and thorough.*

I wrote MORAL INVENTORY at the top of the page and, underneath that, "To thy own self be true." I thought of my past and started writing.

Quickly, memories seemed to download from the ether. My anger at being overweight and teased about it when I was younger. My fear of moving from New Jersey to Florida. My fear of not being good enough or liked. My pride in how I looked now. My anger toward the family business. My pride in my position in the business. My fear of people, religions, and government. My pride at thinking that I was Superman. My fear that I wouldn't get what I wanted. Pride, anger, and fear dominated me.

I sat there, hunched over, scribbling down every contrite recollection. I wrote and wrote and wrote. During those hours, I frequently sighed heavily, looked up at the sky, covered my face with my hands, and cracked my neck. But I didn't stop writing. I needed to clear this hurdle.

A common theme emerged: I lied. I lied a lot. I lied to make people like me more. I lied to get people off my back. I lied to gain respect and admiration. I lied so that I could do what I wanted. But mostly, I lied to cover up my alcoholism and addictions.

Three hours later, I was done. I stood up and stretched. I swallowed hard. I'd digested some huge chunks of truth about myself, things I had to change. I tore off some bread and threw it to the turtles. When I spotted Spike and Taz, I chucked a few pieces their way and winked at them. *Did I just wink at turtles?* I burst into uncontrollable laughter. *Relief. I feel free.* I thought about Gaga. Goosebumps ran up and down my arm. *She's proud of me.*

A CALL TO ACTION

- In Chapter 19 I started writing down my personal inventory. Anger, resentment, dishonesty, fears, shame, guilt, sexual conduct, and harms to myself and others. This exercise is very cathartic and healing. It also allows you the opportunity to NOT BE A VICTIM of your own life! I'd like you to start writing down your personal inventory. Take this opportunity for a long hard look at yourself.

CHAPTER 20

UP, UP, AND AWAY!

FINALLY, IT WAS TIME for me to leave the Hanley Center.

I went to morning meditation for the last time. There were so many new faces. I felt like a seasoned athlete, and these guys were the rookies. They were men about to learn and discover what it took to be a pro, to get sober. The experience was surreal.

After breakfast, I made my rounds of farewells, stopping at the nurses' station to see Kat; at the psychology wing of the cafeteria building to see Dr. J; at the wellness center to see Robert and Cynthia; at the family program office to see Winona; and then back to the men's unit to see Ben. I strolled through the campus, taking in everything around me—the colors, the sounds of the fountain, the new patients shuffling from one building to another.

I was especially excited about one stop in particular—the chapel.

"Come in, son." Father Ron waved me into his office.

I walked in and he greeted me with a hug.

He put his hand on my cheek. "You look good, young man. I cannot believe you are leaving us."

"I know. It's gone by so fast."

"I have something for you."

He pulled out a sheet of paper. As he handed it to me, he said, "I want you to keep this and read it often."

We sat down.

"Please read it out loud to me," Father Ron said.

I looked down at the paper in my hands. In big, black writing at the top of the page was the title A LITTLE BIT OF HANGIN'.

I read, "Abraham Lincoln once listened to the pleas of a soldier's mother who had been sentenced to hang for treason. She begged the president to grant him a pardon. Lincoln agreed. Yet he is reported to have left the woman with the following words: 'I wish we could have taught him a lesson and given him just a little bit of hangin'.'"

I chuckled and then resumed reading.

"There are times when we could all use a little bit of hangin'—times when the stool is kicked out from under our feet and the rope jerked around our necks just long enough to remind us of who and what really matters. Perhaps the wake-up calls of life can be looked at as divine slaps, knocks on the head, glimpses of awful mercy. Because of these, we come face-to-face with one of the underground's slyest agents: familiarity."

"You getting this so far?" Father Ron raised his eyebrows.

I shook my head.

"Please continue."

"His vision is clear and fatal: 'Take nothing from the victim; cause him only to take everything for granted.' We need to note his tactics and detect his presence, for his aim is deadly. Familiarity's goal is nothing less than to take what is most precious to us and make it appear most common."

I thought about Michelle's love and support and my past behavior. All the evenings I'd passed out, wasted. All the apology letters, in which I'd sworn over and over again that I'd stop drinking. I'd presumed that she'd love me and tolerate me no matter how crazy I got.

I again resumed reading.

"To say this agent of familiarity breeds contempt is to let him off easy. He also breeds broken hearts, wasted hours, and a greedy desire for more. He is an expert in robbing the sparkle and replacing it with the drab. He invented the yawn and put the 'hum' in humdrum. And, yes, his strategy is to never tell the truth."

Every word resonated in me. *This is true. I take life for granted.*

"He will not steal away your life; he will just make you forget what it means to be alive. With the passing of time, familiarity will infiltrate your heart with boredom and cover your mind with resistance to change. Score one for the agent of familiarity."

I thought of how robotic and repetitive my life had become. Just a few weeks earlier, I would have thrown on workout clothes and an iPod, not even thinking that I could be talking with a friend during my morning walk. I thought of how I easily got bored with the wonderful gifts in my life—my marriage, my daughter, my family, the family business, exercise, my home, my Hummer—and how every day I ate the same foods—oatmeal, egg whites, chicken breasts, brown rice—rather than trying something new. I had become a creature of habit.

Again, I resumed my reading.

"He won't take away your home; he will do something far worse. Familiarity will paint your home with a drab coat of dullness. He will replace evening gowns with bathrobes, nights on the town with evenings in the recliner, and romance with routine. He will scatter dust on your family photos until they become a memory of another family.

"He will not kidnap your children; he will make you too busy to notice them. He will whisper to you not to take time out for them. He will say that there is plenty of time, that there will always be next summer to go camping, next month to attend the symphony, next week to worship together, and tomorrow to tell someone you love them or forgive them.

"Hence, books will go unread, games will go unplayed, hearts will go unexpressed, and opportunities will go ignored. All because the poison of the ordinary has deadened your senses to the magic of the moment. Now, unless something changes, unless something or someone wakes you up, you will believe the lie that only the extraordinary is important and you will overlook the ordinary."

Father Ron grasped my hands in his.

"Adam, you'll be battling this demon very soon. You will be back in your house with your family, back at your job in

your office. You will be surrounded by the life you had before coming here, with the same daily chores, business tasks, questions, text messages, e-mails, errands, responsibilities. . . . You get the picture? You must be careful of familiarity."

He let go of my hands and became more animated. "Try new things. Eat a different food. Wear a different color. Drive a different way to and from work. Find a hobby—drawing, painting, or maybe writing. Take walks with Michelle. Try different restaurants. Watch different shows. Keep life new, fresh, and exciting. Have a bowl of ice cream once in a while!"

He smiled and lightly slapped my face. "Get it?"

"Got it."

When I walked out of Father Ron's office, I felt like a free man. I closed my eyes and looked up at the sun. I felt the warmth on my face. *I'm sober.*

The time had finally come. I'd completed twenty-eight days of rehab. Grant helped me take my bags to Michelle's car. They embraced each other warmly, having grown close during the family program.

I opened the back door and gave Sloan, in her car seat, a big kiss. "Hi, baby girl. Daddy's coming home."

Her face lit up and she spoke to me in baby talk.

Brent came outside, and Michelle gave him a warm hug.

Then Michelle cleared her throat. "Thank you. Thank you for saving him! For saving us."

Brent rose up slightly on his heels, as if to emphasize his words. "You guys did all the work. I'm just a guide." He patted my back and looked at Michelle. "You mind if I borrow him for just a few minutes?"

Michelle nodded.

Brent and I walked back to the curb, and then he looked me directly in the eyes.

"Adam, this is very important. At every recovery meeting you attend, I want you to raise your hand and share. In the beginning, I want you to introduce yourself and ask for help and telephone numbers. But, after that, I want you to continue sharing every single day."

I rubbed the base of my neck. "Every single day?" My voice cracked. "Why?"

"Because, inside, you still think you're Superman. You'll start comparing yourself to everyone in the meetings. You'll start to compete and see how you're better or smarter or wealthier or more charismatic. You'll begin to think you're different than everybody else. Then, you'll begin to feel uncomfortable. You'll stop going to meetings altogether. You'll think you can do it alone. But you can't. Eventually, you'll drink, and we'll see you back here . . . or worse."

A CALL TO ACTION

- We could all use a, "little bit of a hangin'." Examine your life and where things have become too FAMILIAR. Maybe play with your kids more. Drive a different way to work. Read instead of watch TV. Watch a movie instead of read. Mix it up!
- Share with somebody what's really going on in your life. Yes—again! Because you also think you're Superman. We all need help!

PART II

CHAPTER 21

ATTACKING SOBRIETY

THERE'S ONLY ONE THING I had to change when I got sober—everything! And that's exactly what I did. I questioned every situation and how it related to my sobriety. Will this restaurant make me want to drink? Can I go to my pal's wedding? Is it a good idea for me to read this magazine that has ads for liquor and diet pills? Will this pharmacy bring back my old yearnings? Will this movie, with all the celebrities partying, make we want to revert to my old ways? Does this have any alcohol in it? Are there any chemicals in it that could trigger me to relapse? I changed even the most minor things. I switched from Listerine mouthwash, which contains alcohol, to Crest mouthwash. I learned to HALT (hungry, angry, lonely, or tired) all triggers for getting loaded. My life continued. It was both the same and completely different. I felt as if I were learning to write with my opposite hand.

Social situations were the hardest. In the beginning, I tried to fly under the radar, hoping that nobody would talk to me, but it never worked. The most uncomfortable questions were "What have you been up to?" and "What did you do this weekend?" When I heard those, I pressed my lips together and grimaced slightly. *Oh, I went to recovery meetings, prayed, meditated, met with my sponsor, read some spiritual stuff, and did some self-examination work. You?* "Spent time with the baby" became my mantra.

I went to recovery meetings and asked questions whenever I got stumped. "Hi, I'm Adam, and I'm an alcoholic. Um, what do you say when . . . ?" Fill in the blank: when a person asks what you'd like to drink or why you don't drink anymore or when you stopped drinking.

I analyzed every relationship, with a magnifying glass. Is this person good or bad for my sobriety? I changed all the little things of my life in order to make the bigger picture turn out right.

I slowly acclimated to the world. I felt like Neo going back into the Matrix for the first time and meeting the Oracle and seeing his old stomping grounds. Everything was familiar yet foreign. Things like beer commercials and liquor billboards slowly changed from giant monsters out to get me to normal advertisements. Watching friends and others drink gradually became more tolerable, but I found it hard not to judge heavy drinkers.

One evening, Michelle and I were dining at a trendy, local restaurant. The hostess told us that our table would be ready in a few minutes and asked us to please wait at the bar. The place was packed and buzzing with nightlife, good food, and drinks. We made our way through the festive crowd to the stylish, funky, modern bar. I waved my finger to get the bartender's attention. Out of the corner of my eye, I saw our old, crazy party friends getting loaded. *Please don't see us. Please don't look this way.*

"Adam!" *Damn it.*

Joel stumbled toward us. "C'mon, guys! Join us. Let us buy you a round of shots," he shouted as his eyes searched for a server.

He leaned against me so that he wouldn't fall over. He reeked of booze. The smell made me sick. I looked at Michelle and mimed gagging.

I raised my hands in surrender and backed away slowly. "No, thanks. We're good. We're taking it easy tonight."

"You guys don't go out anymore. C'mon, Adam, you pussy! Have a drink on me." He slurred his words and groped me as he spoke. Toxic sweat was pouring out of his pores.

"No, thanks, Joel. You guys have fun. We'll catch up with you next time."

There will never be a next time.

Anytime somebody got drunk in my presence or shared a story about a crazy night, I silently questioned the person in my head (*Are you an alcoholic? An addict? Do you need help?*). I had this one thought over and over again: *I've been so privileged to learn the universal lessons of how to live. I wish I could share them with you.*

Luckily for me, all my close family members stopped drinking around me, in the beginning, out of love and support. Michelle and I changed the vast majority of our people, places, and things so that I wouldn't have to be around the party lifestyle. Instead of going out to bars, we attended barbeques; wild drinking nights became quiet evenings of dinner and a movie. Those changes made my life a hell of a lot easier, and I enjoyed every second of it.

South Florida is the capital of the recovery world. One can find a meeting just about anywhere, anytime. Within a couple weeks, I discovered a popular, enthusiastic meeting that took place during my lunch hour and only about five miles from my office. It was a group of people I could relate to. They all had years of sobriety and welcomed me with open arms.

I approached my program of recovery like I had my drinking and drugging. This was life or death. Cancer patients need chemotherapy and radiation, diabetics need insulin and diet changes, and alcoholics and addicts need spirituality and other supports for their sobriety. Plus, I still could hear Brent's last words of advice: "You'll think you can do it alone. But you can't. Eventually, you'll drink, and we'll see you back here . . . or worse."

It wasn't easy.

In my usual fashion, I structured my life, even in recovery, to be demanding. My new way of living—spirituality combined with my fast-paced, get-it-done mentality—made me feel like the new kid in school: afraid, unsettled, and a little lost. My daily schedule basically consisted of 5:30 AM morning meditation, 6:30 AM breakfast, 7:30–11:30 AM office, 12:00–1:00 PM twelve-step meeting, 1:00–5:30 PM office, 6:00 PM workout, 7:30 PM dinner with family, and 9:00 PM twelve-step work and readings. I didn't give myself time to breathe. The extreme side of me was still in action, believing more is better.

I trained myself to think like a sober warrior, a recovery warrior. In his book *The Way of the* SEAL, Mark Divine, the famous, retired U.S. Navy SEAL commander, best-selling author, and founder and CEO of SEALFIT, defines a warrior as someone who is committed to becoming a master, who grows to be courageous and serves others. As a recovery warrior, I did all the things to stay sober. I went to meetings, found a sponsor, and worked the twelve steps. I called my sponsor every single day. I performed service work for the twelve-step meeting—making coffee, arriving early to help set up, and staying late to clean up and get to know everybody. I picked up people from rehab centers, detox centers, and halfway houses and took them to meetings. I threw myself into recovery, just like I had at the gym during my bodybuilding days.

Meetings of my regular group became my second home. I loved the camaraderie. Having friends who understood the way my brain worked felt like . . . well, home.

"Yo, Merv, Steve, Scotty, how are you guys?" I asked when I bounced in the door.

"Very good, handsome. How are ya?" Merv asked in his British accent that sounded like a Beatle from Liverpool. Merv was a portly sixty-year-old from London, with a loud, charming personality and decades of sobriety. He wore a youthful, trendy, fitted T-shirt that revealed his belly and a ridiculously loud Swatch watch. There was something rebellious and cool about him.

I sat down next to Merv and leaned toward him. "What's with the watch?"

"Oh, my good boy, you noticed!" He slammed his loud, red penny loafers on the floor and patted my back. "I'll tell you why I do it. It's one of my secrets to staying sober. I do things that make me uncomfortable, to change things up and remind me to stay present in the game of life. I know I'm just one drink away from flushing it all down the toilet."

When Merv shared in meetings, he drew everyone into his elaborate stories. His message was "If you're here in one of these meetings, your drinking is screwed, so just forget about backing out."

Merv also helped with the meetings and welcoming new people. "Adam, have you met Timothy here? He's new."

He pointed to a young kid, fresh out of rehab, who was continually shifting in his seat.

"Hi, Tim." I reached out for a handshake. "Nice to meet you. I'm Adam."

He blinked rapidly at me and then looked around the room.

"Umm . . . is everyone always so happy here?"

I chuckled. "That takes a while. Just keep an open mind, follow some of the suggestions and, most importantly, keep coming back."

That was one thing I'd learned early in recovery—always welcome the new person coming through the doors. I always remembered how afraid I'd felt walking into the Hanley Center.

At the meetings, I listened to other people's stories and how they incorporated the twelve steps into their daily lives. I learned to live by famous slogans "First things first" (Keep my sobriety first, meaning, Don't drink), "Easy does it" (Stop rushing around and pushing my willpower), "Remember your

last drunk" (Tell my drunk stories, not my fun ASU partying stories), "Live and let live" (People will speak and behave in ways I don't like, but I have to move on).

I kept my commitment to Brent: I shared almost every single day. Doing that kept me real and transparent to the others in the group. I raised my hand and purged what was going on in my life. If work and my customers drove me crazy or I was angry with my sloppy neighbors, I let it all out in the meeting. And guess what? It worked. Sharing cut the problem in half. A 2011 University of Chicago study "Writing About Testing Worries Boosts Exam Performance in the Classroom," proved that students who talked or wrote about their worries immediately before taking an exam performed significantly better on that exam than did those who didn't unload their anxieties. The same is true in life. Sharing how I felt kept me healthy and sane. More importantly, in sharing I found my voice. That find was a gift. I discovered a knack for communicating and connecting with other people. It was a special ability that would launch the next level of my sobriety as well as more lessons.

DURING THIS TIME, in my first year of sobriety, I started running outdoors. I began slowly, with a mile or two a few times a week. I liked that running made me feel lean, light, and healthy. Running provided a great sweat and kicked my endorphins into high gear—the runner's high—so, of course, I wanted a lot more of that. Before I knew it, I was up to seven to twelve miles six days a week. And I still craved more. I was experiencing cross-addiction, the substitution of one mood-altering drug or behavior for another.

Michelle could see my disease coming from a mile away, pun intended. I was high as a kite, walking around in sweaty running gear, snacking on almonds, and listening to new age books such as *The Secret* and *The Law of Attraction* on my iPod. I remember one time when she found me stretching in the middle of the kitchen and asked, "How many times did you run this week?"

My nostrils flared. "I've changed myself dramatically. Monday isn't for back and biceps anymore. Tuesday isn't for legs. I do yoga. I work out with weights only three times a week now. I'm more diverse. I'm keeping my vibrations high. What do you want from me?"

Michelle shot me a look of despair. "Keeping your vibrations high? What the hell does that mean?" She shook her head. "You're always pushing yourself to the limit. How much can your body take? You look perfect. I just wish—"

"Enough!" I felt my face go red. I couldn't control my emotions. I took a deep breath and focused on settling down. "Look, I'm trying, baby. Cut me some slack. Please."

I didn't want to examine my new behavior (exercise, spiritual intoxication, and no moderation of either) quite yet, but it was bursting at the seams.

I found a local half-marathon and justified my new obsession by tying it to my recovery. "I'm trying new things, honey. See? I'm believing in myself." Poor Michelle.

That half-marathon rocketed me into high gear. I rummaged around tons of running-related websites, searching for the perfect training regimen. I skipped over the beginner and intermediate regimens and jumped right into the advanced ones. I devoured every piece of literature I could get my hands

on. One day, when I was looking at the *Runner's World* website (runnersworld.com), I found Dean Karnazes and bought his book *Ultramarathon Man: Confessions of an All-Night Runner.* He was famous for running distances thought to not be humanly possible—more than three hundred miles. I read the whole book in four hours straight, fixating on every word.

In typical compulsive fashion, I copied his training philosophies and diet. I tried my hardest to transform myself into a machine like him overnight. Dean had trained himself to wake up at 4:00 AM and run insane mileage every day. So, I woke up at 4:00 AM and upped my runs to twelve miles a day five days a week. I ran longer on weekends, covering anywhere from fifteen to twenty-four miles at a time. If Dean ran over three hundred miles in one session, I thought that I could at least do a marathon (*It's only twenty-six miles!*). I picked the Miami Marathon, which takes place each January. That gave me twenty weeks to train.

I continued to attend daily twelve-step meetings. At home, I spoke my new recovery language to Michelle.

I'll never forget the day I was upset with her and stood at our kitchen table pouting like a baby. I shook my head, disappointed that she wasn't a mind reader.

She raised her eyebrows and crossed her arms. "You okay?"

I glared back at her. "No, I have a resentment toward you."

She tilted her head. "A what?"

"A resentment!"

Michelle's posture stiffened. "A resentment? Who talks like this? You mean you're mad at me. Just say that."

She mimicked how I was standing, scrunched her face and, in a whiny voice, wailed, "I have a resentment toward you." She put her hands on her hips. "You sound like a crazy person!"

Since I had gotten sober, every word that came out of my mouth was in my new recovery lingo or somehow related to the twelve steps, energy, vibrations, attractions, the universe, or God. I relentlessly tried to find some deep, hidden message for me in every single occurrence in my life. *This is all a reflection of what's going on inside me. A consequence of my choices. What is God trying to show me?* Rather than trying to figure out myself—my own thoughts and beliefs, I tried to figure out God and how the laws of the universe operated. Now that I had substituted running and recovery for alcohol, pills, and supplements, I had lost my balance yet again.

I thought Dean Karnazes had found *it*—the meaning of life. That's what I was really seeking. Michelle and I spent less intimate time together than we had when I drank. My new crazy regimen exhausted me so much that I passed out by nine thirty most nights, leaving no time for us to cuddle, talk, and be a couple. My disease had simply outplayed me. It was even using that sneaky voice in my head: *Hey, this isn't familiar, Adam! Just like Father Ron said . . . this is new, fresh, and exciting. You should be proud of what you're doing.*

Like the relentless, liquid-metal T-1000 cyborg in *Terminator 2: Judgment Day,* my disease had morphed into yet another addiction. It was prepared to kill me by any means necessary.

Yet through the arguments and uneasiness of our home, I still ran like a lunatic. I ran, and I ran, and I ran. I even ran from the office to my recovery meetings. I sat through

meetings, sweating like a pig. Then, I'd run back to the office. You know—to bang out some extra mileage. Over time, calluses developed on my feet. I eventually got shin splints from pounding the pavement so much. In my downtime, I constantly studied marathon training programs and protocols. I tried various diets. I tore through sneakers. I had a new running wardrobe. Yeah, I was obsessed.

One evening, a month before the Miami Marathon, when I got home, Michelle was cleaning, jamming and cramming things away violently. I took one look at her reddened face and knew I was in for it.

She rubbed the back of her neck. "This new life of yours. The running, the yoga in the morning, the constant push-ups and sit-ups—It's getting to me, and it's killing us."

"But I'm just—"

"Just listen to me, please," she said in a softer tone. "You're an amazing father. You do everything—bath time, diapers, making the bottles."

She sighed and clasped her hands together. "On top of that, you're a loyal hard worker for the business and you spend all that time going to recovery meetings and talking with your sponsor."

She raised her hands up in defense. "That, I'm one hundred percent behind. Look, it's just nonstop. You work all day, and then you walk the dog. Shower, eat dinner—Boom, you're passed out on the couch. And then, early in the morning, you go for such a long run."

She shook her head. "Where's time for me? For us?"

What does she expect of you, Adam? You're trying your hardest. You're sober now! You have a lot of responsibilities, and running is healthy and makes you feel good. Tell her this is your new life, take it or leave it!

That voice. *My disease is so clever, so manipulative.* Deep down, I knew Michelle was right. The truth was that I missed her, too. I was ashamed and confused. *How do I balance it all?* I was trying to fill a "God-shaped" hole in my heart with running and exercise. Early recovery was so strange. I had all this bunched-up energy inside; a cluster of happiness, vitality, and passion intertwined with lack of self-esteem, desperation, and fear was spinning inside my new, clean body. The experience was like an acid trip.

"You're right," I said. "I think I need some extra help. I want to start seeing that therapist Brent suggested."

Michelle handed me a card.

I looked down at it: GENE ABELSON, P.A. BOARD CERTIFIED ADDICTIONS PROFESSIONAL.

She gave me a giant hug and kiss. "I've been waiting to hear you say that ever since you left Hanley."

A WEEK LATER, I was sitting in Dr. Gene Abelson's office, bouncing my foot up and down and studying him. Gene looked taller than his six feet of height, due to his perfect posture. His grown-out, long, gray locks gave him a rock 'n' roll vibe. He was lean, but he also had well-defined muscles that were apparent through his button-down shirt. From our introductions to each other, I found out that he took immaculate care of himself, eating a healthy diet, following a dedicated swimming regimen, and doing other intense endurance exercise. We had something in common right off

the bat. But, even more importantly, Gene was thirty-three years sober.

After a few sessions, I gave him the full rundown on what was going on with me. Adjusting his glasses, he said, "Adam, you need a constant challenge. You can't stop pushing yourself. It's a sign you're not happy. Your disease goes a lot deeper than just alcohol and pills. Those are just the symptoms."

"I'm happy! I'm one of the happiest people you'll ever meet!"

"You're happy on the outside. Inside, you're still that little boy who wants everybody to like him. You're still that little boy who doesn't want to be called chubby, who's starving for positive attention, begging, 'Look at me. Look at me. I can do whatever is put in front of me. Just watch.' The muscles, the work ethic, and the nonstop extremes . . . we need to get you to like who Adam Jablin *really* is. Then you'll feel balanced, happy, joyous, and free. We just need to get you to believe in. . . . Are you ready for it?"

How many times do I have to go over this? I do believe in Higher Power. How much do I have to talk about God?

I rolled my eyes. "Yeah, I'm ready for it, Gene. Go ahead."

He leaned forward in his chair and rubbed his knees. "Yourself."

Silence.

"We need you to believe in yourself. Not that you can help run a family business. Not that you're a great father and husband. Not that you can run a marathon or lift hundreds of pounds over your head. That's still all the outside stuff. We need you to start believing in your insides. It's an inside job."

DURING THE NEXT few months, with the help of Michelle, my family, my recovery meetings, weekly therapy sessions with Gene, my sponsor, and my twelve-step program, I dove into working on my mind. First, I cut down the exercise to once a day and only five days a week. *Only* five. That eliminated nine workouts.

That change was a huge shock to my system. The sudden halt of constant activity, combined with less endorphin high, pushed my true feelings and emotions to the surface.

I learned about my personality and behavior on a deeper level. For instance, I have a habit of "playing" old tapes in my head. What I mean by that is that when something bothers me—say, I make a mistake on a project at work—I play the old tape of "You're not good enough, Chubby" or "You'll never be as good as your old man. You should just give up" or "What are you? An idiot?" Playing these old, negative tapes over and over again in my head, because I wasn't perfect, drove me to go to extremes of working hard or quitting. Those tapes reinforced my lack of happiness, my dissatisfaction, and my extremely competitive personality.

I also began to recognize my passive-aggressive behaviors. In order to keep the peace and make everybody like me, I tended not to speak up for myself. On the outside, to other people, nothing appeared to bother me; but inside I raged. I was terrified of other people's opinions and I always wanted their approval, so I apologized incessantly. Meanwhile, I stored every little memory that pissed me off, in a compartment in my head, just waiting for the right time to unleash hell on some unlucky person. Gene called that storing behavior *stamp collecting*. I collected stamps in my mind, full of grievances, for every person I cared about. In order to avoid confrontation, I didn't speak to people about things that bothered me. But, eventually, when that person pissed me off for the nth time . . . wham, I cashed in their stamp book and went to town on them about every single incident I'd stored away. I broke some people's spirits doing that. In my sick mind, it was redemption. Afterward, though, I went back to them and apologized—not exactly the right way to resolve situations.

During my first year of recovery, I gained some control over my emotions and learned how to communicate in a healthy manner. Nine out of ten times (or at least seven or eight times) that I got angry, I grinded my teeth and waited to speak to my sponsor before jumping to conclusions. If I was disturbed, I took a walk, wrote in my journal, or simply went to a recovery meeting. When happy, I became able to simply smile calmly without experiencing euphoric highs. I learned how to restrain myself and build in some time between thinking a thought and acting on it. I calmed down.

A CALL TO ACTION

- In Chapter 21, I was newly getting sober, but still very extreme! Examine your life. Where can you calm down? Where are you taking yourself too seriously? Where are you acting like a Lotsaholic?
- I'd like for you start meditating. Start with one minute! Sit down in a quiet room. Put the timer on for sixty seconds. Close your eyes. Slowly, breathe in through your nose, and out through your mouth. You can download an app, or use a guided meditation from YouTube. This is a practice that will pay dividends that you won't believe!

CHAPTER 22

BECOMING ADAM

MY FIRST YEAR OF sobriety came full circle when I returned to the Hanley Center for my one-year medallion ceremony.

On July 14, 2007, Grant, Brent, Michael Walsh (my interventionist), my entire family, and I sat in the gazebo. Michelle had planned this special family ceremony in celebration of my having been sober for one year. She read from a sheet of paper that she had brought:

"Like a butterfly emerges
And unfolds its graceful wings,
Adam has grown and developed
With so many important things.
We are so thankful that
You had the courage to try,
Because, Adam, you always had the wings,

But now you have learned to fly.

We know butterflies became important to you during your recovery, symbolizing comfort, beauty, and joy. So, today, as we celebrate your one-year anniversary and your recovery, we also celebrate life, strength, and hope with a live butterfly release."

Michelle turned to pick up the little brown boxes that she had brought. She handed them to me and asked me to pass them out while she continued reading.

"Butterflies symbolize growth and one of nature's most beautiful metamorphoses. We have watched you grow and change this past year, and we are all very proud of you. When I think about where we all were just one year ago—the intervention—I feel grateful. I thank each and every one of you for your love and support. It had made all the difference for this past year and for our future."

Michelle looked around at our family. I wiggled my eyebrows and then winked at her.

"Get ready, guys!"

She beamed as she gestured for all of us to wait and then looked back down at the paper and continued reading.

"When you open the box, your butterfly will emerge from its envelope and land on your hand for a moment before flying away. There is an Indian legend that says that if you capture a butterfly and whisper a wish to it the silent butterfly will carry your wish to the heavens and grant it. . . . Please add your own silent wish before you release your butterfly. Aaand . . . three . . . two . . . one, go!"

We opened our boxes, and the amazing creatures emerged.

After that private ceremony in the gazebo, we walked to the auditorium, where Michelle stood in front of an audience of about eighty people, including those from the small ceremony as well as Kat, Ben, Charlotte, John Dyben, Dr. J, Father Ron, Cynthia, Robert, some of my buddies from my stay at Hanley, and the new friends I'd met since leaving Hanley. She spoke movingly about having witnessed my transformation. She handed me what I'd waited a year for—the one-fourth medallion that completed the three-fourths medallion I'd received on my last day of treatment at Hanley. We hugged and, as she was about to take her seat, I grabbed her hand tightly and made her remain standing with me.

I described how Michelle was the true definition of love, truth, and perseverance. I spoke about what a magical place Hanley was. I told the stories of how, when I had first walked into the lounge, I had seen Morty painting himself in a dress; about how I had met a mobster I loved and a famous musician I adored; about flying kites and feeding turtles; how I had thought I was in Hanley for only a ten-day evaluation; how I had freaked out about alcoholic, cracked-out volleyball; how I had surrendered; and other stories of my time there and how grateful and happy I was now. I still couldn't believe how easy it was for me to speak about all of that in front of large groups of people. It was a gift of sobriety. During the previous year, I had spoken in front of as many as five hundred people at a time, and I loved it.

Bye-bye, running. Hello, speaking!

TEN DAYS LATER, I spoke in front of fifteen hundred people at a twelve-step convention. As I waited in the wings,

I tapped my foot. When I stepped into the center of the stage, I felt the heat of the lights. I looked out at the audience and felt chills at the realization that they were waiting to and wanting to receive my message. I didn't have a guitar to play or a song to sing. I didn't have a thought in my mind about what they expected from me. I just gave them me. I felt a rush of energy—an electric buzz, my adrenaline pumping, and a sense of clarity and power. I felt like a star while I was on that stage. I realized that was because I was speaking my truth. I had no more secrets and nothing to hide. I said a quick prayer, hoping that they were getting my message, and the words just flowed.

After my speech, I was mobbed by what seemed to be hundreds of people.

One guy shouted, "Oh, my God, man! I loved what you said about spirituality—that it's like having muscles. That we have all the muscles we need. We just need to strengthen them."

Somebody else chimed in. "And your experiences with Father Ron—the fingerprints with UV light. That really helped me!"

I heard a woman yell, "I loved that you stopped judging people, that your wife kept telling you to say you're no better than anyone else."

I shook hands, gave hugs, bumped fists, and slapped high-fives. I stood tall, my chin held high, shoulders back, and chest thrust out. I had never touched so many people by just being myself.

Somebody asked, "Are you a motivational speaker?"

I couldn't believe I was even getting that question. "No, no, nothing like that. I'm just one of you all, one of the gang."

"Who are you?" I heard someone ask, in the background, as I continued to thank people and shake hands.

"Yeah. Who are you?" I heard again.

Who am I? Hmm. Who am I? That was the question—the question I'd been asking myself my whole life. *Adam Jablin, who are you?*

Woosh! The answer flew into my mind. I envisioned Margot Kidder as Lois Lane asking Christopher Reeve as Superman, on the rooftop of *The Daily Planet,* "Who are you?"

I gazed out at the crowd and answered, "I'm a friend."

I had tapped into a hidden power—the ability to speak in public. The energy that pumped through me was euphoric but also provided clarity and wisdom. I felt connected to my listeners. Like radar, I could pick up on their signals, which were being transmitted to me, and know what they needed to hear. This heightened sense was intoxicating.

This gift gave me access to another dimension, where I could watch my life as a movie and, during speeches, pick out specific memories that I could share in order to help the audience. I could feel the sensations—the old thoughts and emotions—from the time I was recounting. Then I could convey those feelings in my own words and push them out through the filter of my enthusiastic personality. I had become a channel.

SHORTLY AFTER that convention, one of my recovery friends introduced me to a program called Living Skills in the Schools (LSIS), in which I could share my story with students in elementary school through and including college and teach them about substance abuse prevention and the importance of maintaining an addiction-free lifestyle. On top of my normal recovery commitments and LSIS, I went north to the Hanley Center and south to the Drug Abuse Foundation once a month to tell my story. Then I added jails and prisons. Being heard and helping people felt good to me. Public speaking became my new addiction. Soon, I was speaking five to eight times a week. I chased it—more, more, more. Every single time I was asked to speak to a group, I said yes, never taking into account my family, business, and life's other demands.

This continued for months and months.

Looking back, a lot of the public speaking was fueled by my ego. Yes, a healing had occurred, but my motives for public speaking were not only to serve but also to receive the adulation. The attention made me feel confident, strong, and wanted.

I was my own booking agent, and I got sloppy. I made appointments that I couldn't keep. I told myself that missing a few speaking commitments here or there was okay because I was doing so many of them and doing them so well. Sharing my story became about my reputation more than helping others suffering from this terminal disease.

One day, James Lehman, a recovery icon, pulled me aside. James was a sixty-year-old man with short-cropped hair, steel-blue eyes, and a big, burly mustache on his thin, chiseled face. He reminded me of the Western actor Sam Elliott in the movies *Tombstone* and *Butch Cassidy and the Sundance Kid*. His voice was deep, raspy, and intimidating. He always said, "Thank God for AA, 'cause I couldn't stop drinking." It was such a simple slogan, but it held so much weight. James

had gone through decades of torture from his alcoholism and drug addictions. He had spent seven years in jails and prisons as a result of burglary attempts to get money for booze or dope. But, in 1984, he had sobered up and turned his life around. Through the power of recovery, James had gone on to get his doctorate and develop a program called The Total Transformation to help parents with kids that have behavioral problems, like those he had as a child. I idolized him in many ways.

When, James pulled me aside that day, he placed his hand on my shoulder and said, "Adam, you've got the gift—the gift of enthusiastic recovery—and you can help many, many people."

I beamed with pride.

"But . . ."

My smile quickly disappeared.

"I sponsor a lot of men, and I've been hearing that you've been cancelling or breaking commitments."

Did he just question my integrity? How dare he! The angry, defensive alcoholic reared his ugly head. "James, you don't understand. I have a lot of obligations. I—"

"Kid, I don't want to hear your excuses. I've been around a long time, and I've seen great men with amazing sobriety go back to drinking or using drugs. When I was younger, my sponsor told me if I continued to live a brutally honest life, go to meetings, and help others, I'd stay sober. And then, he proved it to me. He stopped being honest, stopped picking up his phone, and stopped going to meetings. After twenty-one years of sobriety, he relapsed!"

He squeezed my trapezius muscle. "But it all starts with breaking commitments, not keeping your word, not being accountable."

My shoulders slumped. *He's right.* Like Maverick in the movie *Top Gun*, my ego had been writing checks that my body couldn't cash. I felt like a child being reprimanded by his father, and the reprimand stung.

"I know I just bruised your ego, kid, but keep your head up. So many people in recovery love you, and I truly respect you. Being sober over a year is a big deal, but it's a drop in the bucket. You have enthusiastic sobriety, and it's contagious. People want what you have. So, go help more people, be of service. You don't always need to speak to do that, though. Guide men from the pain and suffering of addictions to the freedom you and I have. Concentrate on your relationship with a Higher Power and doing more for people. Trust God. Clean house—that means keeping your affairs in order, Adam. Throw away the bad, and keep the good. And help others."

I learned from that painful moment, and I turned my entire life around. I stopped making my recovery all about me. Instead, I made it about getting closer to Spirit and helping people. First, I humbled myself and called all the people I had let down by cancelling and made sincere amends to them. An amend is more than saying "I'm sorry." I had used up all my sorries while I was active in my alcoholism and addictions. No, amending a situation is repairing it by making it right and whole. An amend is a three-stage process. In the first stage, I admitted I was wrong. This admission made people more open to listening to what I had to say, because I wasn't being defensive or making lame excuses. In the second stage,

I asked what I could do to make it right. Ninety-nine percent of the time, the person was so touched with my honesty and sincerity that a simple apology was enough. But if the person wanted reparation, I took the proper actions, such as speaking in place of him or her at a later date or taking him or her out for coffee. In the third and final stage, I asked whether the person could find it in his or her heart to forgive me.

Although most of my amends may have seemed as if they were for the benefit of the other person, they also were for my benefit. A proper amend always taught me a good lesson or two. That was true of what transpired after my son Miles was born, in my fifth year of sobriety.

I HAD PROMISED MICHELLE that with Miles I'd do every night feeding—as an amend for leaving her with all the parental duties for Sloan while I was at Hanley. I had thought, *Hey, if mothers who breast-feed can do it, so can I!*

In my mind, not only would I be bonding with my baby boy, but I would be making it right with Michelle and Sloan for having been away for those twenty-eight days.

I averaged three to five hours of sleep per night, and those hours weren't consecutive. I kept up my usual, hardcore daily pace of working at the office, going to recovery meetings, doing service work, and exercising. Over time, maintaining that schedule beat me down. Exhausted, I literally saw stars—small, white, flickering lights drizzled in front of my eyes. Whenever that happened, I shook my head rapidly and they went away temporarily. I was so tired that the room spun, and my hearing faded away, as if life's volume had been turned down. Everything felt far away. I could pass out anywhere. I fully understood why sleep deprivation is used as torture. I was battered, and my guard was down. That's not good for an alcoholic and addict.

One evening, it all hit me, and I almost picked up a drink. Michelle and I went out to a fund-raiser, which she had helped to organize, for Sloan's school. I was drained and I didn't want to go, but I felt that I had to make an appearance. After I'd had a few cups of coffee, we were on our way.

The second we walked in, I felt as if we'd been transported to Bourbon Street in New Orleans. Amazing alcohol displays had been set up. Directly to my right was a beautiful, sleek, modern bar of fine wines. Parallel to that was the tequila tasting station. I tilted my head to the left and saw a gigantic, ice-sculptured vodka bar in the center of the room. Across from the entrance was an enormous beer garden. Diagonal from the beer garden stood a scotch and whiskey bar, including cigars.

For the old Adam, this was heaven. But for the new Adam, this was hell.

I wasn't in the mood to be there. I was tired and cranky. All of a sudden, the drinks started talking to me.

Hey, Adam. It's me. Your old friend Santa Margherita pinot grigio. Remember those good times we had in Italy? Come over here, ya' old bastard. I'll help you out.

I shook it off.

A few minutes into the party, some annoying guy who I'd met several times but whose name I couldn't remember for the life of me walked over and started to yap on and on about his kids. I tried to be polite and make small talk with him, but then it happened again.

Yo, Adam! Over here, buddy. It's your old pal Grey Goose. I'm ice-cold. I'll wake you up.

Whoa.

I walked away from that babbling clown to try to find Michelle. I needed support. I spotted her talking to a bunch of our friends on the other side of the room. I was trying to make my way to her when I felt a hand on my shoulder.

"Hey, Adam! It's me. Jay."

I stared at him blankly.

"You don't remember? Jay from high school."

Envision the scene in the *Groundhog Day* movie, the one when Bill Murray bumps into Ned Ryerson, his annoying high school classmate who's now an insurance salesman. It was aggravating. I had no idea who this guy was.

"What's up, buddy?" I smiled and we made pleasantries.

But then *she* called to me. *Yoo hoo, Addy. Are you going to ignore me all night?*

I know that voice. That craving. I'd know it anywhere.

Addy, please. For old times' sake! You'll feel so much better.

Patron Silver. So sweet. So smooth.

While Jay from high school blabbed away, I thought, *No!*

Oh, come on. Remember what a blast we had. All the memories. Arizona State University. Your wedding.

No. I can't. I'm sober now.

It's been a few years. You're all better now. You can have just one.

And then . . .

I shouted . . .

Out loud,

"I can't!"

Jay stopped dead in his tracks. "You can't what?"

Oh, my God. I just yelled at Patron Silver tequila?

I bit my lip and quickly pointed at my iPhone, indicating that it had vibrated (*Nice cover, Adam!*). I jogged over to an empty area at the side of the room, to get my head on straight. I leaned against the wall and closed my eyes. *God, grant me the serenity . . . to accept the things I cannot change, the courage to change the things I can . . . and the wisdom to know the difference.* I took a few more deep breaths, and then I opened my eyes. And that was when the miracle happened.

I recognized a familiar woman from my recovery meetings. On the other side of the room, she was mingling. We locked eyes. She seemed to glide toward me. Before I knew it, she had put her hand on my shoulder.

"Adam, it's me. Stephanie. Are you okay?"

Everything inside me wanted to act cool. *Yeah, I'm great. Never better. Just a little tired. Have a new baby son at home. You know how it is.*

I smiled, and then I was honest with her.

"No, I'm really not. You're going to think I'm crazy, but I swear the alcohol is talking to me. I mean, actually speaking to me!"

She looked me in the eye. "I don't think you're crazy. I've had that happen to me many a time." She smiled.

Something changed inside me. I felt safe and protected again.

"You have how much time now?"

I looked down at the floor. "Five years. Why would this happen to me?"

She rubbed my back, like a mother. "Well, I have thirty-one years, and I still get the thoughts every now and then. I get the desire, just not the obsession. Have you been stressed lately?"

I nodded.

She grabbed my hand and squeezed it. "Come with me. I'm here with some great people in recovery."

That moment, my entire life changed. I truly believe that I was in danger of taking a drink that night. But I didn't, because I was honest.

That was the lesson!

A FEW DAYS LATER, I met with Jack Stebbins, my sponsor. Jack was a wise, old man with eyebrows and smile like Jack Nicholson's and elegant white hair. As I had continued my recovery, Jack had become my Yoda. We were sitting outside, at his favorite spot for spiritual work: overlooking a serene, inviting lake.

I rubbed my eyes. "I don't know how much longer I can do this, Jack! I can't see straight. I can't concentrate or recall anything. My memory is shot. I never feel rested. I don't really sleep. I swear I almost drank the other night." I stared out at the lake. "I'm making my daily meetings. I'm praying. What's wrong with me?"

Jack slid his black Ray-Ban Original Wayfarer sunglasses down his nose and peered over them. "Adam, my boy, you're an alcoholic. But when are you going to start letting your *sobriety* work for you rather than *you* work for your sobriety?"

"What do you mean?"

"Your recovery program is supposed to *help* you in life, not *harm* you. You're pushing too hard." Jack rubbed the whiskers on his chin. "How many meetings you making a week?"

"Seven. I go every day."

"That's too many, Adam, with a business, a wife, a daughter, and now a newborn son. Cut that back to five. Your weekends are for your wife and children. They're your priority."

I couldn't believe what I was hearing. They had drilled into my head "Meeting makers make it."

"But where will everybody think I went? How will meetings be without me there?"

Jack laughed. "Don't worry about that, kiddo. The meetings will be just fine."

Again, I noticed that I was worried about other people's perceptions of my recovery.

Jack tapped the table with his index finger. "How many men are you helping to get sober?"

"Six."

"Cut that down to two or three, pronto. Tell the others you need to balance your life, that they need to find a new sponsor."

I jerked my head back and furrowed my brow. "Are you serious?"

He nodded slowly and smirked. And then he folded his legs and took a sip of coffee. He looked out at the lake and gestured toward the beauty around us. "I really want you to be in the moment, not in your head, planning, working, and worrying." He paused and then lowered his voice. "Look

at this, right now. It's magnificent. Just relax. Stop trying to force everything. Enjoy your life."

Jack had reminded me of a quote from my favorite basketball player, Michael Jordan. Jordan said, about being in the moment of big games, "I tend to be calm; things tend to slow down as I go into situations that people don't know the outcome of. I already experienced them in my mind, just playing tricks with myself. So, it didn't seem new to me, and I wasn't afraid to fail with it. Once I started to understand that, I became a master of the game of basketball." Jack was a master of life.

He took off his glasses and then looked deeply into my eyes. "I want you to start gauging your serenity ratio."

Whenever anybody asked Jack how he was doing, he always answered between 90 and 98 percent. One day early in my recovery, I finally asked him what exactly he meant by that.

"Ah, my dear Adam. You've asked the golden question. It's my serenity ratio. I try to never allow it to go below ninety-five. I've been through divorce, losing my business, filing bankruptcy, children troubles, major operations, and cancer, but I've learned to be comfortable in all things, because I seek that spiritual power daily."

I nodded now, remembering that day.

Then I thought about Miles and the work it takes to be a good father to a young baby. Sloan's homework and dance schedule. Running the lace factory. Customer meetings. My physical fitness routine. One-on-one time with Michelle. My serenity ratio was at about 40 percent.

"My life's so busy. How do I do that?"

Jack grinned. "Through prayer and meditation, my boy."

There it was again—prayer and meditation.

Cue the Rocky music.

I doubled down on my spiritual connection. I recommitted to daily prayer, following the "diet" that Father Ron had prescribed for me at Hanley. I also started a serious meditation practice. But I found training my mind to be much, much tougher than training my body.

In the beginning, when I tried to meditate I couldn't stop my thoughts. But I kept trying. I chanted. I counted my breaths. I repeated mantras. Sometimes, doing all that relaxed me and put me to sleep! But I stuck with it day in, day out. Practice, practice, practice. I applied my sports background to my spirituality. How does a shooter get out of a shooting slump? Keep shooting. How does a muscle get stronger? Countless reps and failures. I decided that it must be the same with meditation. Repetition! I read numerous books about various types of meditation, including awareness of breath meditation, Zen meditation, mindfulness meditation, and transcendental meditation. I developed my own meditation practice by combining a bunch of types with some visualization techniques. The zealousness that I demonstrated in my spiritual practice actually calmed down all the other areas of my life, including being a husband, father, son, boss, employee, team leader, friend, recovery warrior, speaker, and fitness enthusiast.

Here is the meditation practice that I developed for myself: First, I get comfortable in a seated position. I take a slow, deep breath in through my nose and then exhale completely. My mind may try to wander, but again I inhale, focusing on my breath. After a few minutes, I start to relax. Then, I scan my body with my pretend X-ray vision. I start at my feet, on the floor, and send a healing, golden light all the way from calves up to my thighs, into my hips, through my lower back and abdomen, up to my chest, out to my shoulders and arms and finally up to the top of my head.

Then I watch thoughts drive through my brain like passing cars. One thought may be about what type of exercise I'll do later that day. If I actually get into that car, I'd see all my options: weight training, swimming, running, cycling, CrossFit, yoga, P90X, high-intensity interval training, and so on. That trip would take me down various roads, such as Diet Drive, where macronutrients (macros), micronutrients (micros), calories, the Paleo diet, the ketogenic (keto) diet, the vegan diet, the raw diet, and other diets and nutrition-related concepts are located; Supplements Street, where preworkout drinks, protein powders, vitamins, and other supplements are located; and Vanity Lane, where thoughts such as *How does my body look?, How does my face look?* and *Am I lean or retaining water?* come to mind. If I get into one of the thought cars, in a few short minutes I can be miles away from my original goal of being centered. Over time, however, I have developed the discipline of being still in my mind. I finally found my way to Zen Avenue, but getting there was a process.

Like a muscle, my intuition grew stronger. Things I had thought of as supernatural became part of everyday life.

More and more often, synchronistic things happened. I might be thinking about my uncle, and he'd call me. I might be reminiscing about my Gaga, and a Lady Gaga commercial would come on the TV. I might be thinking a deep thought about Father Ron or God, and a butterfly would appear. I might be upset, and I'd hear a song that would remind me that I'm not alone. One time I was in an airport, going crazy with a flight delay, and Dion and the Belmont's song "A Teenager in Love" came on.

I met Dion when I was twelve years old and he performed at my school. His timeless hits include "The Wanderer," "Runaround Sue," "I Wonder Why," "Abraham, Martin and John," and "Ruby Baby," which happens to have been John Lennon's favorite song. In fact, Dion's face is on the cover (in the second row) of The Beatles's *Sgt. Pepper's Lonely Hearts Club Band* album. In 1989, Dion was inducted into the Rock and Roll Hall of Fame.

During my second week out of rehab, at my favorite recovery meeting, I introduced myself to Dion. I was so scared, worried that he would think I was asking for an autograph. We were in a large, popular meeting hall, and I saw him from across the room. I slowly walked up to him. I felt as if I were approaching royalty. *This is stupid. He won't remember me. That was so many years ago. Why am I doing this?*

He was sitting there, completely relaxed, with his legs crossed in front of him. He was laughing and having a good time. He was chatting with a striking-looking man who resembled Clint Eastwood's Dirty Harry character and was wearing sunglasses and chewing gum. Dion was wearing a black-on-black New York Yankees baseball cap, a black cotton T-shirt, and black jeans. He had a razor-sharp, salt-and-pepper goatee. He epitomized rock 'n' roll.

I finally reached his chair. My eyes widened. "Excuse me. . . . Umm . . . hello, Dion."

He looked up at me and smiled.

"Well, umm. I don't know if this is appropriate, but . . ." My hands were sweaty. "When I was a kid, you came and played at my school. It's one of my best memories from my childhood. I just wanted to say hello and thank you, after all these years." *I'm an idiot.*

"Oh, yeah?" he said in his Bronx Italian accent. "I remember that day. Here kid, take a seat."

He patted the empty chair on his right. "What's your name?"

"Adam."

"Adam. What a blessed name! First man in the Bible." He winked at me. "Adam, meet my dear friend Ben."

Ben's silver hair matched his tie and slacks. When he reached out to shake my hand, I could see that he was no stranger to the gym.

"Adam, nice to meet you."

"Nice to meet you, Ben."

"Well, young man, buckle up your seatbelt. It's a hell of a ride. You're in the land of miracles."

He and Dion nodded in unison.

I pushed out my chest. "I will!"

Dion patted my knee. "Yo, Adam, sit here next to me during the meeting, and we'll talk after."

That day, Dion took me under his wing. We went to lunch together and talked about God, spirituality, alcoholism, addiction, and our families. He was so open with me, so loving. Anything this man said, I did. During the years since, he has become like a second father to me.

When Ben shared with the group, you almost could hear a pin drop. He'd been blessed with a unique gift for explaining philosophy, spirituality, religion, and relationships in a way that opened even the most closed mind. It's the gift given to a prophet, which I'm convinced he is.

And when Dion shared, it was as if God had a microphone and guitar.

Surrounded by men like James, Merv, Ben, Jack, and Dion, I felt protected. I had a solid foundation and a strong team for my recovery. These were men who would keep me accountable, whom I could lean on for support. And Dion was a man I could emulate.

What really made a huge difference in my life was helping other people through the steps of recovery. Like Father Ron taught me during my treatment at Hanley, I followed the commandment "Love your neighbor as yourself." At first, I often wanted them to get sober more than they did. I took it personally when somebody refused to work the recovery program as hard or as passionately as I did, but in time I found a balance. I realized that the same principles exist everywhere—the gym, work, and recovery. I don't have the power to make people train harder or work more intelligently. I could teach, demonstrate, guide, or lead, but I couldn't control what the other person did. Yet each time I tried to help someone find the gift of recovery it helped to keep me sober.

I'd been given a second chance at life.

A gift.

A do-over.

One by one, I let go of my addictions—alcohol and drugs, of course, but also supplements, running, other exercise, and public speaking.

I finally knew my purpose—to help heal people and to give people hope. For years, I had thought that I had to work for my purpose, but, in reality, I had to allow my purpose to work for me. Having the strength to be around alcohol and not crave it could only be described as a miracle. As long as I stayed centered, honest, and true to myself, some mystical power gave me magical experiences with incredible people and kept me safe. I made a deal with the Creator that if I did my part by trying to help more people in the world He would give me a life worth living.

Being clean and sober gave me benefits such as more time in the day, stronger relationships, new adventures, reunions with old friends, the privilege of watching my beautiful children grow up, and a marriage full of love. I felt fulfilled, and it spilled into every area of my life.

At work, where my father was Michael Jordan, I became Phil Jackson. I saw how to lead our super staff by example. I knew how to inspire, with my unique emotional approach to business. I had the ability to see people's strengths and weaknesses and figure out where they'd thrive. I knew when to call time-out. I knew when to substitute players. I knew when to let our team on the floor play out their mistakes. I found the power within myself to create momentum. Most of all, I showed love and respect to each and every employee.

And it was all due to my recovery!

Recovery shifted my identity. It made me comfortable in my own skin. I no longer carried around resentments. I had faith. I built strong boundaries around myself. I no longer wore multiple hats of Work Adam, Dad Adam, Husband Adam, Gym Adam, Sober Adam, Son Adam, Uncle Adam, and so on. I was just Adam. I became authentic. I became real. I became the man I wanted to become.

A CALL TO ACTION

- In Chapter 22 I introduce you to my mentor and spiritual father, Dion! I'd like for you to look for a mentor. A reliable, trust-worthy, outside source of information you can lean on that will guide you to your personal goals. You're going to be afraid of asking, just like I was terrified to introduce myself to Dion. But, just on the other side of fear, is everything you ever wanted. Dion helped me to become Adam Jablin.
- Look back on your life and take ownership of where you feel like you owe a proper amends. Remember, this is not, "I'm sorry." It's the three-stage process I outlined in this chapter.
  1. Admit you were wrong.
  2. Ask what you can do to make things right.
  3. Ask if the person can find it in their heart to forgive you.

EPILOGUE

SUPERMAN

ON JULY 14, 2016, Michelle and I sat quietly, holding hands, in the auditorium at the Hanley Center. We watched as other people picked up their sober anniversary medallions, and we listened to their heartfelt speeches. I looked at my beautiful wife and thought about the many changes in my life since my intervention in 2006.

I was the only man left standing from the class of July–August 2006. Over the years, the men had been picked off, one by one, by the disease. Bruce had died from an overdose. Tony had hanged himself. Jeremy had gotten fired from Stalker and still was trying to get sober. Morty had gone to rehab three more times before giving up and vanishing. Jack had been sentenced to ten years in prison for trafficking in illegal controlled substances. I had heard from Matt once. He had stayed in treatment for three more years because, as he told me, he never was able to stay sober on his own. I have no idea what happened to him.

"And now, Adam J. is celebrating ten years, and his wife, Michelle, will present him with his medallion."

Michelle approached the podium, stood tall and proud, and smiled. She winked at me and took out two special medallions that she had handpicked—a shiny black onyx one with a giant gold X in the center and a shiny gold one engraved with SERENITY ISN'T FREEDOM FROM THE STORM; IT'S THE PEACE WITHIN THE STORM, which, of course, represented the painting of peace that John Dyben had told me about.

Michelle's voice had a warm, caring tone. I took a deep breath, proud of both of us. The years had matured us and relaxed us. We now lived and learned together as a team. The worst days didn't break us or make me have to drink, and the best days didn't make us or make me have to pop a bottle of champagne. As I sat listening to her speak so beautifully, I thought about our dear friend, my roommate Grant.

> It was back in October 2012. I kissed the kids goodnight and entered the bedroom where Michelle was folding laundry, the news playing on the TV in the background. We gave each other the kind of exhausted nod that parents give each other after a long day—We had made it through the day. As I headed to the shower, a commercial for the Hanley Center came on the TV.
>
> Michelle perked up and pointed at the TV. "Oh, that reminds me. Yesterday, I got a random phone call from Mothers Against Drunk Driving. I felt like it was God or Spirit, in a way, reminding us how grateful we should be, so I made a donation." She flipped her long, silky, brown hair

back and out of her eyes. Her voice went down an octave. "I wonder how Grant is. I think about him so much."

"Let's look him up. Maybe he joined Facebook or LinkedIn."

I grabbed my iPhone and searched the Internet for Grant Ness. Within seconds, his name popped up. A chill traveled down my spine. Only three days earlier. Each result of the search confirmed the first result, the one that pointed to an article titled "Grant Allen Ness Obituary; Man who crashed into St. Augustine Beach house has died; 3 injured after Jeep crashes into house."

It knocked the wind out of me, and I lowered my head.

"What is it? Adam?"

I raised my hand and put up my index finger to show that I needed a minute.

I continued reading. "Investigators said alcohol and speed are considered factors in the crash, and Ness was not wearing a seat belt."

I read a little farther down the page. "In 2004 he got a DUI. In 2006 he got another DUI, and over the last three years, he's been given five speeding tickets in St. Johns County." 2006—that was when we were at Hanley together.

I sat down and rested my hand on my stomach. I had to tell Michelle. "Grant . . . umm . . ."

It was hard to say out loud.

"Grant's dead."

I handed the phone to Michelle, and she silently read the article. I studied her as her eyes welled up.

> My dear friend. My rehab roommate. I remembered him telling me that recovery meetings where he lived were boring. I'd checked on him a few times over the years, but each call he'd had less to say. We'd talked about his work and how he felt bored at night. He'd always asked about Michelle and mentioned how he'd like to meet someone just like her. I guess I'd never thought—or wanted to believe—that he'd relapse. At Hanley, they'd taught us that going back to drinking would mean jails, institutions, or death. A part of me had thought they were saying that just to scare us, but now I knew it was true. Grant's passing had made me realize that I'd already been in jail, when I got the DUI during college, and in an institution, Hanley. Next for me would be death.
>
> I felt that Grant's spirit was letting us know what had happened to him, that he was now on the other side, and warning me to stay sober. By that time, I believed in the world of spirit as much as the physical world.

Now, three-and-a-half years after Grant's death, Michelle was asking me to stand up and go to the podium to receive my ten-year medallion. I gave her a giant, warm hug and kissed her on the lips. I told the audience how the Hanley Center had changed my life, how I finally had discovered who I was, what I was, and what I had to do to get better from my terminal disease. "Today, I'm grateful to be an alcoholic and addict. Without it, I'd never have found recovery, you—my new family—the spiritual life, and God. I'm certain I'd be dead."

I looked at Michelle. "Thank you for saving my life."

EPILOGUE: SUPERMAN

A FEW WEEKS LATER, while my father and I pushed Sloan and Miles on the swings at the park, I spoke to him about some of the men I'd been helping to stay sober and some of the recovery talks I'd given recently.

My father, the tough cowboy, leaned toward me with a soft expression on his face. "You know, pal, you're finally like Superman."

"Um, what do you mean?"

"Well, you always thought being Superman was about having muscles or incredible powers. But you know what Superman really does?"

I rubbed my chin and smiled. "What?"

He took a deep, satisfied breath. "Superman saves lives."

ACKNOWLEDGMENTS

I HAVE MANY PEOPLE, from all stages of my life, to thank. Please forgive me if your name isn't in here, and know that you're in my heart. I honor, love, and respect each of you.

Thank you, Lisa Tener, writing coach! I still remember calling you, in 2007, with this crazy, enthusiastic, energetic belief that I had a story that must be heard. You somehow slowed me down and worked with me patiently, draft after draft, teaching me the basics. You taught me how to SHOW, not tell. You helped me feel confident in my writing voice. You calmed me down when I wanted my book done yesterday and told you, "Stallone wrote Rocky in one night!" WOW, I can be a lot to take! Ha ha ha. Thank you, my sister in the literary world. You also introduced me to so many cool people on this amazing journey. People like Stuart Horwitz.

To Stuart Horwitz, the book architect! He's a creative genius who shares my sense of humor (thank God!). Brother, thank you! You showed me what was working and, more importantly, what wasn't working. Writing weighed down at me at times, and you gave me the much-needed energy to attack this book again. You taught me the concepts of *series* and *narrative arcs;* you guided me and helped me find the overall theme of my work. You helped me and hopefully the readers to HEAL! Timing is everything, and I craved your knowledge. But I got much more from you. I feel like I found a real brother in life. You gave me the courage to see what I'll be like after this book is launched. I'm so grateful to you, brother. Thank you for all the long hours and attention you gave me. The best people in the world know what their skill set is and when to pass the ball. Stuart wanted my book as perfect as I did and so, when he had done all he could, he passed the rock to Louann Pope.

Louann Pope, the greatest copyeditor of all time! Honestly, I believe that your eye for detail could unravel and discover the greatest mysteries of the world, let alone my book. When I received the first round of copyediting, which included not just one document but a set of documents, screenshots, and instructions, my eyes popped out of my head. After reviewing the materials several times (measure twice, cut once, I always say), I jumped in. Your precision regarding the most minute characteristics and your accuracy with dates and timeline, made my work more authentic. Your exactness challenged me to go back into my memory and recall aspects of my life that had been buried for a while. My dear friend, I thank you!

Thank you, Molly Regan of Logica Design. You truly brought the LOTSAHOLIC logo to life...you branded the message of HOPE!

1106 Design and Ronda Rawlins. Thank you for being so professional and enthusiastic with my work. I truly am grateful.

Steve and Laura Weatherford. Thank you for coming into my life at the perfect time. For telling me that my voice is important and to stop apologizing. Steve—Divine

Fingerprints, Wow! You both taught me to teach from the mountain and not the valley. You guys are the best. "God will do for you what you can't do for yourself."

Los Silva and the SVG Media Group. Thank you for helping me develop my message and vision to help others on a greater scale. Los, you are truly my brother. "God won't do for you what you can do for yourself." Roddy, thank you so much for all the help with social media. Octavio Cifuentes, thank you so much for your brotherhood and special introductions. You are one in a million.

The Tenafly, New Jersey crew. The Stillman years. We had the greatest childhood, and we were a family. My favorite teachers, Mrs. Williams and Mrs. Bany, thank you for all the love. All my friends from there. I'd like to name a few: David Fisher, David Ross, Alex Wolcoff, Jenny Wasserman, Danielle Lasenna, Vanessa Solomon, Cindy Laser Hoffman, Chris Bray, and Kenny Tanner. The list goes on and on. The Bernstiens—Paul, Barbara, Matty, and Jeremy—thank you for your friendship, the Yankees games we've gone to together and, most of all, introducing me to the Wam. Randi Bauer Lipton, what can I say about you? You're the very definition of a friend. Steven Bounogorio, we still share a special bond. I love you more than words can say. And the Aronoffs. Rob, I'll always love you, and I miss you tons. I hope you're having a great time with Gaga, on the other side. Sheila, thank you for being a second mommy to me for all those years. Matty, I'm very proud of you. Most of all, my brother Jonno, our bond is what songs are written about. "I'll keep movin' through the dark with you in my heart."

My Camp Wigwam brotherhood. I wouldn't be the Adam "Jabbin'" Jablin, aka "Jabber," that I am today without the Wam. Bob and Jane Strauss, what can I say about you? Thank you for coming to my house in 1984 and convincing my parents that Wigwam would become a home for me, a transition before our move to Florida. I owe you so much. Stan and Carol Rothenberg. Peter and Margie Farber. The Balsams. The Verhelsts. The Crolls—Bobby and Kamran Javafizadeh. My favorite counselors, Jordan Steinberg and Rob "Shap" Shapiro. Will "Ruby" Rubenstein, I know that you and Shap cheat at Spades. Jack Chaffin, Jono Lapat, Charlie Kahn, Tom "Sully" Sullivan, and Ned Sader. Gregg Levy, a special thank-you for teaching me about bodybuilding. The one and only, Lucas Almour, my main man, I love you tons. My crew—Tom Skorupski, David "Star!" Starman, and Zachy Rothenberg. And a special huge loving thank-you to my big brothers in life—Hawk Cabin, Robby "Stupid Clod" Simon, Dave "Daaaaaave" Bott, Ken "Deek" Deckinger, and Andy "Guido" Novak. I love you guys with all my heart. "All hail to Camp Wigwam. Ra!"

Mr. and Mrs. Wing. Thanks for putting up with me! Honestly, thank you for always being there and guiding me as a young man. Coach Mark Totovian, thank you for helping me build the confidence that I so desperately needed.

Spanish River 1994! Thank you for the memories. We were so lucky. I love you all. My brothers, just to name a few: Andy Lazarus, Steven Mueller, Ralph Mauro, Guido Liuzzo, Mike "Moosey" Morrison, Wade McCalin, Scotty Gelbart, John "Web" Webberly, Brett "Hairy" Marks, Lance "Axel" Scida, and Erik "Arnold" Szabo.

Arizona State University. Manzanita Hall '94. My Sigma Phi Epsilon brothers and especially my pledge brothers. I love you all. I'd like to name just a few people from those days: My dear handsome brother—Damian Mendell, Gregg Morrow, Joel Fleet, Steve Kushnir, Jeremy Hafner, Jason Hersh, Todd Gherke, Todd Chesney, Todd Benrud, Nate Brelig, CJ, Danny Pritchard, Mitch Bell, Drew Senner, and Rabih Gholam. My pledge class of Spring 95. This is for Donnnie! My brothers in iron at Beauvais Gym. Abbas Khatami, IFBB pro, thank you for taking me under your wing and showing me the ropes. A big hug and kiss to Nick Gagliano. Love you Nicky! The entire Enclave Crew. Ben Ashely, John Palmieri, and Johnny "G" Graham. I'll be a Sun Devil 'til the day I die.

Kevin and Danielle Wilen. A sincere, genuine thank-you for your friendship through the years but, most of all, for introducing me to my bride, my soul mate. You two will always have a very special place in my heart.

The entire super staff of Metritek LLLP. You make going to work every day a joy. You've seen me grow into the man I am today. We're the greatest team in the world. I love you all. An extra heartfelt thank-you to Adriana Baltar, Sheli Lopez, Raquel Fraga, Beverly Richardt (Mom of Metritek), Rob Robles, Rosita Bravo, Paulina Bellocchio, Zuky Jerez, Angie Piccinelli, Julianne Belffi, Steven Silverman, Javier Cano, Fabio Zuluaga, Andres Almonte, Carlos Restrepo, Juan Gomez, Andres Laverde, Juan Aguirre, William Rojas and Mario Flores. You guys mean the world to me.

Michael Walsh, Gene Abelson, Brent Bevelhymer, John Dyben, Father Ron Bersha, Ben Harrison, John Wirth and the entire staff at the Hanley Center from July 2006 to now. Thank you for saving my life. This book is a testimony to your work. I love you all.

Dr. Leslie Levine and Dr. George Kolletis, thank you from the bottom of my heart. It's safe to say, without you I wouldn't have a story to write.

My brothers and sisters in and around recovery. Where would I be without you? Thank you for being with me during this journey. Thank you for your encouragement and love. Many of your names are anonymous, but you know who you are. But I can name a few: Scott Schmaren, Dr. Chris Baker, David Kweller, Russel S., Grant Ness, Chris Smiley M., Geoff K., Gordo G. and Steph A., Nick and Stacie D., John "Sarge", Kyle and Jen C., Eric D., Aaron M., Mike and Katie S., Thatcher S., Brian M., Christopher N., Mike H., Dustin J., Tim L., Brandon K., Bobby H., Peter S., Raphael Wendell, Joe D., Anushka F., Dr. Jeremy S., Drew C., John H., David S., Tommy Z., Myles P., Drew C., Paul H., Mark S., Lisa M., Gene McGovern, Mike Brady, Danny T., Michael H., Brad Abramson, Big-Book George G., Marc M., Les A., Donovan O., Michael "Rambo" C., Harvey B., Troy G., Spike, Wendell M., Si Levine, Carol, Montana G., Jenny A., Alcoholic-Jay M., Chris and Danny S., Gabe, John P., Tony S., Rob M., Jason K., Kent Paul, "You don't know?" Bob D., Sandy B., and the Jets, Snow P., Sameer M., Zach L., Arnold W., Sam B., Aaron T., David L., Energy-Kev., Nick S., Cubby "Biscuit-Brother" Kramer, Justin "Batman" M., Sal and Linda R., Kyle L., John M., Barry Rabkin, Chef-Don, Peter and Bev W., Big "Hobo" Steve, and the one and only Steve Kennedy. To all my sponsees throughout the years, thank you for keeping me sober.

Matt and Chelsea Williams. I cannot begin to express my gratitude for you both. I love you both so much, and the entire FroPro family, including F. Timothy, Rudy Acara and

John Binford. Robert William, Vaun Robin, Tim Kassouf and the Pit Fit Crew, you guys rock!

Zacky Cohen, my little brother from another mother. I love our special time together and thank you for all your support. Red Rum Society forever. Steve Celi aka Dunk Life. Our special bond is truly from the heavens.

Steven Glover, aka Mr. O. Our special bond, our brotherhood truly lifts my spirits. You show me what real faith, courage (in crazy ways), humility and sobriety are all about. Stopping to take pictures with every single fan. Veganism. I can go on and on. Our special conversations and bro-downs have helped me so much over the years. You are family. I love you from the bottom of my heart. I am so proud of you in all areas of life. An honorable mention to international star, Dr. Scott Randolph, I love you too!

David Avidon. Where to begin? You inspire me and we are doing this together. We are burning the ships and moving forward with courage, faith, and love. You, Randi, and the kids are simply amazing and I thank God for putting us together. My dear brother, thank you for having my back. I love you.

Scotty Jeffries. On paper, we are completely polar opposites. Yet, if one listens to us share, we are one spirit. One day at a time, one month at a time, one year at a time… We are doing it—together! From "Have confidence in your sobriety" to "Just be Adam" our special bond has shaped who I am as a sober man. Your art and your heart inspire me (scottyjart.com). Thank you, my dear brother. I love you with all of my heart, Scotty. Momentum!

Mervin Fogell, I'm so thankful to you for welcoming me home and for all your love throughout the years. Steven

Solomon, thank you for all your love and support. Mike Apter, thank you for leading by example. Elliot Broffman, thank you for showing me how to keep physically, spiritually, and emotionally fit as I get older. Rickey Felberbaum, thank you for your friendship and brilliant humor. Ric Newman, thank you for demonstrating true faith and perseverance, you're one of my best teachers and I cherish our special times together. Paul Efron, a very special, heartfelt hug and kiss to you.

Ben Troxell—my Ben! Thank you for all your love, teachings, wisdom, and experience, and for connecting the dots for me. I love you so much. You have no idea how much you mean to me. I hope that over the years I've shown you and Kathy how much and made you proud.

Jack and David Stebbins. A very special thank-you to you both. Your humor and wit keep me wanting to come back and hear more. Thank you for your honesty and for making me a better writer. James Lehman, thank you. Your memory lives on inside this book, inside me, and inside all who knew you. I thank both David and James for guiding me to Jack Stebbins, my sponsor. Jack, I honestly don't know where I'd be without you. I know that you just love all this mushy, sensitive stuff. Ha! Thank you, Jack. My serenity is in the nineties (or at least the high eighties).

Alex Binstock. Thank you for always being there for me and my entire family and for encouraging me in the business, in my marriage, in life, and in my sobriety. I love you. You're family. Marvin Gutter, we miss you.

Tim Braun. Your unique gift has healed my family in so many ways. Thank you for all the love and support you've given us throughout the years. Thank you helping me connect with spirit. Thank you for being my brother. You taught me how to become a Super-Man. I love you Tim.

Alex and Courtney Bafer. What a beautiful friendship based on truth, trust, respect and love. Doesn't matter how much we see each other; the bond is strong as oak. I love you guys and will always be here for you.

Michael and Dana Yormark! What a journey we have been on together. I can't begin to express my gratitude for all your support. Dana, you have been the best confidant and truest of friends. Michael, you are a rock. You are such a special man with a humility and confidence that are unparalleled. I love you both very much.

The Shapblinkel crew—King Scott, Dana Frankel, Seth (Doc.), and the beautiful Dari Shapiro. My sincerest gratitude to you. The experiences—the ups and downs—that we and our kids have shared on holidays and vacations, and the loving bonds that we've formed are nothing short of miraculous. I could write a page on each of you. You have a very special place in my heart. You've enriched my life and always kept my sobriety first. I love you guys so much. Thank you from the bottom of my heart. Shapblinkel, dammit!

Nino and Lew, you're my best pals in the world.

Anthony "Nino" and Rosie Alagna. Through the years, you've been my truest friends. You're family. I was able to talk with you about things that I knew nobody else would understand: relationships, the family business, marriage, and parenthood. Rosie, thank you for taking care of my brother. Nino, I love you and your entire family so much. "O-Kay!"—Scarface voice.

Lewis Davis. My best-man, where do I begin? The greatest stories, throughout history, about love, life, and friendship pale in comparison to what we've been through together. Our brotherhood is a part of our DNA. It's been battle-tested, and it remains as strong as ever. I'm sending all my love to the entire Davis family.

Uncle Peter, Aunt Patty, cousin John, and Melissa Racanello. You guys have been there for me every step of the way. You're my family. You always have been and you always will be. I love you with every inch of my heart and soul.

Amy Jablin, my cousin, I love you to pieces. Thanks for always having my back, for your love and support, for introducing me to Bruuuuuuce! Uncle Mel and Aunt Bernice Jablin, I miss you and will love you forever.

My brother and sister-in-law. To try to express my gratitude to my family in just a few sentences is a gut-wrenching task. There aren't enough pages in a book to write down all that I am grateful for. Thank you for all your love, support, and patience throughout the years. I know I put you guys through a lot. Thank you for being a part of the intervention. I'll never be able to express to you my full appreciation for everything. I was like Emilio! Most of all, thank you for my nephews, my boys.

My nephews. Being your uncle is a privilege. I love you like sons. Watching you grow up has been such a joy. Sharing inside jokes with you, watching the Miami Heat with you, watching Will Ferrell movies with you, and talking U.S. politics, I feed off your energy. I love you boys, and I'll always be there for you. Always!

My in-laws. Thank you for always believing in me, for always having my back, for loving me and treating me like a son, and for teaching me about life, family, and commitment. I can count on you guys for anything. I feel so lucky to be able to say you're my father and mother. A loving and honorable mention to Sydney and Caroline Rubin and the Spillert and Lockett families. I'd also like to thank Grandpa Sydney Lubin for watching over me from the other side. I love you, Papa. And, of course, my girl Grandma Mimi. God must be getting a kick out of all your opinions and humor. I miss you.

My namesake grandfather who I never knew, Moshe Maschiach, and my grandma Safta Maschiach. Thank you for having my back and never giving up on me. Thank you for inspiring Mom to come to America and give life to my sister and me. I'm indebted to you. A special loving shout-out to my Aunt Elana, Uncle Mome, and all the Maschiachs and Labrozas.

Cue the Superman theme song, please. Dun, dun, dun, dun, dun.

Uncle David and Aunt Linda. Where do I begin? May 19th? Superman? We share one soul, one love, one heart. This book is a reflection of our love. I carry you inside me. This book is a symbol of us, like the "S" on Superman's chest. I'm so proud of the man I've become, and you guys have been my safe place, my fortress. Uncle David, we did it! I love you both from the bottom of my heart.

Poppa and Gaga, Morton and Charlotte Jablin, thank you for being the best grandparents in the world. I feel you guys in my heart with every decision I make. The effect you've had on me is immeasurable. I'm the luckiest man in the world. Poppa, thank you for everything you do for my family here on Earth. Gaga, thanks for everything you do on the other side of the veil. I love you both so much. I hope I've made you proud.

Dion DiMucci, my main man, my beloved teacher, my mentor, my inspiration. Thank you for everything! And I mean everything—for taking me under your wing and showing me the ropes, for showing me how to be a man, for teaching me the difference between love and approval, for instructing me in how to uplift my wife and my children and make them feel loved and cherished, for coaching me in how to walk the walk and talk the talk, for tutoring me in how to set boundaries and love more by caring less, and for enlightening me about how to truly trust God. I value every minute that we spend together. Susan DiMucci, thank you for all of the love and support throughout the years. You guys have shown me how to keep and nourish a beautiful marriage and family in recovery! I love you like a father, Dion.

My beloved parents, Robert and Varda Jablin. Boy, do I love you guys! Thank you for instilling in me the values of family, love, generosity, responsibility, drive, and determination. Thank you for supporting me in life and in the writing of this book. Thank you for entrusting me with running the family business. Thank you for being there the countless times I needed you. Dad, you'll always be my hero, my cowboy. I'm so proud of you. You taught me to Cowboy Up! Mom, I love you more than words can say. There's a special bond between a mother and a son, and it can't be put into words. Thank you for teaching me how to love and have enthusiasm for life. My sister, Kimberly, through thick and thin, you've always had a special piece of my heart.

And, of course, my heart-stopping, pants-dropping, house-rocking, earth-quaking, booty-shaking, true loves of my life, my beautiful children. You guys give my life meaning and purpose. You own my heart. You have no idea what an honor and privilege it is to be your father. I cherish every moment I get to spend with you guys. We're the luckiest family in the universe. You two are my world! You've taught me more than I'll ever teach you. My love is unconditional. Like Superman says, you guys will make my strength your own. You'll see my life through your eyes, just as I'll see your lives through my eyes. The daughter and son become the father, and the father becomes his kids. I look forward to watching you grow up and loving you every step of the way. Thank you, babies. Daddy loves you so much!

Above all, my wife. Thank you for EVERYTHING! Thank you for giving birth to the two greatest kids in the world. Thank you for saving my life. Thank you for pushing me to grow and become a confident, sober man. Thank you for reining me in when I needed it. Thank you being my anchor, keeping me grounded to what's truly important in life. The stresses of my getting sober and the challenges of my writing this very book have been immeasurable. You always mean what you say and say what you mean. You're defined by how big your heart is. Your honesty is as strong as a mighty oak. You're simply the BEST! I know I can depend on you for anything. Thank you for loving me.

Thank you to everyone I've met on my journey. This book is for all of you and for the sick, suffering souls that need to be healed or are looking for a friend to connect with. If you're in the darkness, lost, and frightened, I'm always around.